A beginning teacher's guide to special educational needs

A beginning teacher's guide to special educational needs

Janice Wearmouth

Open University Press

Open University Press
McGraw-Hill Education
McGraw-Hill House
Shoppenhangers Road
Maidenhead
Berkshire
England
SL6 2QL

email: enquiries@openup.co.uk
world wide web: www.openup.co.uk

and Two Penn Plaza, New York, NY 10121–2289, USA

First published 2009

A catalogue record of this book is available from the British Library

ISBN 13: 978 0 335 23354 0 (pb) 978 0 335 23352 6 (hb)
ISBN 10: 0 335 23354 6 (pb) 0 335 23352 X (hb)

Library of Congress Cataloging-in-Publication Data
CIP data applied for

Typeset by YHT Ltd, London
Printed in the UK by Bell and Bain Ltd, Glasgow

Fictitious names of companies, products, people, characters and/or data that may be used herein (in case studies or in examples) are not intended to represent any real individual, company, product or event.

The **McGraw·Hill** Companies

This book is for my beloved family, past, present and future

Contents

Preface

Special needs provision in schools continues to be a major source of anxiety for teachers and other educators, politicians and parents. The whole area of 'special educational needs' and 'inclusion' is often shrouded with uncertainty about what it means, either in theory or in practice, or what it entails. Stories in the national press and questions asked in Parliament about the quality of special needs provision in schools have served to heighten awareness of the need for an improved level of teacher awareness and expertise in this area of education, and for improved communication with parents and others about the issues involved. In light of this degree of public concern, for newly qualified teachers particularly, but for other teachers and school governors as well, being faced with students labelled as 'having special educational needs' can be a daunting prospect. The current text addresses these issues in a straightforward, intelligible and practical way.

This book draws on research-based practice that is known to be effective in supporting groups of students identified as having special learning needs in different settings and phases to inform and equip teachers and others interested in this area of education. Each chapter has been deliberately written to incorporate:

- questions for reflection;
- personal thinking around some of the contentious issues in the special educational needs area of education;
- illustrations of real-life experiences, my own and those of others;
- examples of good practice;
- techniques and strategies that have been shown to work.

In Section I, the introductory chapter sets the scene by discussing the whole issue of how children learn, and illustrates the kinds of challenges all new (as well as more experienced) teachers are likely to face in ensuring that all students can learn effectively in their classrooms. The following chapter then focuses on an understanding of the responsibilities of all teachers for the progress of students in their classes, and sets out to make clear how current legislation in relation to difficulties in learning has evolved over time.

Section II is concerned with assessment, planning, teaching and learning. In it, Chapter 3 offers an overview of the four broad areas of need outlined in the *Special Educational Needs Code of Practice* (DfES 2001) together with general strategies appropriate to assessing and addressing each one. Chapter 4 looks at assessment and planning in more detail. It aims to offer an overview of a whole range of different types of assessment, both informal and formal, with a discussion of practical and theoretical issues associated with these. This discussion includes reference to important student, peer and family views and experiences, as well as teachers' own perspectives on students' learning. Clear, focused planning for students' learning is seen as stemming from appropriate rigorous assessment. Almost all teachers are bound, at some time or another, to come across young people in their classrooms who experience particular difficulties in the area of literacy and numeracy, and/or whose behaviour is seen as problematic in some way. The chapter on assessment and planning is therefore followed by discrete chapters focusing on ways to understand and address difficulties in literacy, numeracy and student behaviour in classrooms and schools. These three chapters (5, 6 and 7) aim to foster understanding of the difficulties that are experienced in ways that offer clear, straightforward strategies for intervention.

Section III of the book focuses on support for students' learning. There is currently a great deal of interest in the applications and uses of information and communications technology (ICT) in schools. Chapter 8 therefore focuses on the range of ICT that is available in schools to support students' special learning needs. Many approaches to addressing students' special learning, physical or behavioural needs include working with other educators such as teaching assistants or learning support personnel. Chapter 9 discusses practicalities and challenges in relation to this kind of partnership work – with examples of what can happen in practice. It also highlights the whole issue of child protection and welfare, and teachers' and schools' responsibilities to work in partnership with other agencies in support of the 'Every Child Matters' agenda.

SECTION I

SPECIAL EDUCATIONAL NEEDS: POLICY AND CONTEXT

All of us, as teachers, are bound at some time or another to come across young people in our classrooms who experience difficulties in learning, or some kind of sensory or physical difficulty that impedes their learning, and/or whose behaviour is seen as problematic in some way. There can be challenges, but also huge personal rewards, for teachers in knowing that they can be instrumental in opening up children's life chances and changing their future prospects for the better by deliberately and proactively problem-solving barriers to learning and good behaviour in schools.

The way in which 'special educational needs' are talked about in government publications, regulations, official circulars, consultation, advice and guidance documents, academic texts and articles, often gives the impression that we all know what this means. Is this really the case?

Question for reflection

From your own experience, how far would you consider these children as having special educational needs:

- a child who is otherwise very successful in school but experiences great difficulty with spelling accurately;
- a child with partial sight;
- a child whose behaviour is more disruptive in the classroom more often than that of peers, or a child who is withdrawn and ill at ease talking with others;
- a child with cerebral palsy who experiences difficulty in controlling movement;
- a child with Down syndrome who is developing language, comprehension and physical skills more slowly than typical peers;
- a child with profound and multiple disabilities, who cannot move, eat or drink independently nor communicate with words?

Section I looks at ways to understand the whole area of special educational needs as it relates to learning and behaviour in schools. Chapter 1 considers the concept of what we mean by 'needs', and who defines a 'need'. It discusses what we know about how people learn and whether children with special educational needs learn differently from others. It then reflects on ways of including all children in classroom activities. Chapter 2 looks at the historical development of 'special' provision for the few against which current provision can be understood. It outlines the law within which schools are currently required to operate, and offers an overview of the four areas of 'need' as they are defined in the *Special Educational Needs Code of Practice* (DfES 2001). Section I concludes with general considerations for responding to students' learning needs in schools.

1 Making sense of learning and difficulties in learning

> **Questions addressed in this chapter**
>
> What we mean by 'needs'?
> Who defines what might constitute a 'need'?
> What do we know about how people learn?
> Do children with special educational needs learn differently from others?
> How can we include all children in classroom activities?

Introduction

In schools, the expression 'special educational needs' is intended to relate very clearly to students' learning. We might ask ourselves whether the learning of children identified as having 'special educational needs' might be understood in the same way as that of other children. These days, with inclusion in mainstream schools in such high focus, the practical consequences of our answer to this question is very important for classroom teachers.

Defining 'need'

Labelling students as 'special needs' children, or children 'with special educational needs', is highly problematic for a number of reasons.

What is a 'need'?

We can define 'need' in different ways. For example it can be seen as a lack of something in an individual, which gives rise to difficulty. For example, hunger will constitute a need for someone who is starving. 'Need' can also mean the thing the individual requires to satisfy that lack. Food and drink would satisfy an immediate need for sustenance for the starving. In the educational context, for the student without sight, the need might be for text in Braille, 'talking books' or support from a classroom assistant to enable access to the school curriculum.

What does the label 'special educational needs' tell us about children?

As we shall see in Chapter 2, the term 'special educational needs' (SEN) covers a range of areas – learning, behavioural, sensory, and so on. To give a child the label 'special educational needs' therefore tells us nothing specific about a student and his or her learning.

How 'neutral' is the label?

The SEN label carries with it a connotation that often (but not always) is not very complimentary.

Who has the say?

On the surface, the notion of fulfilling a 'need' conveys a sense of kindliness. In practice, however, the kind of special or additional provision that is made often implies a value placed on students which they are deemed to 'need' – or deserve (Salmon 1998). There may be an assumption of agreement between all the interested parties about what is 'needed', which often (but not always, of course) ignores 'crucial issues' of the lack of power that may be allowed to pupils and parents in the decision-making process.

What are the connotations of SEN?

The use of the word 'need' is extremely sensitive in the context of education. It is not simply the word itself but the expectations that go with it. There is a strong relationship between teachers' expectations and student achievement, self-esteem and development that has been well documented (Rosenthal and Jacobson 1968). Salmon (1995) comments on her perception that the term is now associated with a sense of failure to come up to the mark. Instead of signifying belonging and entitlement, she sees the terms *special* and *need* as 'weasel words' with connotations of helplessness and inadequacy. They are used to justify relegating the problem to a specialist, while at the same time leaving teachers 'feeling helpless and deskilled' (Salmon 1995: 73–4). In a similar vein, Corbett comments that students with the SEN label can become marginalized rather than valued by schools: 'What does "special" mean? If we detach this word from its anchor in "educational" we can see that "special" does not mean especially good and valued unless we use a phrase like, "you are a special person". It is linked to "needs" which implies dependency, inadequacy and unworthiness' (1996: 3).

Where use of the label 'special educational needs' depends on the sense of deficiency in children, it is often seen as reflecting a 'medical' or 'deficit model' of difficulties in learning and/or behaviour. This model has a sense of being in some way inferior or distant from the norm, for example *dis-, un-, -challenged, difficulty*. This way of looking at the difficulties that students experience in schools may in itself prevent a positive approach to diversity and difference.

Not all educators take the same view, however. Some argue that identifying children's 'special educational needs' has a very humanitarian aim, which is to provide additional resources, develop specialist methods to address particular difficulties in learning, or overcome the effects of a disability in order that children can derive maximum benefit from their education. Without such identification of individual needs it is not possible to justify this level of personal attention.

Questions for reflection

How do you feel about the benefits and drawbacks of identification and labelling?
How can we make sure that children who need additional or different resources or provision generally can receive it without being stigmatized or otherwise marginalized?

In my own experience of teaching in eight different schools, it is very clear that how we view students strongly affects how we treat them. Teachers' views about the root of the difficulties experienced by a student are highly influential on the kind of provision made for him/her.

Interpretations of one student's 'need'

Thirteen-year-old 'Melvin', was small, thin, frequently hungry and often dirty. Several times he was caught stealing from peers, staff, the local shops and people queuing at the bus stop near the school. Some of his teachers saw him as intrinsically bad and wanted him to be excluded permanently because they thought he was a threat to his peers as well as to the smooth functioning of the school. What he 'needed' was expulsion from the mainstream school and treatment in a special school. The educational psychologist thought he 'needed' hypnotherapy, to 'treat' and 'cure' him. Others thought he was an ordinary teenager. His problem was not badness within himself, but neglect by his family. They felt that what he really 'needed' was food and clean clothes, and that then he would be 'sorted out'.

Sometimes personal experiences with students can open our eyes to some of the issues related to the labels we give to students.

Personal reflection

Fairly early in my own teaching career a specific incident made me think about the way in which an easy use of labels can serve to prevent us reflecting on what really causes students to behave the way they do. 'Jamie' was categorized as both disruptive and lazy. He was placed in the bottom band of three, the 'remedial' band, in the comprehensive school in which I was teaching. I taught his class group Classical Studies and shared stories from Greek mythology which Jamie loved. He was always the first with the answer to everything and was verbally very articulate. At the end of one year, a particular incident with him in class led to me consciously reflecting on the fact that the category 'remedial' as it related to Jamie certainly did not mean slow-learning, and that 'behaviour difficulties' were not always attributable to the student alone. I was telling the tale of Minos, King of Crete, and his pursuit of the escaping inventor, Daedalus. I had reached the point of describing Minos's undignified death when Jamie suddenly corrected me. He reminded me that I had given a different version of Minos's death nearly three terms previously. He was correct. I had forgotten. He then related, in detail, the whole of my previous account. I reflected on this piece of evidence for a very long time after the event. I was fairly new to teaching and not in a position at that particular school to influence his categorization as 'remedial' or his placement in the bottom, 'remedial' band. However, the disjunction between the label 'remedial' and my perception of him as articulate, interested and engaged in his learning forced me to rethink my conceptualization of him as both a slow learner, termed a student 'with moderate learning difficulties' at that time, and as 'disruptive' as he had been described to me. I reconceptualized the challenges that he presented to teachers from a slowness in his thinking and from pathological resistance to anything teachers said or wanted him to do, to literacy difficulties of a dyslexic nature which had gone unrecognized by teachers and had led to profound frustration in his inability to cope with written text or to express himself in writing.

Hence it was unsurprising if he loudly resisted writing tasks. Jamie's disaffection seemed to me to be the product of the learning environment in which he found himself. To be disaffected a person must be feeling alienated from something. In some lessons Jamie was expressing this feelings in obviously hostile behaviour. In my lessons I was relying largely on narrative so his hostility to having pressure placed on him to cope with text did not apply. In school, students are in a very different position from professionals in the hierarchy of power and influence. Those with a professional responsibility for sustaining existing organizational structures may well experience the rejection of school provision by students such as Jamie as challenging to the existing order as well as to themselves. They may then go on to interpret the behaviour of these students, and the students themselves, as deviant and as 'needing' to be cured by a special intervention programme.

Currently, questions about 'underachievement' are being raised at a national level. It is pertinent, therefore, to examine what might lie at the root of difficulties in learning faced by individuals and groups of students in a broader context. One might ask, for example, what part factors associated with the child and the particular teaching approaches and curriculum play in creating these learning difficulties.

Experiencing difficulty in learning

Questions for reflection

What is the hardest text you have ever tried to read?
What was it that made it so hard?

The hardest text I ever tried to read was the text of Shakespeare's *Macbeth* in school at the age of 13 – with no introduction or explanation. I remember being bemused, and then frustrated, by the unfamiliar language and vocabulary of the play. I became completely hostile to the suggestion of anything Shakespearean for years afterwards – until a very good live production of another Shakespeare play undid the damage. We can only make sense of new ideas and information in terms of what we already know. It is hard to learn unless what we are reading about, listening to or looking at makes sense to us. What would have helped me to make more sense of *Macbeth* was a clear introduction at the beginning, perhaps watching a film of the play (had it been available at the time) and teacher explanation of the vocabulary.

Without a way of a way of relating to the words and the ideas in a passage we are not likely to be interested in it.

Learning happens in the same way for all students of any age. They can make sense of new ideas only by relating them to what they already know.

Making sense

All of us draw on existing knowledge to make sense of a new experience. Even so, misconceptions may be very common.

Misconceptions in the classroom

Luke and the talking cards

Luke, a young primary pupil, had often heard his teacher ask in reading lessons, 'What does this say', as she held up a card to the class on which was written a letter of the alphabet. One day, at the end of playtime, the teacher came into the classroom to see Luke in floods of tears with a letter card pressed close to each ear. 'What's the matter, Luke?' the teacher asked. 'I can't hear them saying anything to me,' the boy sobbed. Luke's way of making his own sense from what he heard was to take the teacher's words literally.

Nikki's subtraction errors

Nikki, in a bottom mathematics set in a comprehensive school, at the age of 14 repeatedly made subtraction errors of the following kind:

$$\begin{array}{r} 9842 \\ -1357 \\ \hline 8515 \end{array}$$

She thought that the subtraction rule was always to subtract the lower from the higher figure, whether the figure appeared in the upper or lower line.

Upper and lower case confusions

As a teacher in a secondary school, I frequently noticed the following kinds of errors in the written work of a number of pupils who experienced difficulties in literacy acquisition and expression:

aBle; saiD

For a long time I simply corrected these errors. However, after a long time when they persisted I asked the pupils to write the words in front of me, and talk through what they were doing. They all said that they knew that 'B' and 'D' were upper case, but could not remember the difference between them in lower case. When I looked to see how they were writing these letters they made no difference between lower case bs and ds, starting them both at the top and running down to the curve, left or right, at the bottom. It is no wonder that they could not remember the difference. They tried to show that they knew the correct spellings by using upper case that they could clearly distinguish.

What these examples illustrate is how learners try to make sense of a new experience or solve a new problem. They try to fit it to similar experiences of problems they have met before. If there is a good fit then it is more likely that the learner will understand the current experience or solve the problem correctly. If the gap between the existing knowledge or experience and what is needed to understand the current problem or experience is too great, however, this is unlikely to happen.

Supporting learning in schools

Teachers and other adults in schools are responsible for finding ways to support learners to make connections with what they already know. One straightforward way to do this is to talk with learners of any age about what they do or do not know and encourage them not to be embarrassed to discuss difficulties they might be experiencing. Young people have a right to be heard (Council of Europe 1966). At the same time listening to what they say is an important part of the process of supporting learning. If the teacher had not listened to Luke crying because he could not 'hear' the alphabet cards 'talking' to him, she would not have understood his difficulty. Nikki had gone on making the same subtraction errors because, as she later explained, she was 'useless' at mathematics and was too embarrassed to explain her reasoning. I had simply never thought to ask the boys why they used upper case letters in the middle of words because it did not occur to me that they might have chosen to do this deliberately. Concentrating only on the right answer can mean losing the chance to gain insights into learners' understandings and misunderstandings and, therefore, the opportunities to support learning at the right moment.

Understanding learning and behaviour

Adults in schools have to be concerned all the time with the sense that children are making of their worlds, their experiences, tasks in classrooms, and so on. Being open to this demands careful and sensitive listening, observation and reflection. How young people think of themselves in school has an enormous impact on their learning and behaviour:

> Some may be highly anxious and continually under-value themselves. Others may seem over-confident and extremely resilient. Some may be very well aware of their own strengths and weaknesses whilst others may seem to have relatively naïve views of themselves. Children may be gregarious, or loners, or they may be lonely.
>
> (Pollard 2002: 97–8)

The experience of loneliness and social isolation

In every school I have taught, I have encountered students with whom communication has been difficult, who have, seemingly, shut themselves off from teachers. Many have been socially isolated and, to judge by body language, feel appalled at their own loneliness yet just cannot do anything about it. I well remember the case of Paul, undernourished, dirty, smelly, and always alone, but hovering as close to the entrance of the school building as he could manage. Deliberation on the situation led me to try to get him involved in a lunchtime mutual-support group of students, but was told on the phone by his father: 'I'm not having my son associating with a load of drongos. He's not a drongo. I don't want him labelled.' I experienced his father's reaction as extremely offensive and rude. I could never find a way to communicate with Paul to see if there was anything the school could do to support him better.

(Wearmouth, unpublished manuscript)

We are all much more likely to engage in activities that carry a positive outcome than those that will result in no benefit. In schools, like the rest of us, children come to decisions about what learning is worth investing in. They judge whether the benefits of any given learning situation outweigh the time, effort and (in some classrooms) the risk of being wrong and exposing themselves to public humiliation in being thought stupid. Questions of value-to-oneself are at the heart of the learning process. Young people may not make the effort if they do not perceive it as worthwhile in relation to the effort that is required.

The influence of lack of value to oneself

Arnold was another student about whom I had many concerns. Over the two years I worked with him in a comprehensive upper (13–18) school his written work showed just how little progress he seemed to have made in literacy skills. He just did not seem to care. He came to school in a shirt that was always dirty. He smelled of body odour and nicotine. I never knew what Arnold was thinking. I never knew what he felt about his own lack of literacy. If we had known, it might have made a difference either to our approach or to the outcome educationally. Arnold left school functionally illiterate.

(Wearmouth, unpublished manuscript)

All learners are active, all learners think about their learning, all have views about it and all have feelings about it, no matter what the context. Allowing learners some degree of choice in, or power over, what they learn and how they learn invites them to take control over their learning. This is not always easy in busy classrooms. However, for young people in schools, feeling that they have some control over their learning, for example, having some control over what they learn, understanding why they are learning something, choosing how to do it and when to do it, may be important.

Needing to be able to participate in learning

All of us, as human beings, have a fundamental need to belong and to feel valued as a member of a community or group. In schools this means being included in its activities:

- learning;
- acquiring knowledge;
- gaining a sense of oneself as able to achieve;
- having a sense of belonging.

In many parts of the world there is a national curriculum that describes what children at various stages of their schooling are expected to know and understand and be able to do. This gives a very strong steer to the kind of learning that is seen in schools as really mattering. While learning related to national curriculum requirements is important, how students in schools learn is at least as important as what they learn. Learning is a highly complex human activity and much is known about it that is useful for supporting learning in classrooms.

Constructing understanding

A number of researchers have contributed to the way we often think about children's learning in the twenty-first century. Two of the foremost theorists are Jean Piaget (1896–1980) and Lev Vygotsky (1896–1934).

Jean Piaget

Jean Piaget, a Swiss psychologist, was one of the theorists who contributed a lot to the thinking that led primary schools to organize their classrooms with the children in mind, and provide a rich learning environment with concrete materials and resources. His research evidence led him to conclude that learners construct knowledge by interacting with their environment and what it is in it. When children have a new experience, Piaget suggested, they reconstruct their thoughts in the light of it. As they grow older, learners develop more detailed and accurate understandings or constructions of the things they experience. Children's direct experience with their environment is therefore vitally important to their learning.

Lev Vygotsky

Ideas of the learner as actively making sense of experiences together with knowledge of the particular situations and social practices in which experiences occur are important in understanding learning. However, as the Russian psychologist, Lev Vygotsky, suggested, language is also important in the sense-making process. This means that relationships among learners themselves and between learners and adults that are bound up with the learning environment are also important. Vygotsky concluded that it is through inter-acting with others, especially a more able other, that learning mainly occurs and is developed.

Linked with this idea is the concept of the 'zone of proximal development' or ZPD. This refers to the range of knowledge and skills that learners are not yet ready to learn on their own but can learn with support from, and in interaction with, more informed and experienced others, for example adults. Within the zone the more experienced other is central. Learning involves practice below the zone, for example to encourage the development of skills to automatic level. Learning is also about participating, for example having the chance to behave as a reader, writer and so on, alongside other readers and writers. Learning is often highly charged with emotion. Feelings accompanying success can be very pleasant and/or exciting. The sense of failure can be very upsetting and/or disturbing, especially when it is a frequent occurrence. Feelings are therefore very powerful in supporting or inhibiting learning, as we saw in the case of Arnold.

The view of learning just described emphasizes the social and cultural context of learning and the role that adults play in supporting that learning, and is often called 'socio-constructivism' (the construction of knowledge in a social context), or referred to as taking a sociocultural perspective on learning. Other leading educationalists, for example Jerome Bruner, have picked up and developed Vygotsky's ideas. The ideas from this view of learning underpin much of the current work on formative assessment – 'assessment for learning' – which is discussed in Chapter 4 of this book.

Scaffolding learning

One of the ideas that has been developed from a sociocultural view is that of 'scaffolding' (Wood et al. 1976) to support learning. Rogoff (1990) identifies six elements in scaffolding learning:

- engaging the learners' interest in the task;
- demonstrating (modelling) how to do the task;
- where possible, reducing the number of steps required to complete the task so learners can recognize ongoing progress;
- controlling frustration;
- providing feedback that will enable learners to understand how they are making progress;
- motivating the learners so they continue to engage with the task.

To be successful, the interaction must be collaborative between student and the more knowledgeable other. The scaffolding must operate within the learner's zone of proximal development. The scaffolder must access the learner's level of comprehension and then work at slightly beyond that level, drawing the learner into new areas of learning. The scaffold should be withdrawn in stages as the learner becomes more competent. In schools, the final goal is for the learner to become autonomous, secure enough in the knowledge required to complete the task.

Not all learning requires the physical presence of an adult. Learners need scaffolding from more knowledgeable others, but not too much. Getting the balance right is crucial. This is often especially difficult in school where there is a tendency in most classrooms for the adults to talk too much and for the learners to talk too little. Other resources, apart from adults, can also scaffold learning: information technologies, peers, books, materials, pop music and so on.

Other views of learning

From the discussion so far it should be clear how important it is to listen to what students have to say. From a constructivist or sociocultural view of learning, in order to work within the learner's zone of proximal development, engage the learner's interest, scaffold new learning and provide meaningful feedback of a sort that will enable the learners to move on, the scaffolder must be able to access the learner's current level of understanding. It is therefore crucial to understand, as far as we can, how students are thinking and constructing their worlds.

Views of students as learners have not always taken account of active agency in knowledge construction, however. One very commonly applied approach, what is often known as 'operant conditioning', is from behavioural psychology and assumes a passive rather than active view of students as learners. Operant conditioning – reinforcing what teachers want their students to do again, ignoring or punishing what they want students to stop doing – has been widely applied in teaching in UK classrooms since the 1970s (Merrett 1985).

Understanding learning from a behaviourist view

We discuss this view of learning in more detail in Section II, Chapter 7. Suffice it to say for now that almost all the principles associated with a behavioural model have been derived from work with laboratory animals, for example Skinner (1953). These same principles have been applied to behavioural interactions between teachers and pupils in classroom and school contexts. The behavioural model works on the principle that behaviour is learned, and that responses (or behaviours) are strengthened or weakened by the consequences of those behaviours. Learning and behaviour can therefore be modified through intervening in the environment. This model has often been used in, for example, classroom management, and in programmed instruction where tasks like learning multiplication tables, spelling, phonic work and word recognition are repetitive and can be broken down into small steps. Each one can be reinforced with some kind of reward. The behavioural approach to generating interventions when things are seen to have gone wrong in terms of learning and behaviour has often dominated thinking in educational institutions (Dwivedi and Gupta 2000). It is particularly important, therefore, to be familiar with this approach.

Classroom and school rules are examples of antecedent conditions (or setting events) that are intended to signify behaviour that is acceptable or appropriate. Such rules can also serve as antecedent conditions for teacher monitoring and providing punishing consequences for behaviour that is unacceptable.

Different types of reinforcers for learning and behaviour can be used by teachers and parents, such as tangible rewards, token reinforcers (for example, points exchangeable for desirable rewards) and social reinforcers (for example, smiles, praise, social attention but also access to enjoyable social interaction or shared activities with adults or peers).

Practical applications of a behavioural approach

A number of behavioural principles can be applied when devising programmes for learning:

- Positive reinforcement means behaviour will reoccur.
- Student responses need to be reinforced. For this to happen consistently, information should be presented in small amounts so that each response to each piece of information can be reinforced (shaping).
- Reinforcements will generalize across similar stimuli.

The requirement for information to be broken down into small steps and for each response to be reinforced immediately restricts what can be learned through this approach. Not everything can be broken down into small steps in a clear sequence, and that is one of the concerns about the approach. However, where this is possible, a learning sequence might be structured as follows:

- Practice might consist of teacher questions and student answers which expose the student to the new learning in gradual stages.
- The learner responds to every question and receives immediate feedback.
- The difficulty level of the questions is graded so the learner's response is always correct and the learner receives positive reinforcement.
- Good performance in the lesson is followed by reinforcers such as verbal praise, prizes and good grades.

Challenges for the behavioural approach

There is criticism of this approach that it can be rigid and mechanical. Although it is useful in learning repetitive tasks like multiplication tables and those work skills that require a great deal of practice and can be broken down into small stages, higher-order learning is not involved. Some educators, for example Hanko (1994), feel that behavioural approaches also fail to address adequately either the emotions or students' sense of self-efficacy and ability to reflect on their own behaviour and achievement. Potentially, behavioural approaches may serve teachers' wishes to manage students rather than encouraging teachers to teach their students through responding to individual needs.

Even so, behavioural approaches have been very commonly adopted in schools and can still be identified – for example in 'Assertive Discipline' (Canter and Canter 1992) and in many software programmes intended to encourage awareness of phonics and designed to provide immediate feedback and reinforcement of learning.

Active and passive views of mind

There is an important, though in some ways simplistic, distinction that we can make between the views of students' learning discussed above that is crucial to any discussion of difficulties in learning and ways to address these:

- Constructivist and sociocultural views take a view of the human mind as active in reaching out and constructing meaning.
- Behavioural views assume a passive view of the human mind. The learner is 'done to' by a reinforcer that shapes learning and behaviour.

In the world of special needs provision there has often been a sense of interventions and individual education plans that are 'done to' the child. We should all be very aware of our own understanding of learning, how this happens and how we, as teachers, can most effectively support our students, whether they experience difficulties or not.

The influence of teachers' beliefs about students' learning

An interview held with 22-year-old 'James' to elicit his reconstruction of his educational experience illustrates some of the issues related to the influence of teachers' beliefs and understandings about students' learning (Wearmouth 2004a: 60–7). On account of serious difficulties in literacy acquisition, in his primary school 'James' was placed in the lowest ability groups for reading and writing in his class and withdrawn for special lessons. Separation from competent literacy learners in the classroom and tuition in low-level 'remedial' literacy activities that he felt were irrelevant and meaningless resulted in feelings of hopelessness, helplessness and frustration. Great feelings of anger, defiance and frustration resulted from the conflict between the provision made by the school, what he felt he needed, and by his own impotence in the situation:

> ... first of all, when I went to the lessons, I was called out in front of the class, and they were referred to as special lessons, and politically correct as the teacher thought that was, it really wasn't. Kids are cruel, and I felt really targeted and singled out ... the lessons that they gave seemed very simple. They were like obvious repetitive stuff, going over stuff that I found simple ... I think the type of work that it was, was perhaps, writing out a page of like, a hundred, you know a full page worth of say a letter at a time, say D, repeating it over and over again and although my hand writing wasn't fantastic, I could write the letter D, but then that seemed to bear no relation to me writing a word.

The category of slow learner, created in order to manage special literacy provision in the school, hovered in the air ready to 'gobble up' likely candidates (Mehan 1996).

James's experiences in secondary school were very different. Teachers responded to his difficulties in a way that suited his individual learning needs and he was encouraged to see himself as an active agent in his own learning, capable of making sense of his own world and learning needs. With the added motivation of teachers expecting that he could and would learn, despite extreme tiredness every day James began to look for ways to achieve and overcome the difficulties he experienced: 'I was still slow and it was still hard work ... I'd be in bed by eight thirty, up until fifteen almost. I was exhausted ... and I felt like I came home and it would take me about twice three times as long as anyone else to finish the work, homework or whatever but I was coping.'

James's secondary teachers established a more 'responsive' approach where James and his teachers engaged in two-way discussion about the best ways to address his learning needs:

'Well by that time, I'd started to get quite good at coping ... I did have problems, but my note taking started to become a bit more efficient. I also worked a lot with books, with a [published examination] syllabus. I found that I could use the syllabus to have an advantage. Basically for the sciences, I could get a book, and just work through each point of the syllabus, and if I knew it then that was fine and I didn't almost need the lessons ... So, if there was something that I missed in class or couldn't keep up with ... I basically listed each point of the syllabus, and found the relevant piece of information and picked it out ... Basically, I'd know that ... a question would be awarded five or ten marks, and I know for ten marks they give you five points and I'd cut out the waffle. I became very strategic ... it was a strategy I worked out for myself, but for me it seemed blatantly obvious. If the course provides a syllabus, and the examiners can only ask you on that syllabus, then why not learn everything in the syllabus, and keep to that?

Self-taught study skills, supported by sensitive, aware teachers who responded to James's initiatives and a growing sense of agency enabled James to achieve academic success at the General Certificate of Secondary Education level (GCSE): 'before then it was blips, because the rest of my work was terrible. But when I did my GCSEs, I think all told I took 13 GCSEs, and I got two A stars, six As and five Bs. By then people were like, "Bloody hell!" and then it got to my A levels, and in the three sciences I got three B grades which was quite good.'

These skills, refined for study at degree level, enabled James to extend responsibility for his own learning until his graduation with an Upper Second Honours degree.

In the next chapter we look specifically at the legal obligations of all teachers for the learning of all students in their classrooms. In particular we will focus on those defined as having 'special educational needs'.

Effective teaching for all students

Recent research confirms that strategies recommended for particular special educational needs are useful for most, if not all, students. Lewis and Norwich (2000) point out that there is little evidence that staff should use entirely different teaching approaches for most students with SEN. Instead they point to research suggesting that staff should give students:

- more time to solve problems;
- more chances to practise their skills;
- more examples to learn from;
- more experience of using knowledge and skills in different situations;
- more strategies to help learn information and skills;
- more preparation for the next stage of their learning;
- more frequent assessment of what is and what is not being learned, and why.

It might therefore be sensible for newly qualified teachers to concentrate at first on strategies which improve the learning environment and increase the range of teaching strategies rather than assuming that something different has to be organized for every individual.

Conclusion

How we understand learning and how we see what lies at the root of a 'learning difficulty' in school has a very strong influence on how we respond. Over the years, different social or psychological understandings about the root of the difficulty have given rise to different approaches.

In schools, staff may react to children's difficulties in a number of different ways. Some people might focus on 'what is wrong with a child'. They may talk about how this 'problem with the child' can be dealt with. They might be concerned with finding out what is wrong within an individual, finding ways of measuring the problem and coming up with a set of planned responses to 'make them better', or as well as possible or so that 'they will fit in'. Other people in the school might be more concerned about their welfare. They may worry about the child and want other people to feel sympathy for the child's struggles. They may focus upon their moral duty to help them.

Focusing on what is wrong with a person means emphasizing ways in which s/he is different or deficient, where 'deficiencies' can be 'treated' like an illness. It can often be experienced, especially by the learners themselves, as a very negative way of meeting needs. In some situations, the difficulties that children experience may be seen as a tragedy for the individual and/or the family, and the children treated like 'charity cases'. Within school settings we can often see all these views of the difficulties experienced by children.

Another way of looking at difficulties is by examining the social context in which learning takes place. By doing this we can see how the context itself – the physical environment, resources, teaching approaches, the difficulty and/or interest level of the task or activity – can act as a facilitator or barrier to learning. The focus here is on a person's surroundings and what may be creating the barrier s/he is struggling to overcome. If we acknowledge that all people have differences, then it is social factors that turn some differences into disabilities. Economic factors, government policy, institutional practices, broader social attitudes or inappropriate physical surroundings might stop people from doing things.

As Peacey and Wearmouth (2007) comment, asking for guidance and help is a very good way to learn and to build confidence:

- In schools, mentors can be an important route to support.
- Students themselves who experience difficulties may tell teachers what works best for them.
- Parents and carers can often give valuable insights.
- The special educational needs co-ordinator (SENCO) and other teachers can advise and help those new to the profession to learn from outside experts like educational psychologists and therapists.
- A number of organizations, for example the British Educational and Communications and Technology Agency (BECTA), host discussion groups on Internet e-fora on many areas of special educational needs.

Problem-solving special needs provision

There is no golden formula for addressing the special learning needs of every student who experiences difficulties of some sort in schools. There are some general principles, however. For example:

- Every student who experiences difficulties in learning is different.
- Every situation is different.

Addressing difficulties is a question of problem-solving:

- Find out about the learner and the expectations of the particular curriculum area.
- Find out about the difficulties s/he experiences.
- Think about the barriers to learning in the classroom environment.
- Reflect on what will best address those barriers to help the learner to achieve in the classroom.

The extent to which children qualify under the legal definition as children 'with special educational needs' depends to a large extent on the policies and resources within their local authorities (LAs) and educational settings as well as on the wording of particular Education Acts. In the next chapter we look at teachers' current legal responsibilities in teaching all children, including those identified as having special educational needs, set against the context of a historical perspective on special education.

2 A historical perspective and the current legal position

Questions addressed in this chapter

What is the historical background to special educational provision?

What is the law relating to education within which schools are currently required to operate?

What interpretations of 'special' and 'different' are associated with current legal definitions?

What are the four areas of 'need' that are defined in the *Special Educational Needs Code of Practice* (DfES 2001)?

What is good practice in responding to students' learning needs in schools?

Introduction

Why some students fail to make good progress in their learning can be explained in a range of ways, for example:

- deficiency in learning and behaviour;
- the influence of social factors, such as family poverty and unemployment or in cultural differences between family and school in understandings and expectations;
- inappropriate teaching methods or texts, or inadequate school resources.

These days 'learning difficulty' is probably most commonly spoken about in schools as a general, overall, global 'difficulty in learning', a slowness to grasp new concepts and ideas.

However, there are other, less obvious, interpretations of this term in law. Learning difficulty and '*special* educational need' are, in law, not synonymous.

Development of the 'special' education sector for the few: a historical perspective

The way in which educational provision is currently organized is a product both of its own history and of the values, beliefs and political ideology of our society. In the current system, most students are expected to be able to cope with the curriculum offered in mainstream schools. The inclusion of all students in mainstream schools wherever possible is now enshrined in public policy in the UK and in many other countries.

Questions for reflection

How can we provide an education that takes account of the 'sameness' of all students and, at the same time, pays clear and respectful regard to 'difference' and 'diversity' among individuals (Norwich 1996)?

How can education policy-makers cope with this fundamental dilemma?

Focusing on difference can lead to discrimination. At the same time, failing to acknowledge difference can be seen as disrespectful to life experiences and may mean that individual learning needs are ignored.

Warnock (1978) outlines the stages at which special schools were introduced for the various groups of students seen as 'different' and the kind of education seen as appropriate at various times. The structure of special education that developed grew out of voluntary enterprise. The first 'special' schools were founded at a time when child labour was the norm in society; thus these schools were intended to be solely vocational. The first groups for whom special schools were founded were the blind and the deaf. Then came schools for students with a physical disability, then schools for 'mentally handicapped' students and, finally, special schools for the 'maladjusted' and for those having speech impairments.

Compulsory education for (almost) all

In England and Wales the Elementary Education Act of 1870 marked the beginning of compulsory state education. Subsequent education laws expanded the system. The view of who was entitled to schooling also expanded. Consequently, there was pressure on schools to evolve as institutions capable of educating all students. After the 1870 Act made attendance at school compulsory, the question of what to do with children who made little or no progress and whose presence in the classroom was felt to be holding others back became important. Local education authorities responded to the challenge of compulsory education for (almost all) students by creating and maintaining a dual system of mainstream and special schooling, built upon the structure that already existed.

In 1896 a Committee on Defective and Epileptic Children issued its recommendations on the kind of provision thought to be appropriate for students identified as having some kind of cognitive difficulty, that is, difficulty in the area of language, problem-solving, memory and perception. Three groups were defined as coming under this general heading: 'feeble-minded', 'imbeciles' and 'idiots'. The changing nature of society and the education system within it has meant that many labels once attached to students ('imbeciles', 'feeble minded') have become unacceptable. However, in the nineteenth century there was a big difference in status and respect given to those groups of students who had been identified as 'different' from the rest. 'Idiots', 'feeble-minded' and 'imbeciles' should be separated off from the rest for the good of the majority. 'Imbeciles' were considered to need admission to an asylum, while the 'feeble-minded' were deemed in need of education in special schools or classes. 'Idiots' were not thought to be educable.

After the old school boards were abolished and the two-tier system of local education authorities for elementary and secondary education was established in 1902, as Warnock

(1978) comments, the statutory foundation of special provision continued broadly until the 1944 Act. Responsibility for special education was transferred to the authorities for elementary education, although the authorities dealing with secondary education also had the power to provide for blind, deaf, defective (the physically disabled) and epileptic children.

Developments in differentiated curricula for different learners

Towards the end of the Second World War, a coalition government reorganized the education system through the 1944 Education Act in England and Wales, in which they sought to develop a common national framework for the education of a diverse student population. The creators of the 1944 Act formalized a system of selection and segregation based on the results of assessment techniques that, they believed, could differentiate different 'types' of learners. They believed it was possible to design different curricula for different learning 'types' who could be educated in separate sectors of the system.

The educational hierarchy that developed was seen by many as both fair, because students appeared to be able to rise to a level which reflected their ability, and stable because it was based on psychometric testing which a lot of people at that time thought was reliable and valid. In mainstream, students took an examination at the age of 11 and were selected into different types of secondary school: grammar, technical and secondary modern. Within individual mainstream schools students were selected into ability 'streams'. Students might be directed into academic or work-related programmes according to measured 'ability'. Many students identified as having difficulties of various kinds were separated off into special schools.

In the area of special education, the 1944 Education Act, Sections 33 and 34, set out the legal basis for subsequent provision. The difficulties in learning experienced by students were seen as disabilities of body and mind, and intrinsic to the students themselves. These days we might call this way of viewing difficulties in learning as the 'medical' or 'deficit model'. It implies that students fail in schools because they have deficiencies in body and/or mind which should be treated rather like a disease. The Handicapped Students and School Health Service Regulations 1945 developed a new framework of 11 categories of students, including that of 'maladjusted' for the first time. Local education authorities (LEAs) were required to ascertain the needs of children in their areas for special educational treatment. Blind, deaf, epileptic, physically handicapped and aphasic children were deemed educable only in special schools; those children thought to have a severe mental handicap were perceived as ineducable and dealt with by health authorities.

During the years which followed, the two groups which continually expanded in numbers were those students considered 'educationally sub-normal' and those identified as 'maladjusted' (Warnock 1978). Student 'maladjustment' is an invention of the second part of the twentieth century. The 'maladjusted' label is one with a powerful history of stigma and association with objectionable personal and social characteristics (Galloway et al. 1994).

The case of 'maladjustment'

The term 'maladjusted' no longer exists as a formal descriptor of student behaviour in schools. Examination of the rise and demise of the category 'maladjustment' shows how the use of labels attaching problems to children can pervade the education system to suit the existing national context and, if used unwisely, can be damaging.

Until 1945 there was no formal category of 'maladjustment' enshrined in Ministry of Education regulations. It had its origins in the 1913 Mental Deficiency Act which created a category of moral imbeciles or defectives. Children who displayed emotionally disturbed or disruptive behaviour came to be associated with both mental defect and moral defect (Galloway et al. 1994: 110). Board of Education Reports in the 1920s, for example, identified 'unstable', 'nervous', 'difficult and maladjusted' children as in need of child guidance (Galloway et al. 1994: 112).

After 1945 all LEAs had a responsibility to establish special educational treatment in special or ordinary schools for students defined as 'maladjusted'. The concept was still relatively new when the Underwood Committee was set up in 1950 to enquire into 'maladjusted' students' medical, educational and social problems. The Underwood Report (1955: ch. 4, para. 96) lists six symptoms of 'maladjustment' requiring professional help from psychologists, child guidance clinics or doctors:

- nervous disorders, for example, fears, depression, apathy, excitability;
- habit disorders, for example, speech defects, sleep-walking, twitching and incontinence;
- behaviour disorders, for example, defiance, aggression, jealousy and stealing;
- organic disorders, for example, cerebral tumours;
- psychotic behaviour, for example, delusions, bizarre behaviour;
- educational and vocational difficulties, for example, inability to concentrate or keep jobs.

An overall definition proved difficult. There has never been a consensus on what defines 'problem behaviour', of the sort categorized by the term 'maladjusted'. As Galloway and Goodwin (1987, p. 32) comment: 'the common point to emerge from attempts to clarify behavioural disorders and types of maladjustment is that it is a ragbag term describing any kind of behaviour that teachers and parents find disturbing'.

'Maladjustment' was often used pragmatically to justify special educational provision for those students for whom segregation from peers has been seen as necessary. Invent the category, create the student. Between 1945 and 1960, the numbers of students classified as maladjusted rose from 0 to 1742. In 1979, Rutter's attempted to assess the prevalence of specific categories of difficulties in the school student population. Estimates of maladjustment in the child population varied across the country from 5 to 25 per cent. 'Most investigations have shown that between 5 per cent and 12 per cent of children are "maladjusted" or show some kind of psychiatric disorder (Underwood 1955), but rates of up to 25 per cent have occasionally been reported (Brandon 1961)' (Rutter et al. 1979: 178). Furlong (1985) notes that, by 1975, there were 13,000 students labelled as 'maladjusted'.

The term is no longer used. It has been replaced by descriptors such as 'emotional and behavioural difficulties' (EBD), first formally by Warnock (1978), or 'social, emotional and behavioural difficulties, (SEBD), which suffer from the same lack of clear definition as maladjusted but which still enables the removal of students from mainstream on occasions.

Education for all

The system initiated after 1944 seemed stable. However, as Clark et al. (1997) note, many commentators in education began to see that the system of selection into grammar, technical and secondary modern schools was not as fair as was first thought:

- Differing proportions of students were selected for each type of school in different areas of the country.
- Considerable doubt was increasingly thrown on the reliability and validity of the psychometric tests that were used to discriminate between children.
- There was obvious overlap between the learning needs of students in mainstream and special schools (Wearmouth 1986).
- Movement between school types was very difficult, regardless of the amount of progress made by individual students.

In addition, there was a growing concern for equality of opportunity and social cohesion in society at large. Some commented that the system was divisive and functioned to sustain the position of some already advantaged societal groups over others. For example, there was a disproportionate number of middle-class children in grammar schools (Douglas 1967; Hargreaves 1967).

The result of all this was, beginning in the 1960s and increasingly in the 1970s, the establishment of comprehensive schools in mainstream, the introduction of special classes and 'remedial' provision, and the integration of some children from special to mainstream schools. In the special sector, the 1970 Handicapped Children Education Act transferred responsibility for children with multiple and profound difficulties in learning from health to education authorities. For the first time, children seen as having severe cognitive disabilities were entitled to a school-based education.

Introduction of the concept of special educational needs

In 1978 a review of educational provision in Great Britain for children and young people who, up to that time, were considered 'handicapped by disabilities of body or mind' was published in the Warnock Report. It introduced a new concept of 'special educational needs' to replace the previous categorization of handicap. Prior to this report, a study by Rutter et al. (1970) had enquired into the incidence of difficulties in learning in the school population. The report from this study showed teachers' perceptions that, on average, 20 per cent of their students were experiencing difficulty of some kind. Since that time, the figure of 20 per cent has been used to estimate the number of children nationally who might experience difficulties. Of the total number of students, approximately 2 per cent are seen by policy-makers as likely to have difficulties which require additional or extra resources to be provided for them. This figure of 2 per cent is clearly useful to resource-providers, for example local education authorities, to estimate what proportion of their resources they are likely to have to set aside to support individual students' educational needs. However, it is an arbitrary figure, drawn from a count of students in special schools in 1944. The law, focusing as it does on individual need, gives no such figures for the incidence of children likely to need statutory assessment. However, LAs, whose duty it is to implement legislation, have used such government guidance to establish general criteria for assessment.

The 1981 Education Act attempted to translate the Warnock Report into legislation. The eleven categories of handicap were replaced with the view that:

- difficulties occur on a continuum;
- a 'special educational need' exists if a child has 'significantly greater difficulty in learning' than peers, or a disability that hinders him or her from using educational facilities normally available in the local school.

Local authorities were given responsibilities to identify needs which called for special provision, that is, provision in addition to that normally available in the school. Parents should be consulted about provision for their child, and could appeal against a local authority's decisions. All children should be educated in mainstream schools but with certain provisos:

- that their needs could be met there;
- that it was compatible with the education of other children and with the 'efficient use of resources'.

Differences in views

Locally and nationally there is a wide variety of conflicting goals being pursued by different pressure groups. For instance, many people within the deaf community feel that it is vital to their culture that their children go to their own schools. They want them to be allowed to learn within a signing environment which draws upon a rich heritage and sense of self-identity. Some organizations too, such as Barnados and Scope, run their own schools. In many local authorities, too, it is possible to find campaigns run by schools and parents to keep special schools open. Equally, organizations such as the Centre for Studies on Inclusive Education (CSIE), Parents for Inclusion, and the Alliance for Inclusion work to promote the closure of special school provision and the development of mainstream schools that are open to all. Similarly, it is possible to find individual parents and children involved in comparable battles. The press and the Internet are full of stories of people fighting to get their child into (or back into) a mainstream setting or fighting for them to be removed from the mainstream and placed in a special school.

Local and regional differences

Around the UK the different practices and policies of local education authorities (library boards, in Northern Ireland) as well as issues of ethnicity and socio-economic factors associated with the family, age and gender have resulted in very different levels and kinds of provision for students:

- in 2000 students in Wales were nearly twice as likely to have statements of SEN as in the numbers of students with 'Records of Need' (the equivalent of statements) in Scotland
- throughout the UK girls receive less SEN support
- middle-class children are more likely than working-class children to receive the label of dyslexia
- African Caribbean students are far more likely than their white peers to be labeled as having Emotional, Behavioural and Social Difficulties (EBSD).

(Open University 2005: 8)

There is enormous variation in the development of policy and funding priorities.

- some LAs ration provision and define special educational needs according to available resources;
- some LAs support inclusive schools on the one hand, others special schools and Pupil Referral Units (PRUs).

There is no consistency across the UK and no requirement from government for consistency. In 2001, for example, in Manchester, a disabled student was more than seven times as likely to be placed in a segregated special school than a child in the London Borough of Newham, which has actively pursued a policy of inclusion since 1985 (DfES 2002).

Inclusive or special schools?

Decisions about whether inclusive mainstream, or special schools are more likely to meet children's learning needs are not always clear-cut.

Questions for reflection

Should the principle of inclusion in mainstream always be the overriding factor in considerations about children's placement?
Can you think of instances where mainstream schools are obviously not suitable for some students?

Two groups of students about whom teachers often express very serious concerns are those who experience profound and complex difficulties in learning who may also have acute physical disabilities, and those whose behaviour is perceived as very threatening and disruptive. It may be that some students are so vulnerable that the overriding consideration for them is a protective environment where their individual care needs can be considered together with their education. Whether the actual location is a mainstream or special site may be of less relevance than other considerations. The quality of the specialist facilities to support children's physical requirements, the level of understanding between students and staff and the effectiveness of the system of communication between home and school are very important irrespective of location. In relation to the second, the proviso that students 'with special educational needs' should be educated in mainstream schools provided that this is compatible with the education of peers is often seen as the justification for placement in an alternative location.

Parental views

In 1997 the government issued a Green Paper, *Excellence for All Children* (DfEE 1997), which took a strongly inclusive perspective. Over 3000 parents/carers responded to it. The ratio of parental responses favouring special as opposed to mainstream provision for students who have Statements of Special Educational Needs was 20:1. The sample of parents responding cannot be considered a cross-section of those whose children have a statement. Mostly these statements referred to educational needs arising from sensory impairments or multiple and complex difficulties in learning. Some of the reasons given for supporting special provision were:

- bullying in mainstream. Physically disabled children are often perceived to suffer at the hands of non-disabled peers. 'Children can be treated like, and feel like, a freak if they are integrated as individual disabled children' (letter from parent). One parent wrote: 'The worry caused when your child is being bullied or feeling depressed affects the whole family. Taking an Asperger child out of that environment greatly increases the quality of the child's life as well as the family';
- a perception that, although the same opportunities are often not available to students in special schools as those in mainstream, this does not mean these opportunities automatically become available if the child is moved into mainstream schooling. These opportunities must be made available within the special schools rather than transferring the children to mainstream;
- a perception of intolerance by children and staff;
- a perception that special schools constitute a 'reservoir of shared knowledge and expertise in teaching' of students with specialist needs;
- huge dissatisfaction with perception of levels of resourcing, staff training, awareness and understanding in mainstream.

The minority of parents wanting a mainstream education for their children had equally strong views on their children's rights to be respected as full members of society. In preparation for this they felt it most appropriate that they should be included in local mainstream schools with additional provision to meet their individual needs. In an interview (Wearmouth, unpublished manuscript) the mother of a blind child was very upset when it was suggested that her daughter should be transferred from mainstream to a special boarding school. She expressed her very firm opinion that her daughter who had been supported through local lower and middle schools by a very competent classroom assistant should continue to be educated in her local neighbourhood upper school. She had developed close friendships with peers living close by and attending the same school. Her mother saw the development of these relationships as an essential part of her child's education and was concerned that these friendships would weaken and her daughter would no longer be seen as an accepted member of the local community if she was forced into a special school.

Learning difficulties, disabilities and the law

In law, the learning difficulty creates the need. The need is 'special' if the provision required to satisfy that need is 'special'. A student might have a 'learning difficulty', for example, if he or she has a physical disability which makes it hard to move around the school to engage in the same learning activities as other students.

The law and special educational needs: the 1996 Education Act

In England and Wales, the aspect of law currently relating to special educational needs is Part 1V of the 1996 Education Act (Part 11 of the Education Order 1996 in Northern Ireland). Under the terms of this Act a child 'has *special educational needs* if he or she has a *learning difficulty* which calls for *special educational provision* to be made for him or her'. That is, a child only has 'special educational needs' when special provision is required to meet them: learning difficulties do not in themselves constitute such a need.

In understanding the legal definition of SEN fully, we need to understand what is meant by 'learning difficulty'. In the parts of the UK governed by Education Acts passed by Parliament in London, a child has a learning difficulty if:

   a)   he has a significantly greater difficulty in learning than the majority of children of his age,
   b)   he has a disability which either prevents or hinders him from making use of educational facilities of a kind generally provided for children of his age in schools within the area of the local education authority.

(Education Act 1996: S. 312; DENI 1998: para. 1.4)

In law, then, the learning difficulty creates the need. The need is 'special' if the provision required to satisfy that need is 'special'. A student might have a 'learning difficulty', for example, if he or she has a physical disability which makes it hard to move around the school to engage in the same learning activities as other students.

This way of defining a learning difficulty raises a number of questions. Included in them are:

- how to measure 'significantly greater difficulty in learning';
- how to compare one student to the majority. Comparing individuals against what we feel most people at that age should be learning and the way they should be learning it is bound to lead to mistakes, leaving some children without support and others with support that is unnecessary;
- how to gauge the contexts in which a difficulty becomes significant, for example whether remembering names is difficult only in examinations, or in everyday learning situations also;
- what is meant by a general level of provision. Some schools have space for particular sporting activities, others do not, for example. All teaching staff tend to adapt their classrooms to suit their way of working.

The majority of those who might be defined as having learning difficulties will experience difficulties of a mild nature. Whether they are identified as needing additional support is very variable in different parts of the country. It is not unusual for schools to use formal curriculum attainment levels as a general marker in an attempt to identify children with learning difficulties or disabilities. In England, for example, practitioners will often identify someone as having learning difficulties if they are working two or more National Curriculum levels below the majority of their age group. The danger here is that this allows assessment designed for a different purpose to validate decisions which affect provision and children's learning. Inevitably, whatever system is used to define students' needs, the professional, resource and policy judgements involved in the decision-making process will always leave room for inequality.

The second part of the definition in the 1996 Education Act refers to a 'disability' as causing learning difficulties. This means that, by law, a person with a visual impairment has a learning difficulty if the individual cannot access the same facilities as peers. This aspect of the definition of learning difficulty means that if LAs and schools provide appropriate learning opportunities, then no child would be hindered 'from making use of educational facilities generally provided' (Education Act 1996: S. 312; DENI 1998: para. 1.4), and therefore no child would have special educational needs.

Special Educational Needs and Disability Act 2001 (SENDA)

Another piece of legislation may well affect the teaching role in schools. This is the Special Educational Needs and Disability Act 2001 (SENDA). In 1981 the law said that all children should attend mainstream schools, provided three conditions were met:

- the child must receive the special provision that he or she requires;
- the child's placement must be compatible with the 'efficient education' of other children in the same school;
- the child's placement must be compatible with efficient use of available resources.

Although there was a legal duty to include children in mainstream schools, these three conditions meant that some LEAs were able to argue that some children should go to special schools, even if their parents wanted them to go to a mainstream school. This law has now been changed. The SENDA has taken away two of the conditions and this has increased children's rights to be educated in mainstream schools. The law now says that a child who has special educational needs and a statement of special educational needs must be educated in mainstream school unless this would be incompatible with:

- the wishes of the child's parents;
- the provision of efficient education of other children.

Children described in law as having 'special educational needs' have been given stronger rights to a place in a mainstream school, making it unlawful for schools and LEAs to discriminate against disabled students, particularly in relation to admission arrangements and the educational provision in school. The SENDA gives parents (not children) the right of appeal to the Special Educational Needs and Disability Tribunal, if they feel their child has suffered discrimination. Parents have a right to say where they want their child to go to school, but they do not have the right to insist on their own choice of school.

The Disability Discrimination Act (DDA) 2005

One other piece of legislation, the DDA (2005), is pertinent to the work of teachers in classrooms. In this Act the definition of disability in Section 1 says:

A disabled person has a physical or mental disability which has an effect on their ability to carry out normal day-to-day activities The effect must be:

- substantial (that is more than a minor or trivial) and
- adverse and
- long term (has lasted or is likely to last at least a year or for the rest of the life of the person affected)

The DDA:

- stresses planned approaches to eliminating discrimination and improving access;
- is nationwide (including private education) – duties on schools and local authorities;
- places a duty on public bodies to promote disability equality.

Responding to individual needs

When a teacher is seriously concerned about the progress made by a child in a classroom, it is very important to be aware of the process that should be followed to maintain the child's access to education.

The Code of Practice

In 1994, the government published a *Code of Practice for the Identification and Assessment of Special Educational Needs* (DfE 1994). This was designed to offer 'statutory guidance' to schools in England and Wales to address issues of how to provide appropriate support to those with learning difficulties. A similar publication was produced later in Northern Ireland (DENI 1998).

In 2001, a revised *Special Educational Needs Code of Practice* (DfES 2001; National Assembly of Wales 2004) was implemented, offering statutory guidance to LEAs, governing bodies and schools. The guidance suggests that children's learning needs may fall generally into one of four areas:

> Children will have their needs and requirements which may fall into at least one of four areas. Many children will have inter-related needs. The impact of these combinations on the child's ability to function, learn and succeed should be taken into account. The areas of need are:
>
> - communication and interaction
> - cognition and learning
> - behaviour, emotional and social development
> - sensory and/or physical
>
> (DfES 2001: 74)

A list of the types of support appropriate to each area is outlined in the code. We return to this in Chapter 3.

The Code of Practice makes the assumption that teachers will offer differentiated learning opportunities, and that 'the culture, practice, management and deployment of resources in a school or setting are designed to ensure all children's needs are met (DfES 2001: para.1:6, 2). If, however, a child fails to make adequate progress then additional or different action should be taken.

> Adequate progress can be defined in a number of ways. It might, for instance, be progress which:
>
> - closes the attainment gap between the child and their peers;
> - is similar to that of peers starting from the same attainment base-line, but less than that of the majority of peers;
> - matches or betters the child's previous rate of progress;
> - ensures access to the full curriculum;
> - demonstrates an improvement in self-help, social or personal skills;
> - demonstrates improvements in the child's behaviour;
> - prevents the attainment gap growing wider.
>
> (DfES 2001: para. 4.14)

The 2001 Code of Practice recommends a graduated approach to individualized interventions through provision at School Action or School Action Plus. School Action begins when a class teacher, special educational needs co-ordinator or teaching assistant identifies a child as having special educational needs and requiring individual provision. This provision should be additional to or different from an adapted, or differentiated curriculum and strategies that are usually provided in the class. The school receives no additional funding for the child. School Action is likely to involve:

- consultation between the class teacher, the school's SENCO and the parents;
- collation of information already available about the child's progress, and possibly collection of more information;
- closer attention to the child's programme of work in the classroom, and closer monitoring of progress.

School Action Plus is for children who are likely to need support from specialists outside the school. The most likely sources of advice and support are a teacher from the LA's special needs support service, and an educational psychologist. Others might include:

- speech therapists;
- physiotherapists;
- occupational therapists;
- the school nurse;
- health visitors;
- doctors, especially the school doctor and the child's general practitioner (GP);
- education welfare officers;

- social workers;
- member of the local child guidance or family guidance team;
- the special needs adviser or inspector;
- peripatetic teachers for children with physical or visual disabilities or hearing impairments.

School Action and School Action Plus are the responsibility of the school. All class teachers are expected to:

- know which children have been identified at School Action and School Action Plus;
- contribute information about children's progress at each stage;
- be aware of the content of children's individual education plans (IEPs) at School Action and School Action Plus;
- take a leading role in monitoring and recording of children's progress;
- work with the school's SENCO at School Action and School Action Plus and beyond;
- work with professionals from outside the school.

After the stage of School Action Plus, a request for a statutory assessment might be made. If so, the process is handled by the school and the LA, and may result in a Statement of Special Educational Needs that outlines special educational provision determined by the LA.

Statutory assessment of special educational needs

Of the large number of children that schools identify as having special educational needs, a small proportion are the subject of a Statement of Special Educational Need. This is a legal document and provisions specified on it are mandatory. Around 2–3 per cent of all children of school age have a statement.

Children with such statements tend to be those who have longer-term or more severe disabilities or difficulties. They are usually made the subject of a Statement of Special Educational Need for one of two reasons:

- they need guaranteed access to special resources and expertise, a special curriculum, or an environment with higher than normal staff support;
- their parents, or the professionals responsible for them, want them to attend a special school, or some other form of special provision such as a resource base in a mainstream school.

By law a statement has to describe the child's special educational needs, and the special educational provision required to meet those needs. This must include:

- the objectives of the special provision;
- the resources that will be provided;
- how the child's progress will be monitored;

- the name of the school that the child will go to;
- any 'non-educational' needs and provision that have been identified. (These might include services to meet the child's medical needs.)

The special provision listed must be provided by law, and the school named must admit the child. Chapter 7, the 'Statutory assessment of special educational needs' in the 2001 *Code of Practice* outlines the assessment and identification process that is required. The LA has to involve parents at many points, and parents have a number of legal rights. The LA must also collect evidence and advice from a number of professionals, including the child's head teacher, a doctor and an educational psychologist.

The Special Educational Needs Co-ordinator

The role of the SENCO (Table 2.1) developed in response to the Education Act 1981.

Table 2.1 The SENCO's responsibilities

In pre-school settings (DfES 2001: para. 4.15)	In primary and secondary schools (DfES 2001: paras 5.32; 6.35)
<ul><li>ensuring liaison with parents and other professionals in respect of children with special educational needs</li><li>advising and supporting other practitioners in the setting</li><li>ensuring the appropriate Individual Education Plans are in place</li><li>ensuring that relevant background information about individual children with special educational needs is collected, recorded and updated</li></ul>	<ul><li>overseeing the day-to-day operation of the school's SEN policy</li><li>co-ordinating provision for students with special educational needs</li><li>liaising with and advising fellow teachers</li><li>managing the SEN team of teachers and learning support assistants</li><li>overseeing the records on all students with special educational needs</li><li>contributing to the in-service training of staff</li><li>liaising with parents of children with special educational needs</li><li>liaising with external agencies including the LEA's support and educational psychology services, health and social service and voluntary bodies</li></ul>

The role of the SENCO in schools varies widely across the country. The role may be allocated to members of the school senior management team, class teachers or teaching assistants (TAs). Special needs co-ordinators may have responsibilities both at the level of the individual children and the whole school. They may take charge of budgeting, resource allocation, timetabling and other managerial and administrative roles. They may also work with individual students, as well as advising, appraising and training staff, and liaising with outside agencies, professionals and parents.

Individual education plans

Current legislation and guidance refers to an individual education plan for recording the nature of a student's difficulties and how they are going to be addressed. The plan for a student might include adaptations to normal classroom activities, or a special programme of individual work for the child, or both. The IEP also includes criteria for judging success, a section for recording outcomes and a date for reviewing the plan. The student's progress can then be reviewed regularly to see if the aims of the IEP are being achieved. It is expected that both parents and students will be actively involved in creating and assessing the effectiveness of the IEP.

A number of criticisms have been levelled at IEPs:

- They can be too bureaucratic.
- They may include targets for the child which can be demotivating if focused only on weaknesses that the student should attempt to overcome.
- Sometimes targets are written by teachers or TAs without any consultation with the individual learner and may not be appropriate or intelligible to the student.
- They may focus only on the student and not take account of the learning environment or the factors that may be impacting on the child's learning or contributing to his or her difficulties.

However, IEPs can also be used very effectively in the process of analysing a student's needs and planning the next steps in a student's learning programme. This process should be negotiated between all those working with a student as well as the student him/herself so that it will be meaningful and have a direct impact on ways of thinking and working.

Summary

Over the years, the ways in which differences between people have been conceptualized, notions of entitlements and human rights have developed, and the focus of, and on, education itself has altered, have all contributed to the complexity and changing nature of the field of special educational needs.

The term used in legislation since 1983, 'special educational needs', is part of the discourse which, according to Salmon (1998) and Corbett (1996), for example, suggests a deficit model. At the same time we must recognize, along with the Disability Movement, that failing to acknowledge difference can be counter-productive to the learning needs of a student and be interpreted as disrespectful to that person's life experiences. Whatever an individual's view, parents, teachers and other professionals in education have to conform to aspects of the official definitions when engaged on formal processes under the Act such as assessment and statementing.

SECTION II

APPROACHES TO ASSESSMENT, PLANNING, TEACHING AND LEARNING

As noted in Section I, the term 'special educational needs' became widely used after the publication of what is commonly known as the Warnock Report (1978). Until then, special education had largely been treated as the province of specialist professionals – especially doctors and educational psychologists – and special schools. One of the Warnock Report's most important conclusions was that we should broaden our idea of who might experience special educational needs, to include any student who might need: 'additional help, wherever it is provided and whether on a full or part-time basis, by which students may be helped to overcome educational difficulties, however they are caused' (1978: 46).

Most students who might be identified as having special educational needs will experience difficulties of a mild nature. However, in the 1996 Education Act there is reference also to a 'disability' as causing learning difficulties. This means that, by law, a person with a physical, for example visual, impairment has a learning difficulty if the individual cannot access the same facilities as peers. Subsequently, legislation to address discrimination as a result of disability increased awareness of individual students' needs in schools. Inevitably, whatever system is used to define a student's needs individual judgements will also be made as a result of personal professional experience, availability of resources and local and national policy at the time the decision is taken, and this will always leave room for differences of opinion.

Section II looks first at the four broad areas of need outlined in the *Special Educational Needs Code of Practice* (DfES 2001) together with general strategies appropriate to each. Chapter 4 then addresses issues of assessment and planning, moves from informal approaches to formal, and takes account of student, peer and family views and experiences, as well as teachers' own perspectives on students' learning.

All teachers are bound, at some time or another, to come across young people in their classrooms who experience particular difficulties in the area of literacy and numeracy, and/or whose behaviour is seen as problematic in some way. Chapter 5 therefore focuses on the difficulties that may be experienced in literacy and offers a range of clear, straightforward strategies for intervention. Chapter 6 takes a similar approach to the experience of difficulties in numeracy. Chapter 7 concludes Section II with a discussion of ways to understand problematic behaviour and describes positive responses to this.

3 Overview of approaches to four areas of need

Questions addressed in this chapter

How can we include all students in classroom activities?

What are the four areas of need outlined in the *Special Education Needs Code of Practice* (DfES 2001)?

How can we understand these four areas of need?

What might be some of the ways of addressing these needs?

Introduction

The 2001 Code of Practice (DfES 2001: para. 7:52) recommends that formal assessment and subsequent provision should address four 'areas of need' which are described in general terms as:

- communication and interaction. 'The range of difficulties will encompass students and young people with speech and language delay, impairments and disorders, specific learning difficulties, such as dyslexia and dyspraxia, hearing impairment and those who demonstrate features within the autistic spectrum; they may also apply to some children and young people with moderate, severe or profound learning difficulties. The range of need will include those for whom language and communication difficulties are the result of permanent sensory or physical impairment' (para. 7:55).
- cognition and learning. 'Children who demonstrate features of moderate, severe or profound learning difficulties or specific learning difficulties, such as dyslexia or dyspraxia, require specific programmes to aid progress in cognition and learning. Such requirements may also apply to some extent to children with physical and sensory impairments and those on the autistic spectrum. Some of these children may have associated sensory, physical and behavioural difficulties that compound their need' (para 7:58);
- behaviour, emotional and social development. 'Children and young people who demonstrate features of emotional and behavioural difficulties, who are withdrawn or isolated, disruptive and disturbing, hyperactive and lack concentration; those with immature social skills; and those presenting challenging behaviours arising from other complex special needs, may require help or counselling . . .' (para. 7:60);
- sensory and/or physical needs. 'There is a wide spectrum of sensory, multi-

sensory and physical difficulties. The sensory range extends from profound and permanent deafness or visual impairment through to lesser levels of loss, which may only be temporary. Physical impairments may arise from physical, neurological or metabolic causes that only require appropriate access to educational facilities and equipment; others may lead to more complex learning and social needs; a few children will have multi-sensory difficulties some with associated physical difficulties. For some children the inability to take part fully in school life causes significant emotional stress or physical fatigue' (para. 7:62).

It is clear that there is a lot of overlap between these areas. For example, in terms of communication and interaction, lack of facility with receptive and expressive language has important implications for cognition and learning. There are a number of teaching approaches seen as appropriate for addressing the learning needs of students who experience difficulties either in communication and interaction or in cognition and learning that are common to both areas:

- flexible teaching arrangements;
- help in/with ... language;
- help ... in acquiring literacy skills;
- help in organising ... help with organisational skills.

(DfES 2001: paras 7:56 and 7:58)

Inclusion in mainstream schools

Question for reflection

How can we increase the participation of all students in the cultures, curricula and communities of schools, particularly those students at risk of being marginalized?

Teachers and schools are expected to implement the National Curriculum inclusion statement (QCA 2000). The inclusion statement sets out three principles:

- setting suitable learning challenges;
- responding to students' diverse learning needs;
- overcoming potential barriers to learning and assessment for individuals and groups of students.

Inclusive teaching means:

- adjusting learning objectives to suit individual students' needs. Not every student is expected to be working on the same learning objectives as every other student in the class;
- teaching that draws on a variety of approaches (open and closed tasks, short and long tasks, visual, auditory or kinaesthetic learning) matched to the needs of individuals;

- understanding that the learning context itself can support, or hinder, learning. For example, science laboratories with high benches and stools, or art rooms with little rooms between tables, chairs and easels may be very difficult for students with restricted movement. The acoustic environment is important for the attainment of all students, but particularly for those who experience auditory difficulties.

Some students who experience difficulties in learning can work on the same learning objectives as others in the class, as long as the teacher plans access strategies to address the barriers to learning experienced by the individual student. For example, a teacher might build in access strategies (such as alternatives to written recording, and/or provision of appropriate age and culturally related resources). Disability legislation, as described in a previous chapter, calls these and other modifications to learning and teaching programmes 'reasonable adjustments'. For example, if a barrier to a mathematics lesson on problem-solving is a dyslexic student's lack of fluent knowledge of number facts, s/he may need to use a calculator. If, however, the barrier is a motor co-ordination difficulty that prevents accurate drawing of shapes and graphs, s/he may need the use of appropriate software which is programmed to draw shapes and graphs. If it is difficulty with use of abstract symbols s/he may benefit from the use of concrete materials of some kind. Teachers will need to try out ideas and assess the results to develop their own practice. Strategies that do not result in improved learning and/or behaviour can be seen as experiments leading teachers towards solutions, not failures.

Creating a positive learning environment for all

Questions for reflection

In your opinion:

- What kind of difficulties in learning might children, newly coping with life in school, experience in any one of the four areas of need?
- How might we induct these children into the practices of a school, for example literacy, in the early years?

Recent research confirms that strategies recommended for particular special educational needs are useful for most, if not all students (Lewis and Norwich 2000). It might therefore be sensible for newly qualified teachers to concentrate at first on strategies which improve the learning environment and increase the range of teaching strategies rather than assuming that something different has to be organized for every individual.

Well-chosen stories told in the classroom by the teacher can 'provide a valuable set of "recipes" for coping with school literacy practices, through acting as unique "scaffolds" to children's learning in a way that conversation cannot' (Gregory 1996: 142). As Gregory (1996: 124–5) notes, you might introduce beginning readers to story-reading sessions by explicitly modelling what fluent readers do:

- Set the context for the story by discussing the place, one or more of the characters and the main theme, and relate these to real life and/or the children's lives.
- Reading the story slowly, clearly, with 'lively intonation' and without interruption.
- Discuss the story and relate the themes and talk about the characters.
- Reread the story if appropriate.

The same principles apply when choosing chapters for reading in classrooms that include children who experience the range of difficulties outlined above. Chapters should include 'memorable stories and texts from all times and places', perhaps containing 'universal truths, values and morals, fear and security' which pertains to students of all levels and ages (Gregory 1996: 122).

Inducting children into story-reading

As Gregory (1996, p 142) describes story-telling to children as bathing them 'in a magic where story and text intertwine and understanding comes somewhere in-between'. Gregory compares two examples of chapters found in infant and primary classrooms to show why some texts are very popular with children even if, at first glance, they might seem complex. The first, 'The Clay Flute' by Mats Rehnman, is set in the Arabian desert and tells the story of a poor boy who suffers many misfortunes but finally 'makes good':

- It portrays universal values of courage and kindness. Children may identify with the little grey monkey or the kind child (two characters in the story).
- It shows the victory of good over evil.
- It shows a world far from present reality, yet with everyday feelings children may experience anywhere.
- Although the language is difficult, it is rich in imagery and uses many words which might be personal 'key words' for children (witch, horrible, grab, scream, kiss, tear, sword, heart, etc).
- The story moves purposefully and clearly.
- The illustrations are inspiring.

(Gregory 1996: 120)

The second is, superficially, simpler: 'Don't Blame Me!' by Paul Rogers. It is intended to make children laugh as it tells the tale of a series of events triggered off by paint from a pub sign dripping on to a man's suit. Gregory notes that the story does not hold the attention of those new to the culture because:

- It is very culture-specific (the pub ... etc)
- The language is very colloquial and the humour rests upon understanding the finer nuances of the language. There is very little sign of any really important words which might form children's personal 'key words'.

- It relies upon humour itself for success as the story is not memorable, nor does it follow a clear path of events.
- The illustrations are not clear from a distance . . .

(1996: 121)

Classroom grouping for effective learning

Student grouping has for a long time been the focus of considerable controversy in schools

Questions for reflection

What, in your experience, are the advantages and disadvantages of mixed attainment teaching for all students?
Do you think grouping by attainment is ever justifiable? If so, when?

Summaries of the evidence about student grouping, for example Ireson and Hallam (1999) and Ireson et al. (2001; 2002) suggest:

- Students should remain in mixed ability classes for the greater part of the time, their point of identification being with a mixed ability class.
- Structured ability grouping should be adopted only where teaching and learning in the subject domain depends on students having shared prior knowledge and levels of attainment.
- To reduce stigmatization, schools should enable greater flexibility of movement between groups and reduce the extent of differentiation between sets.
- Parallel groupings should be adopted, for example five parallel sets rather than ten differentiated sets.
- Progress should be assessed frequently, followed by reassignment of different groups where appropriate.
- Teachers should have high expectations of students in the lower sets.

Mixed ability teaching can:

- provide a means of offering equal opportunities;
- address the negative social consequences of structured ability grouping by encouraging co-operative behaviour and social integration;
- provide positive role models for less able students;
- promote good relations between students;
- enhance student/teacher interactions;
- reduce some of the competition;
- reduce some of the competition engendered by structured grouping.

Conceptualizing a differentiated approach

Overall, there is no golden formula for addressing the special learning needs of every student who experiences each kind of difficulty. As already noted in a previous chapter, there are a number of general considerations in relation to addressing individual students' special educational needs, for example:

- Every student who experiences difficulties in learning is different.
- Every situation is different.

Addressing difficulties is a question of problem-solving:

- Find out about the learner.
- Find out about the difficulties s/he experiences.
- Think about the requirements of the particular curriculum area.
- Barriers to learning in the classroom environment and in the particular curriculum area.
- Reflect on what will best address those barriers to help the learner to achieve in the classroom.

Communication, language and cognition

Students with language impairment
Difficulties in the area of language acquisition may involve receptive (that is, limitations in comprehending what is said) or expressive (that is, difficulty in putting thoughts coherently into words) language impairments. The first of these is less obvious than the second and can create barriers to learning if overlooked. It is really important for teachers to get to know their students very well and to check carefully that what has been said is properly understood.

Addressing receptive language difficulties

When taking account of children's difficulties in receptive language, teachers might consider:

- not always speaking in terms that are immediately understood by students or their language will never develop. Where children experience difficulties with understanding spoken language, they will often get the gist from non-verbal clues;
- ensuring, whenever possible, that students who have a difficulty in language should have direct experience of a concept before it is used. Children learn by doing first;
- allowing students plenty of time before expecting a response. With some, a teacher may wish to explain that s/he will be asking them a question in a minute or so;
- organizing transitions between different activities and different parts of the classroom and school carefully. They should use visual timetables and schedules, prepare students by telling them when and where they are going to move, and go through the transition points in the day with them first thing. Support staff can make a great contribution to this;

- ensuring students know they are being spoken to, and not posing a question in the middle of a string of less relevant talk;
- not assuming one-to-one listening will generalize to listening to whole class instruction or during assembly. Specific teaching may be needed (adapted from Primary National Strategy 2005).

In the classroom, teachers might keep a small audio recorder in a pocket, record all or part of a lesson and check how often:

- they speak during the lesson;
- they use an idea or comment contributed by a student;
- they explain something several different ways if they have not been understood the first time;
- they repeat what students say in discussion or question and answer sessions (in any case, others in the class may not have heard).

To ensure that all students understand what is said, teachers should check that:

- they speak calmly and evenly, and their faces are clearly visible;
- they use visual aids and cues to the topics being discussed;
- the student is appropriately placed to hear and see.

It might be that a trusted colleague is willing to observe a lesson or two and offer feedback.

Expressive language

Students who experience difficulty in expressing themselves need frequent opportunities for exploratory talk in every area of the curriculum in order to put new information and ideas into their own words and link subject matter to what they already know.

Supporting the development of oral language

Strategies that facilitate oral language development might include:

- exploratory talk in small groups;
- oral reports following group discussion;
- problem-solving conducted orally;
- explanations of how something is made, or how and why things happen;
- announcements read by students;
- dramatization and role-playing;
- simulation games;
- interviews (live or taped);
- group discussion where, for example, students choose or are given a scenario such as bullying; role play the situation and then brainstorm and discuss alternative ways of resolving the conflict.

To check opportunities for student teachers might reflect on how often:

- they really listen to what a student says;

- they ask a question I'm really interested in;
- students speak in lessons;
- students speak voluntarily on the topic under discussion;
- there is an opportunity for small group work and discussion.

Coping with written text

It is highly likely that any teacher will meet students who experience difficulties in literacy in classes at some time or another. Having the ability to handle written text with confidence is a key part of coping with the day-to-day expectations of classroom life. Commonly, difficulties in literacy may include barriers experienced in all or any of reading comprehension, reading accuracy, spelling and written expression. Sometimes students are identified as experiencing specific difficulties in literacy of a dyslexic nature.

Reading comprehension

First, it is important to be able to judge the level of difficulty of any text used in class. For this, in general terms, it is important to consider carefully (Lunzer and Gardner 1979):

- the interest level of the text and/or prior knowledge of the subject matter. If students are interested in, or already understand, what they are reading, they can cope with more difficult text;
- sentence length and complexity, word length and familiarity;
- conciseness of explanation of concepts. More students can understand higher level concepts if ideas are expanded and explained step by step.

Strategies for developing reading comprehension

Teachers might foster students' reading comprehension by:

- adding pictures, subheadings and summaries to the text;
- teaching students to take notes, underline key passages or write summaries;
- teaching students to think consciously about the text as they read: whether it fits in with what they already know, whether they have understood it, or what questions they might ask themselves about the meaning of a text as they read it through;
- shortening the amount read before questions are raised. This may mean a page-by-page reading, or even a paragraph by paragraph reading. Close consideration must be given to the constitution of student groups in this case. As students pay more attention to the messages conveyed by text the amount of text read before questions are asked can be lengthened;
- group reading, where students share the reading of a book and meet to discuss topics such as: how did the main character feel? Has anything like this ever happened to you? What happens next?
- use of illustrations. Students can be referred to the appropriate page to draw pictures of the setting, the characters, a plan or a map of the area, or look through magazines to find pictures of people to represent the characters;
- use of Cloze to make sure that students are reading for meaning. Every fifth word or so is

---

deleted from the text, and the student is asked to fill in the gaps with a suitable, meaningful word;

- teaching students to scan the text before reading in depth, including focusing on pictures, diagrams, captions, subheadings and highlighted words.

A number of other very useful strategies for developing comprehension are discussed in Chapter 5.

Often students need to gain more experience in reading in order to increase word identification, knowledge of letter/sound combinations and use of contextual information and inference. Excellent ways in which to develop these skills and the related writing skills of language structure, organization of thought and creative writing are:

- following the text with the eyes while listening to the recording (which has to be word perfect);
- 'paired reading' or 'reading buddies'.

Reading accuracy and spelling

Some students experience a particular difficulty in reading individual words accurately, associating sounds and alphabetic symbols in words, in ordering letters correctly or in letter orientation. In order to reduce errors, and the resulting corrective feedback from teachers, students may limit themselves to writing short, simple, minimal sentences or phrases, so that their writing is of little interest or stimulation to a reader. This is particularly likely if the feedback provided from teachers for writing is contingent only on surface features such as spelling. Whichever subject is taught, the teacher will need to show students *how* to learn to spell words.

Whatever the attitudes of individual teachers might be to the teaching of spelling, there are some adults at least who failed to learn to spell well at school and who come to regret this later in life: ... 'a "public audience" will always make harsh judgements about poor spelling ... good spelling is a vital component of communication through writing' (Rees and the Education Department of Western Australia 2001: 18). One way to strengthen word recognition and spelling is to adopt a multi-sensory approach to teaching, which emphasizes the spelling of the whole word. Students should be encouraged to use every sense – auditory, visual, kinaesthetic and tactile – simultaneously in quick succession to reinforce their learning of new skills. For example, when learning new spellings, students might look at a word, say it out loud, say the letters in the word out loud while simultaneously writing them down, draw the letters on a rough surface while saying them out loud, and so on.

A number of other strategies for encouraging the development of students' spelling skills are included in Chapter 5.

Writing

Learners who experience problems in expressing themselves in writing may often benefit from structured support to help them develop skills for different types of writing. Allowing a student to dictate text onto an audio recorder and then transcribing it for him/her will help the student to get thoughts and ideas down on paper. Alternatively the student can be allowed to dictate text while the teacher/older student/parent scribes.

There is further detailed discussion of the issues involved with addressing students' difficulties in producing written text and ways of addressing these in Chapter 5.

Marking students' work

In school there may be considerable difference of opinion about the extent to which corrections should be made to a script which contains very many mistakes. On the one hand, it can be argued that, for some students, repeatedly receiving back scripts covered with marks indicating errors is very demoralizing. On the other, there has to be a rational, structured approach to ensuring that students make progress in recognizing mistakes and learning how to correct them. Teachers may feel it is appropriate to encourage students to proofread their own, or peers', work before handing it in, and/or, perhaps, to correct only words or sentence structure with which they feel students should already be familiar. Before deciding how to mark individual students' written work, teachers new to a school would be well advised to find out about the school's marking policy.

Dyslexia and literacy difficulties

The most common theory underpinning dyslexic-type literacy difficulty is that it results from a phonological deficit (Snowling 2000). Phonological awareness is both the explicit knowledge that words are made up of sounds and the ability to manipulate those sounds. The ability to develop phonological awareness is innate but development is not spontaneous. Phonological awareness develops over time and is helped by language games and nursery rhymes. According to phonological deficit theory, dyslexic people are specifically impaired in their ability to detect and process speech sounds.

In our present state of knowledge it does not appear to be helpful for teachers to think of some of their students as 'dyslexics' and of others as ordinary poor readers. The research (Rice and Brooks 2004) does not indicate that 'dyslexics' and 'ordinary poor readers' should be taught by different methods. The methods promoted as specialist interventions for dyslexic people are well suited for mainstream teaching, which is how they originated. For example, dyslexic students often benefit from word-processing their scripts because:

- handwriting is eliminated;
- typing gives the writer a chance to think about what s/he is writing unlike handwriting, where established hand movements can produce mistakes;
- it is easier to identify mistakes on the screen;
- the text can be changed, moved around and corrected as often as necessary until the work is acceptable;
- drafting and correcting is less laborious and the printed copy can be corrected away from the machine by the student or the teacher and improved versions created without difficulty;
- everything can be saved and reused easily, allowing work to be done in small amounts;
- presentation is improved, when the final version is printed it is legible and looks good;

- spellcheckers can remove much of the inhibition about writing that comes from poor spelling, as well as the stigma that spelling mistakes incur;
- there are advantages in programmes that offer different styles and sizes of fonts and text display. These can encourage students to think about ways in which the presentation can be adapted to suit the purpose of the writing;
- optical comfort is important. A choice of screen colours can be helpful to students;
- word-processing helps students to overcome their problems with organizing ideas and structuring written work;
- the appearance of the work improves greatly and the students no longer have to concentrate on the physical skill of handwriting;
- spelling often improves when students see the image on the screen;
- the motivational value of computer-assisted learning increases the time that students are willing to practise academic skills so that mastery learning can take place.

Other non-dyslexic students who experience difficulties in literacy acquisition and expression also often benefit from word-processing their work.

'Metacognitive' strategies can help dyslexic and other students to think about their own thinking processes so that those who experience difficulty in particular areas of learning can develop alternative routes to accessing these areas. 'Mind-mapping' is an example of one way to develop a structure for producing extended text. It assumes that the structure and content of the text will be of higher quality if the learner is encouraged first to produce a visual representation of all those areas to be covered in the text before beginning on the written task.

As we see in Chapter 8, there is a very wide range of software on the market which can support different approaches to literacy development. Many students will not become proficient without repetitive practice. Computer-supported instruction can make repetitive practice acceptable. For example programmes are available to encourage the acquisition of 'basic skills' such as phonics. On the other hand, accurate recordings of texts and 'talking word processors' can support a meaning-based approach to reading. Word processors with a spell-checking facility can help to build confidence in writing more extended prose.

Commonly, dyslexic students experience a number of difficulties in mathematics. These include:

- the learning of number bonds;
- the learning of multiplication tables;
- the understanding of concepts involving directionality. Time and spatial concepts can prove difficult;
- sequencing activities;
- orientation. Confusion can arise through having to process different operations in different directions;
- spatial awareness;
- visual discrimination resulting in confusion of signs;

- mental arithmetic (mental manipulation of number/symbols in short-term memory).

When teaching mathematics, therefore, the principles of multi-sensory teaching (visual, auditory, tactile, kinaesthetic) which apply to language work also apply to the mathematics field; for example, introducing new mathematical concepts and processes using concrete materials, diagrams, pictures and verbal explanation, and then asking the student to explain the process, instructions and so on in his or her own words. Progress should be carefully monitored at each stage, checking that a particular concept has been thoroughly mastered and understood before moving on to the next step.

English as an additional language and special educational needs

The *Special Educational Needs Code of Practice* notes that the identification and assessment of the special educational needs of young people whose first language is not English requires particular care. Lack of competence in English cannot be equated with general difficulties in learning, or particular difficulties in language acquisition as understood in this code. Students learning English may say little or nothing for some time, but are learning nevertheless. Like other students, those learning English benefit from high-quality learning environments and may well not need an individual programme.

Having said this, we cannot assume that their language status is the only reason for students who learn English as an additional language to make slow progress. They may also experience general cognitive difficulties. This may be a very sensitive area that requires specialist help.

Difficulties in symbolic understanding

There are ways in which difficulties experienced by some students in the area of communication and interaction, more specifically language acquisition and use, overlap with those in the area of cognition and learning. As Grauberg (2002) notes, probably the most general feature that can be identified in children who experience difficulties such as these is weakness in understanding symbols. Sometimes children without a language impairment also share this difficulty – a difficulty in understanding and remembering that a symbol can 'stand for' something else, for example something concrete or an action. Some children may have a strong inclination to take things very literally, and this is something for a teacher to be aware of.

One way to conceptualize a clear approach to supporting the development of students who experience such difficulties is to consider Bruner's framework for the different modes of representation of reality used by humans as they develop their conceptual understanding of the world. Bruner (1996) outlines three modes:

- enactive, that works through action. We 'do' and then we understand and know. It is a mode that works without the need for verbal and/or written and/or physical symbols;
- iconic, that works through images that can stand for the physical object;
- symbolic, that is an abstract representation of something else.

To some extent movement through the modes is developmental, but it must be said that, as adults, we all habitually use all three modes. Children who experience language difficulties and difficulties in cognition are very likely to need much more time in absorbing concepts using concrete objects and the enactive mode of representation. Very great care must be taken in working out ways to support children's understanding by making clear links from one small step to the next.

Memory problems

There are a number of ways to conceptualize what happens in the human memory system. Often, memory is seen as having two distinctive parts: long-term memory and short-term or 'working' memory. Long-term memory is also often seen as consisting of two parts: knowing *that* (declarative or semantic memory), and knowing *how* (procedural memory). There is clearly a big difference between knowing a fact, for example a date, and knowing how to do something. Memory can be accessed through recall or through recognition. Of these, recognition is usually easier than recall, although if the context in which the initial learning occurred is very similar to the context in which recall is needed and there are strong memory cues, then recall can be easier.

Very poor memory is a problem for a few students. There are a number of common reasons for this:

- unclear grasp of the information in the first place;
- insufficient linking of the new information to previous knowledge;
- lack of differentiation of the new knowledge from what is already known, so that the new information interferes with the old.

Many students with short-term memory difficulties have:

- problems absorbing and recalling information;
- responding to and carrying out instructions within a busy classroom situation;
- copying from the blackboard as they are unable to memorize what they have seen and transpose it to the paper on the desk. As well as this they are required to rotate this visual image through 90 degrees from the vertical to the horizontal and to transpose the size of the letters involved.

All this has clear implications for students' initial learning. It makes sense, as Kirchner and Klatzky (1985) assert, to emphasize meaning and understanding rather than rote learning when students experience difficulties with memory so that they can begin from first principles. Knowing when and how to apply rules is clearly important, but there is a strong argument for asserting that knowing why should be established first.

Young children have to learn sequences of certain items relating to particular areas that are important for everyday living: letters of the alphabet, months of the year, days of the week and numbers, for example. There are many students who, even in secondary schools, cannot recite either the alphabet or the months of the year in the correct order. For some children it may be important to establish the meaning of the individual items first, and then concentrate on the correct sequence afterwards.

Difficulties in this area, however, can be improved with training.

Strategies for memory training

Teachers might try:

- increasing the span of items that are to be remembered;
- increasing the length of time between presenting the sequence and asking for recall by 5-second intervals. As memory span increases, an intervening task can be given between presentation and recall;
- introducing games such as 'I went to the market and bought';
- gradually increasing sequences of instructions, beginning with one or two only: 'Please go to the cupboard and get some pencils', and subsequently, perhaps: 'Please go to the cupboard, get some pencils, give one to Jane and one to Aaron.'
- asking the student to give a verbal message to deliver to another teacher, secretary, administrator. Again, increase the length of the message as the student is successful. It is important to encourage the student to repeat the instruction before carrying it out and use his/her own voice to aid his/her memory;
- at the end of the school day, asking the student to recall three activities in which s/he was engaged, and gradually increasing the number of activities the student is required to recall;
- after a special event, asking the student to sequence the activities that occurred;
- after reading a short story, asking the student to identify the main characters, sequence of events and outcome;
- recording a message on the tape recorder and then asking the student to write the message or recall the message;
- encourage students to think up their own mnemonic and visualization techniques and, if possible, both together;
- repeating aloud and rehearsing items to be remembered;
- using a multi-sensory mode of learning through oral, visual, auditory and kinaesthetic modes. The learner should be able to see, hear, say and, if possible, touch the materials to be learned. This reinforces the input stimuli and helps to consolidate the information for use, meaning and transfer to other areas;
- constructing mind maps, using pictorial images, symbols and different colours. An example of software produced to support students' creation of mind maps is 'Inspiration'. Using this program students can build visual diagrams such as concept maps to support their academic performance and creativity across the curriculum. 'Inspiration' can be used across the curriculum to help structure projects, research or essays (www.inclusive.co.uk/catalogue/acatalog/inspiration_v76.html, accessed 29 June 2008). Students should create their own mind maps to help with both the understanding of key concepts and the retention and recall of associated facts;
- keeping verbal instructions clear and concise and ensuring students are attending before teachers start to speak. It can help to preface instructions with a warning (for example, Peter, in a moment I am going to ask you) to ensure that the student is ready to listen;
- encouraging students to repeat back key points as well as to talk through tasks, using their own voice to help direct their motor movements;
- supplementing auditory verbal material with visual cues and practical demonstrations. In some cases, written checklists or pictorial reminders may be beneficial.

Autism

Autism is a condition that is generally considered to affect communication, cognition and learning. Kanner (1943), noting that a pattern of behaviour in a small group of young children seemed apparently inward-looking, termed this behaviour 'early infantile autism', after the Greek 'autos' (self). Asperger (1944), separately, describing older children whose behaviour was in some ways similar to that commented on by Kanner, used the term 'autistic'. Asperger syndrome now commonly refers to a 'form of autism used to describe people at the higher functioning end of the autistic spectrum' (National Autistic Society 2004).

The National Autistic Society in the UK estimates that 'autistic spectrum disorders are estimated to touch the lives of over 500,000 families throughout the UK'. Autism is defined as:

> a lifelong developmental disability that affects the way a person communicates and relates to people around them. Children and adults with autism are unable to relate to others in a meaningful way. Their ability to develop friendships is impaired as is their capacity to understand other people's feelings.
>
> People with autism can often have accompanying learning disabilities but everyone with the condition shares a difficulty in making sense of the world ...
>
> Reality to an autistic person is a confusing, interacting mass of events, people, places, sounds and sights. There seems to be no clear boundaries, order or meaning to anything. A large part of my life is spent just trying to work out the pattern behind everything.
>
> A person with autism
> (www.nas.org.uk/nas/jsp/polopoly.jsp?d=211, accessed 6 July 2007)

Wing and Gould (1979) identified a 'triad of impairments' in the areas of social interaction, communication and imagination in a broader group of 'autistic' children, about 15 in 10,000:

> **Social interaction** (difficulty with social relationships, for example appearing aloof and indifferent to other people).
> **Social communication** (difficulty with verbal and nonverbal communication, for example not really understanding the meaning of gestures, facial expressions or tone of voice).
> **Imagination** (difficulty in the development of play and imagination, for example having a limited range of imaginative activities, possibly copied and pursued rigidly and repetitively).
>
> In addition to this triad, repetitive behaviour patterns are a notable feature and a resistance to change in routine.
>
> (www.nas.org.uk/nas/jsp/polopoly.jsp?d=211, accessed 6 July 2007)

Typically, autism in young people is identified through agreed diagnostic criteria consisting of a profile of symptoms and characteristics of autistic behaviour. According to the

National Autistic Society in the UK (2004), the exact causes of autism are still not known, although there is evidence that genetic factors are implicated. Research also indicates that a variety of conditions affecting brain development which occur before, at, or soon after birth are associated with autism.

Approaches to autism

According to the UK National Autistic Society, what is needed in educational terms to support the learning of autistic students is a 'specialist' approach and 'structured support' (www.nas.org.uk/nas/jsp/polopoly.jps?d=211; accessed 19 January 2004). An example is applied behavioural analysis which is built on behavioural methods such as reducing identified tasks into small discrete 'teachable' steps reinforcing appropriate behaviours associated with each step, and using highly structured intensive teaching strategies.

Another commonly used approach is 'TEACCH' (Treatment and Education of Autistic and Related Communication Handicapped Students) (TEACCH 1998) in which parental involvement is seen as an important element. TEACCH's approach considers the way the student 'reads' their environment, rather than looking simply for environmental stimuli that might trigger particular behaviours. TEACCH considers the environment in terms of how the student will be able to interact and learn from it, and how the student him/herself will see the environment. Therefore a TEACCH-influenced classroom places a large emphasis on physically structuring the room to facilitate learning interactions within it.

Behaviour, emotional and social development

Student behaviour in schools does not occur in a vacuum. Difficult behaviour which seems to relate to a particular student may be indicative of a range of contextual issues associated with the family, school, classroom, peer group or teacher, as well as the student. Blaming the student and their background alone will not give you confidence to look for ways to manage behaviour that are within your own control. There is much evidence to show that, in the classroom, unacceptable student behaviour is influenced not only by the attributes of individual students, but also by:

- inappropriateness of classroom tasks and activities (for example, reading materials that are too difficult;
- concepts that assume too much prior knowledge and understanding;
- the influence of the classroom peer groups;
- individual teachers' management of classes;
- teacher expectations that are too high or too low;

and so on. To improve behaviour, teachers might be able to intervene effectively in relation to any one of these influences.

For a variety of reasons, students may develop 'extreme behaviours', that is, 'those that significantly and seriously disrupt the functioning and well-being of the student' (Dunckley 1999: 12). Preventing this kind of behaviour from developing is preferable to intervening later on. It makes good sense to implement a range of preventive strategies in the classroom so that incidents of severe behaviour are less likely to appear.

Preventing extreme behaviour

Prevention strategies may include:

- policies and practices that promote non-violence, mutual respect and respect for property.
- interesting programmes that are achievable for all. Students who experience success are less likely to engage in negative behaviour.
- praise and positive reinforcement for effort.
- stable, predictable environments with familiar routines and consistent limits. Students benefit from knowing what is acceptable behaviour, what is required and what will happen if transgressions occur.
- positive environments. Create situations where students will value praise and comments [from teachers or others].
- teaching that reinforces acceptable behaviour. Do not assume that this will be learned incidentally. For example, teach students to put their hands up to gain attention and praise them for following instruction and taking turns. Reinforce students for following the rules of games and activities, and help them cope with both winning and losing.
- defusing incidents through positive comments. Friendly positive direction will encourage cooperation (for example, *When you have removed your hat you can come and join us*). Give choices. Choices reduce the likelihood of outright refusal (for example, *You can finish this work now or at lunchtime*).
- being aware of events that may be stressful for students and teachers. These situations cannot always be avoided, but careful management can reduce the risk of extreme behaviour.
- avoiding situations known to lead to extreme behaviour for individual students. Know the circumstances under which a behaviour is likely to occur and make changes accordingly.
- early intervention. Don't ignore behaviours that are likely to become extreme.

(Dunckley 1999: 13)

For a small minority of students whose behaviour continues to be a focus of teachers' concerns, it may be seen as appropriate to investigate learning and behavioural issues at the level of the individual.

Attention deficit/hyperactivity disorder

One of the conditions for which individual assessment might take place is attention deficit/hyperactivity disorder (AD/HD). According to the British Psychological Society (1996), between 2 and 5 per cent of British school students are believed to experience this condition. It is very likely, therefore, that teachers new to the profession will meet students identified in this way.

Attention deficit/hyperactivity disorder is described by Norwich et al. as:

> a medical diagnosis of the American Psychiatric Association. It is characterised by chronic and pervasive (to home and school) problems of inattention, impulsiveness, and/or excessive motor activity which have seriously debilitating effects on individuals' social, emotional and educational development, and are sometimes disruptive to the home and/or school environment. Between two and five per cent of British school children are believed to experience this condition (BPS, 1996). The coming of this diagnosis has revived traditional conflicts between medical and educational perspectives on EBD, which affect the way in which practitioners approach problems surrounding childhood attention and activity problems . . .
>
> (2002: 182)

There are interesting differences in the reported incidence of AD/HD internationally which are explained by some researchers as related to prevailing variations in cultural practices:

> up to 9% of US children diagnosed as AD/HD in certain regions compared to only 0.007% in the UK (Hinshaw, 1994; Prendergast *et al.*, 1988; Schachar, 1991; Taylor, 1994; Holowenko and Pashute, 2000). These variations reflect several factors, including how the diagnostic systems are interpreted and used in practice by professionals, and cultural practices as regards diagnosis in this field.
>
> (Norwich et al. 2002: 182)

The category AD/HD originates in the USA but is now in widespread international use. The British Psychological Society (BPS) notes, the 'defining features' of AD/HD is students' behaviour which 'appears inattentive, impulsive and overactive to an extent that is unwarranted for their developmental age and is a significant hindrance to their social and educational success' (BPS 1996: 13). In Britain, the tradition has been 'to use the diagnostic systems of the International Classification of Diseases (ICD) published by the World Health Organisation' (BPS 1996: 13) and to assume a 'hyperkinetic disorder'. There is a strict requirement for 'pervasiveness and persistence'. This means that behaviour which is seen largely only in one context does not constitute grounds for a diagnosis.

A medical diagnosis of problematic behaviour may result in a prescription for medication. There is research to indicate that psycho-stimulant medication, combined with psychological, social and educational support, may encourage student behaviour that is socially acceptable in schools. Of the three most commonly used psycho-stimulants, methylphenidate (Ritalin) is most widely prescribed (BPS 1996: 50–2).

We discuss the concept of AD/HD in more detail in Chapter 7. Suffice it to say for now that, on occasion, students may be aggressive, out of control and a danger to themselves and others. Safety is a priority and the goal is to defuse the situation. Teachers should ensure that they are aware of their school policy in this situation. In particular they should take great care to check the school policy on physical restraint.

Sensory and/or physical needs

As noted already in this chapter:

> There is a wide spectrum of sensory, multi-sensory and physical difficulties. The sensory range extends from profound and permanent deafness or visual impairment through to lesser levels of loss, which may only be temporary. Physical impairments may arise from physical, neurological or metabolic causes that only require appropriate access to educational facilities and equipment; others may lead to more complex learning and social needs; a few children will have multi-sensory difficulties some with associated physical difficulties.
>
> (DfES 2001: para. 7:62)

Many of these young people will require:

- flexible teaching arrangements
- appropriate seating, acoustic conditioning and lighting
- adaptations to the physical environment of the school
- adaptations to school policies and procedures
- access to alternative or augmented forms of communication
- provision of tactile and kinaesthetic materials
- access to different amplification systems
- access to low vision aids
- access in all areas of the curriculum through specialist aids, equipment or furniture
- regular and frequent access to specialist support.

(DfES 2001: para 7:62)

Deaf students and those who are hard of hearing

We might choose to exemplify some of the principles of addressing the needs of students who experience sensory or physical difficulties with advice from the Royal National Institute for the Deaf (RNID) about education in mainstream for students who are deaf or hard of hearing. The RNID strongly promotes the message that effective pedagogy for students who experience hearing difficulties is effective pedagogy for a whole range of other students also: 'Reviewing and adapting teaching styles, presentation methods, listening conditions and differentiation of the curriculum to address the needs of deaf pupils will also improve the learning conditions for many other pupils in the school' (2004: 8). As in other areas of special educational needs, the key to successful inclusion is the ethos of the school in which the hearing impaired students are placed.

Recognizing and responding to bullying of deaf children

Some deaf students may be vulnerable to bullying. The RNID (2004: 13) outlines the following warning signs of bullying:

- anxiety about attending school, feigning illness
- clothes ripped, unexplained cuts and bruises
- not eating at school
- arriving late at school
- anxiety at end of the school day (where students travel home alone)
- feigning illness to miss particular classes
- not playing with friends at playtime or after school
- sitting alone in class
- deterioration in quality of school work
- asking to stay inside at break times
- becoming withdrawn.

The following support techniques might be considered for the individual deaf student:

- taking time to listen to the pupil
- supporting other pupils who disapprove of bullying behaviour
- keeping a record of all pupils involved in an incident
- following up all incidents
- taking all complaints seriously
- not dismissing a report of bullying as 'telling tales'
- consulting ToDs [teachers of the deaf] and other professionals who may be able to help.

(RNID 2004: 13)

In mainstream schools there is a diverse range of deaf and hard of hearing students. As the RNID (2004: 15) notes, in 2000 the vast majority of all deaf children in English schools were reported to be using 'auditory-oral' approaches that do 'not use sign language or manually coded elements to support the understanding of spoken language'. These approaches assume that students have enough residual hearing to acquire and use spoken language without needing to use sign language or finger spelling, provided there is sufficient amplification of sound. The listening environment is therefore a crucial consideration. Sound waves reverberate and increase the amount of background noise in rooms with hard surfaces. Soundfield systems and the acoustic treatment of teaching spaces can improve the listening environment for all students. It is important for class teachers to think carefully about the clarity of their spoken language. Teachers should use natural speech patterns and not exaggerate lip movements or shout, highlight key terms and key concepts and place themselves in a position appropriate for students to lip-read or benefit from a hearing aid where the maximum range is often 2 metres. Deaf students may also need to be encouraged to see the faces of peers who are speaking. To acquire spoken and written English, students may also need the support of visual and written forms of language, as well as lip-reading or multi-sensory clues. For example, with video materials, deaf students might benefit from advanced access to a summary of the programme and new vocabulary and concepts explained, as well as sub-titles. In addition, auditory-oral approaches require 'consistent, efficient use of individual hearing aids, radio aids and/or cochlear implant devices' (RNID 2004: 15).

Other students might use a 'sign bilingual' approach: the use of signed and spoken English: 'based on an understanding that deaf people are members of a minority linguistic and cultural group. Deaf children are therefore bilingual and bi-cultural and this must be reflected in the philosophy and structures of the school' (Pickersgill and Gregory 1998, cited in RNID 2004: 17). Where students use sign bilingualism, classroom teachers have to become accustomed to communication support workers (CSWs) in their classes and the visual spatial nature of British Sign Language with syntax that is different from English.

Working with communication support staff in classrooms

The RNID (2004: 22–3) notes that:

- the deaf pupil will be looking at the CSW/interpreter/transliterator and will only occasionally glance at the speaker. The teacher should not be put off by the fact that the pupil's eye contact with them is intermittent
- the deaf pupil needs to sit in a position where they can see the teacher and interpreter simultaneously
- CSWs/interpreters/transliterators will interpret the comments and questions of class members as well as everything that the teacher says
- the CSW/interpreter will use sign at all times when the deaf pupil is present
- CSWs/interpreters will voice over, that is, speak aloud, the comments and questions of the deaf pupil in the first person
- a CSW/interpreter/transliterator may occasionally need to stop a class teacher to ask them to slow down or speed up delivery, or to clarify content
- CSWs/interpreters/transliterators are not there to answer the deaf pupil's questions nor should they be asked questions about the pupils, eg 'How's s/he getting on?' They are there to provide an interpreting service
- questions from the pupil about lesson content should be directed at the teacher, through the CSW/interpreter/transliterator
- the CSW/interpreter/transliterator will always be a few words behind the teacher and needs time to finish. The deaf pupil therefore needs extra time to absorb questions that have been interpreted, before responding
- a CSW/interpreter/transliterator can only interpret for one person at a time, whether from voice to sign or vice versa. The class teacher therefore needs to manage class discussion so that only one person is speaking at a time
- the deaf pupil and CSW/interpreter/transliterator will experience mental, physical and visual fatigue during a very long session. It is helpful is the lesson can be planned to build in breaks, with activities alternating with 'from the front' sessions
- CSWs/interpreters/transliterators can do a better job if they have sight of the lesson notes ahead of the lesson and advance warning of any technical/specialist vocabulary that will be used
- when video/slides are shown, some light is needed so that the deaf pupil can see

> the CSW/interpreter/transliterator and the pupil will need extra time to look at the slide and then at the CSW
> - when a class teacher refers to visual aids it can be difficult for a CSW/interpreter/transliterator to follow. For example, it is helpful if class teachers are encouraged to substitute 'multiply 42 by 46' for 'multiply this by that'.

Liaising with support staff

In general terms, one of the ways of approaching how to support students who experience visual, auditory or physical difficulties is to consider how best to liaise with support staff who may be employed to help address these students' learning needs. As discussed in further detail in Chapter 9, the Education (Specified Work and Registration) (England) Regulations 2003 specify circumstances in which certain school staff – such as support staff – may carry out 'specified work' relating to teaching and learning. 'Specified work' includes planning, preparing and delivering lessons to students, and assessing and reporting on development, for individuals as well as groups.

The role of support staff in the classroom is to help the teacher make sure that each student engages positively in class activities and makes progress. Support staff can help to:

- raise the performance of individual students;
- provide coping strategies for students;
- assist in the management of students' behaviour;
- promote students' independence;
- support the development of differentiated curricular approaches to meet the diversity of students' learning needs. The kind of materials that support staff might help to develop for students who, for example, experience visual difficulties, might well be checked against what the Royal National Institute for the Blind (RNIB) calls its 'See it right checklist'.

The RNIB's checklist for ensuring visual clarity of texts

Simple and clear typeface is used
Type size is 12 point or ideally 14 point
Text is left aligned
Layout is consistent and logical
Words are not split between lines
No large blocks of capital letters
No italics
No words are underlined
No text is laid over the top of an image or texture
Paper, lamination or encapsulation is not glossy
Paper is thick enough to minimise the amount of show through from the other side
Leading is not cramped
Good contrast between the text and the background
Line space between paragraphs

All text is set horizontally

Adequate gutter between columns

No information is conveyed solely through the use of images, diagrams or colour.

(www.rnib.org.uk/xpedio/groups/public/documents/PublicWebsite/

public_printchecklist1.pdf)

Support staff carrying out 'specified work' must be subject to the direction and supervision of a teacher. The teacher of the class has overall responsibility for student learning. Support staff can sometimes impede inclusion by working in isolation with individual students. Too much one-to-one support with a student can have a negative impact on participation. To develop effective classroom practice teachers might:

- review the situation frequently to achieve an appropriate balance of individual and group work and be prepared to make some compromises;
- liaise with support staff to plan ahead and implement programmes of work. Specific time may need to be set aside to discuss/plan together;
- ensure support staff know exactly what is expected of students;
- establish a *number of ground rules* at the outset. For example:
  - the status and title to give an adult helper in the classroom;
  - ways to organize time to talk about any difficulties;
  - how to share information with the adult helper about the classroom rules and the importance of maintaining confidentiality.

There is fuller discussion of the use of support staff in classrooms in Chapter 9.

Planning for learning

If a student cannot work on the same objectives as the class as a whole, the teacher might want to choose learning objectives that are linked to the topic on which the whole class is working, but earlier in a learning progression. If working in literacy or mathematics, it will be possible to 'track back' through the objectives in the National Strategy Frameworks to locate earlier learning objectives. In other subjects guidance will come from the relevant programmes of study.

Planning for learning will need to be informed by the individual priorities for students with special educational needs or disabilities. Normally it will be appropriate for them to work on objectives that are similar and related to the whole-class topic. However, at other times teachers will also have to consider whether the students have other priority needs that are central to their learning, for example a need to concentrate on some key skills such as communication, problem-solving, working with others, managing their own emotions, and so on. These needs may be detailed in the student's individual education plan or a Statement of Special Educational Needs. They can often be met within the whole-class learning; for example relating physiotherapy objectives to the physical education (PE) curriculum, communication to literacy lessons, and problem-solving to mathematics, history or geography. A student with severe learning difficulties can, for example, be learning about turn-taking in the context of collaborative group work in a Year 4 history lesson about Celts and Romans. What the teacher wants the student to learn is distinct and different from the learning objectives for the class, but the activities designed for the class as whole can encompass the student's individual priority need.

Some students may have additional therapeutic or other needs which cannot easily be met through class activities. For these students a teacher may sometimes decide to plan alternative objectives to meet specific needs and give these identified time. For example, a student might be withdrawn for a time-limited number of weeks to take part in group work to develop social, emotional and behavioural skills, or for a one-to-one literacy intervention programme. Or students might work every day in class on a group programme devised by a speech and language therapist and carried out by a teaching assistant. Such alternative activities are legitimate as long as they are in the context of ensuring that, over time, all students receive a broad and balanced curriculum.

An individual education plan may well be used to record the plans for an individual student. The IEP records the nature of the student's difficulties, how they are going to be tackled and progress assessed. This might include adaptations to normal classroom activities, or a special programme of individual work for the student, or both. The IEP also includes a review date, criteria for judging success and a section for recording outcomes. Involvement of parents and students in creating and assessing the IEP is expected. Recently, the government has made clear that IEPs are not necessarily required if a school maintains an effective individual planning system for all students.

Summary

Staff attitudes and students' views of themselves as capable of learning and achieving in schools make for powerful interactions for good or ill. Teachers and others need to work from an understanding that everyone including those with special educational needs or disabilities has strengths and/or interests on which approaches to learning can draw to make them more effective in many situations. In another chapter we discuss the case of a 12-year-old student who was disaffected from school and often disrupted the learning of his peers in the classroom as a result of his frustration at his inability to read and write. He was very dyslexic. In his mainstream school he was fully engaged in one area only: classical studies. On investigation it became clear that he was fascinated by stories from classical Greek mythology, and responded well to a narrative style of teaching – as did many of his peers.

Students in classrooms have rights to additional support based on assessments of their progress in the past. For some students with communication and interaction needs, for students with sensory or physical impairment, for many dyslexic students and for students with behavioural, emotional and social needs it is highly likely that what is needed is adaptations to teaching styles and the use of access strategies, rather than different learning objectives. When planning for individuals, teachers first need to know whether the student or group can, with appropriate access strategies and teaching styles, work on the same learning objectives as the rest of the class. As discussed in the next chapter, getting this right will depend on accurate assessment of what the student knows, understands and can do.

4   Assessment and planning

Questions addressed in this chapter

In the area of special educational needs, are there any concerns associated with standardized forms of assessment which seek to compare students' performance against national or regional age norms? If so, what are they? What might teachers need to know in relation to other forms of assessment commonly used in schools, particularly in relation to special educational needs?

How can we assess barriers in the context in which learning occurs?

How can we be responsive to students' views and the views of parents and families?

What are the major issues related to planning programmes for students' learning?

Introduction

The central focus of this chapter is what a thoughtful, reflective teacher should be aware of, and should do in the area of assessment and planning for students' special learning needs in order that those students can thrive and grow in the context of school. Setting targets for individual students on individual education plans, records or profiles may give the rather misleading impression that addressing learning needs is straightforward. However, there are some very important issues to be considered:

- Different kinds of assessment make different assumptions about how learning takes place and what people are like in general terms. The implications of these assumptions can be very productive in supporting learning, or sometimes be quite damaging to individuals.
- Difficulties in learning and/or behaviour always take place in the context of something. It may be that the learning environment, including teaching method(s), materials and the curriculum in general is contributing to the difficulties the learner is experiencing.
- Each student who experiences difficulties in learning of some sort is an individual.
- Each situation is unique. Each requires its own solution. There is no one easy option.

Teachers need to be fully conversant with test procedures, their aims and rationale. They also need to bear in mind the wider cultural and social factors, the school and curriculum context, and factors related more specifically to the individual child. Difficulties in learning and/or behaviour, for example, which seem to relate to a particular student may be indicative of a range of contextual issues associated with society, the family, ethnic or community group, school, classroom, peer group or teacher, as well as the individual student.

Assumptions underlying assessment, and their consequences

Questions for reflection

Do you feel that particular forms of assessment of students' 'special' learning needs make any kinds of assumptions about the nature of learning, intelligence, and so on? If so, what are they?

What do you think professionals try to achieve in the assessment process?

How, in your experience, does the assessment of learning and behaviour influence achievement?

All students need identities as positive achievers. Assessment processes and systems in schools can be 'inclusive'. However, this depends on the extent to which they support students to feel that they are making positive progress in whichever student group the particular form of assessment is used. Different forms of assessment can act to support the development of students' sense of themselves as learners, or non-learners, in ways that interact with how students already feel about themselves (Murphy 2002). Thus, assessment itself can serve to reinforce or undermine the motivation to strive for future achievement in schools.

Assessment of individual 'special' learning and behavioural needs

A student has a special educational need if s/he has a difficulty in learning that is significantly greater than that of peers. In order to identify the students who are 'different' and, therefore, decide who is eligible for additional services, special educational provision may depend on the results of norm-referenced assessment that is designed to indicate a learner's achievement in comparison with others.

Understanding standardized test results

Some assessments, for example the Neale Analysis of Reading Ability (Neale 1997), are standardized and provide normative scores. These compare a child with standards achieved by children in the population as a whole. Another example is the standardized tests of verbal ability, the *British Picture Vocabulary Scale* (Dunn et al. 1997). This is described by the publishers as the most widely used standardized picture-based test of receptive vocabulary in the UK that does not require any reading, speaking or writing, just responses to picture cards. An example of a standardized test procedure designed to measure a person's ability to form perceptual relations and to reason by analogy rather than to measure language and formal schooling as in the tests above is *Ravens Progressive Matrices* (Raven et al. 1998). Each of the problems within both the standard progressive matrices (SPM) and the advanced progressive matrices (APM) is presented in the form of a sequence (matrix) of symbolic figures. The child is required to understand the nature of the relationships within each sequence and select one figure which completes each sequence. The assumption is that, by so doing, the child demonstrates the degree to which a systematic method of reasoning has been developed.

To understand the use and, potentially, misuse, of standardized testing it is important to be familiar with the test standardization process, including the significance of 'measure of spread' of scores, and a number of important concepts related to standardized tests and test procedures:

- validity and reliability;
- the usefulness of standardized scores;
- interpretations of percentile ranks, confidence bands and reading ages.

The standardization process

One way to make test scores such as 45 out of 100 and 25 out of 44 more readily understandable and comparable would be to convert them to percentages (45 per cent and 57 per cent, to the nearest whole number). However, these percentages on their own do not tell us either the average score of all children or how spread out the scores are.

Standardizing a test score involves setting the mean (average) score at 100, no matter how easy or difficult the assessment may be. It is easy to compare a child's result with this score of 100. Standardized scores therefore enable teachers to compare a learner's test result with a large, nationally representative sample. A standardized test is often used in order to provide a set of national standards against which to make comparisons.

An important concept associated with standardized tests is that of the 'measure of the spread' of scores, the so-called 'standard deviation'. This is usually set to 15 for educational attainment and ability tests. Irrespective of the difficulty of the test, about 68 per cent of students in a national sample will have a standardized score within one standard deviation (15 points) of the average (that is, between 85 and 115) and about 95 per cent will have a standardized score within two standard deviations (30 points) of the average (between 70 and 130). These examples come from a frequency distribution, known as the 'normal distribution', which is shown below.

Validity and reliability

We often refer to 'validity' and 'reliability' of both formal and informal tests. In general terms, we can assess the 'validity' of a test by asking ourselves whether the test actually tests what it is intended to test. We might ask, for example:

- whether a visual test of vocabulary that has been developed and standardized in Britain would be valid for young people from a completely different culture and new to the UK, who have been traumatized by civil conflict in their own country;
- how valid is the concept of 'reading age' and whether we think it would be appropriate with reference to adults (see the discussion below);
- whether a test has 'context validity', that is whether it tests what we expect it to test in the context in which it is being used;

'Reliability', on the other hand, generally means whether we would obtain the same result on the same test with the same cohort of individuals if we did the test procedure again.

Usefulness of standardized scores

The use of standardized scores is often thought to be more useful than of raw scores for three main reasons:

1   *It produces a scale that enables a comparison of results.* Standardized tests allow us to see whether a child is above or below the national average through comparison with a standardized score. It is particularly important to note the date when the test was standardized, however. An old test may no longer be valid in terms of comparisons of individuals with national norms.

2   *To cater for different ages.* When assessing in schools there is a range of ages in any one year group, so there can be up to a 12-month gap in ages. However, in both primary and secondary schools older children almost always score higher than younger children. Standardized scores are often worked out so that the ages of the children are taken into account and children with the same age in years and months are compared.

3   *To compare one test with another.* Using standardized scores allows us to compare one test with another since most tests provide standardized scores which range from 70 to 130 or 140. This enables us to compare a student's standing in tests in one area of the curriculum such as maths with standardized readings scores from another, for example reading comprehension.

Percentile ranks

The percentile rank is often used to enable us to compare the performance of a student with the performance of other students who form the basis of the national standardization sample. The percentage of students in the sample of the same age who gained a score *at the same level or below* that of the child's score is *the percentile rank.*

Figure 4.1 shows that there is a constant relationship between the percentile ranks and standardized scores when the same average score and standard deviation are used. For example, performance at the 50th percentile indicates that the child performed as well as, or better than 50 per cent of the sample when age is taken into account.

Confidence bands

It is never possible to obtain the 'true score', that is the hypothetically perfect measurement of the individual's ability. Among the reasons for this are:

- tests of the sort discussed here measure attainment – that is, the outcome of the student's work at any particular time – and not 'ability';
- no matter how carefully educational tests are put together and administered, errors can result from outside influences such as the child's state of health, fatigue due to the length of the test, and so on.

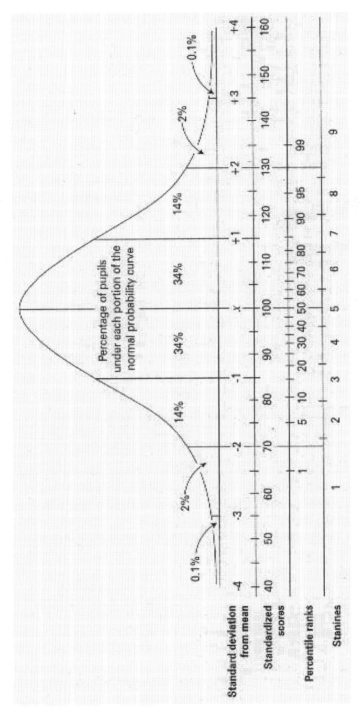

Figure 4.1 The relationship between standardized scores, percentile ranks and stanines under a normal distribution curve

'Confidence bands', therefore, indicate the range of scores within which the accurate assessment of attainment is likely to fall.

Understanding 'reading ages'

One of the most commonly used concepts in relation to norm-referenced assessment in schools, is that of 'reading age'. Reading ages are used in standardized assessments such as the Neale Analysis of Reading Ability (Neale 1997) to indicate the age at which a given raw score was the average. They are obtained by working out for each age group the average raw score of all the children in the sample of that age and then smoothing out any irregularities in the resulting graph. Increases in performance with age are smaller for older age groups. Of course, this raises issues for using this measurement with older students as, according to the model on which they are based, accuracy and rate of reading would show no improvement beyond a certain point.

We, therefore, need to be careful when using reading ages that we do not interpret these as fixed and exact measures of reading attainment as they represent snapshots of a progression in literacy development. It has been argued, however, that if we use these normative scores while taking into account the confidence bands attributed to the known score, we can then view reading ages as estimates of reading ability at the time of testing. There is another issue, too. Nothing fixed is indicated by a given reading age. Reading is a learned behaviour that is closely aligned with development, age, access to appropriate reading material and instruction, and so on. Thus a low reading score does not necessarily suggest general low ability, slow developmental growth, and so on.

Practical issues in using and interpreting formal, standardized tests

Some of the practical issues in the using and interpreting standardized tests are:

- 'fitness for purpose'. The nature and purpose of the test should fit what the student is being tested for. Standardized tests alone are not designed to diagnose the root of the problem. They therefore do not offer a clear route to a solution on their own;
- meticulous preparation. Those carrying out formal test procedures of any kind should:
  - read the instructions;
  - not go into the test situation without knowing what they are going to do;
  - make sure they understand the rationale underpinning the particular test;
- the age of a test which may invalidate it;
- ethical considerations, for example a consideration of whose interests the test is serving, by whom it is carried out, and how and whether the student's and parent's views are taken into account;
- the interval of time within which the same standardized test is used. Too short an interval of time will confound the results.

Issues associated with norm-referencing

While there are practical issues to think about with standardized test procedures, there are also theoretical issues. For example, standardized tests compare one student's results with the whole student cohort. There are also other issues. Some of the principles behind identifying individual difficulties in learning through norm-referenced testing may be seen as contradicting some of the principles of inclusion and equal opportunities in schools:

- Some students may be allocated additional resources after achieving only very low scores on norm-referenced tests. However, there is a very grey area around the cut-off point above which other students will receive no additional provision.
- When an individual student's test score lies within the bottom 'tail' of a normal distribution curve there may be a feeling that the student's actual ability is very low. S/he may be seen as only capable of achieving within the lowest few in the student population. This view can limit teachers' expectations of what to expect of certain students and, therefore, lead to continued poor achievement (Rosenthal and Jacobson 1968).
- Using standardized forms of tests means that we can pinpoint those students whose scores fall into the lowest 2 per cent or so. However, it also means we are not likely to view these same students as having the potential to achieve very highly, even if given the appropriate learning opportunities. Poor scores on normative tests can mean that students' failure to achieve in school is automatically 'blamed' on poor ability, or the family or ethnic group. This view absolves schools from responsibility for that learner's progress in school rather than opening up discussion of how classroom teaching practices and the school curriculum generally can be adapted to suit students' learning and behaviour better. 'Success' and 'failure' on norm-referenced tests are not just the result of children's natural ability, however (Tomlinson 1988). Children's lack of achievement in the education system can be understood as the outcome of the way society works. Some families cannot support their own children adequately as a result of the impoverished circumstances in which they find themselves and the way that schools are structured, as much as of a lack of innate ability in the child.

Ongoing assessment that enhances learning

Assessment is a powerful educational tool for promoting learning. However, assessment activities should be appropriate to the aims of the assessment, to the objectives of the curriculum and to the individual students (Caygill and Elley 2001; Clarke et al. 2003). 'There is no evidence that increasing the amount of testing will enhance learning' (Assessment Reform Group 1999: 2). In many countries there has been a shift in emphasis in recent years from assessment methods that serve only summative or 'assessment *of* learning' purposes. Results from externally imposed summative tests, especially where there are very high stakes attached to these results in countries such as England, can have very negative effects on students. Teachers often feel they have to devote considerable time to practise test-taking rather than to use assessment to support learning. Where this is the case, students, especially lower achievers, tend to become overanxious and demoralized, seeing assessment as something that labels and stigmatizes them among their peers. As the Assessment Reform Group comment, to be successful, learners need to:

- understand the goals they are aiming for;
- be motivated;
- possess the skills to achieve success.

In a seminal piece of work that synthesized research on assessment and classroom learning, Black and Wiliam (1998) demonstrated clearly that student achievement, particularly that of lower achievers, can be raised through formative assessment in the classroom. Improving learning through assessment depends on five, 'deceptively simple', factors:

- The provision of effective feedback;
- The active involvement of students in their own learning;
- Adjusting teaching to take account of the results of assessment;
- A recognition of the profound influence assessment has on the motivation and self-esteem of students, both of which are crucial influences on learning;
- The need for students to be able to assess themselves and understand how to improve.

(Assessment Reform Group 1999: 5)

Black and Wiliam's research synthesis takes the view that learners have active agency in learning. They must, ultimately, be responsible for their own learning. They do it for themselves. Assessment that supports learning must therefore involve students so that they have information about how well they are doing that guides subsequent learning. Much of this information will come as feedback from the teacher. Some may also result from assessment of their own work in a constructive way that shows them what they need to do, and can do, to make progress.

The shift in emphasis in the purpose of day-to-day assessment in classrooms has resulted in a focus on 'Assessment for Learning' (AfL) in some places.

Principles of formative assessment in practice

AfL is:

the ongoing day-to-day formative assessment that takes place to gather information on what a child or group of children understand or do not understand and how future teaching will be adapted to account for this. Effective ongoing day to day assessments would include effective questioning; observations of children during teaching and while they are working; holding discussions with children; analysing work and reporting to children; conducting tests and giving quick feedback and engaging children in the assessment process.

(www.standards.dfes.gov.uk/primary/features/primary/1091819/1092063, accessed 7 May 2008)

Advice given on putting AfL into practice suggests that:

Assessment for learning should:

- be part of effective planning of teaching and learning;
- focus on how students learn;
- be recognised as central to classroom practice;
- be regarded as a key professional skill for teachers;
- be sensitive and constructive because any assessment has an emotional impact;
- take account of the importance of learner motivation;
- promote commitment to learning goals and a shared understanding of the criteria by which students will be assessed;
- provide constructive guidance for learners about how to improve;
- develop learners' capacity for self assessment and recognising their next steps and how to take them;
- recognise the full range of achievement of all learners.

(www.standards.dfes.gov.uk/primary/features/primary/1091819/1092063, accessed 7 May 2008)

Ongoing continuous formative assessment can provide teachers with formal and informal opportunities to:

- notice what is happening during learning activities;
- recognize where the learning of individuals and groups of students is going;
- see how they can help to take that learning further.

Teachers who do this are sometimes called 'reflective practitioners' (Schön 1983; 1987). Reflective practitioners notice what is different or unusual about patterns of progress in student learning. They think carefully and deeply about what assessment information is telling them about student understandings, and more particularly about their own teaching and what they should or can do differently to connect to and respond to the thinking of each student.

Feedback to students is most effective when it:

- focuses on the tasks and the associated learning, not the student;
- confirms for the student that he or she is on the right track;
- includes suggestions that help the student (that is that scaffold their learning);
- is frequent and given when there is opportunity for the student to take action;
- is in the context of a dialogue about the learning.

(Ministry of Education 2005: 16)

Feedback that connects directly to specific and challenging goals related to students' prior knowledge and experience helps those students to focus more productively on new goals and next learning steps.

Assessing learning through classroom observation

In addition to using formative strategies, learning may be assessed in context, and problematic issues can be identified, through classroom observation. It is important, however, that the observer recognizes that observational assessment needs to be implemented in different contexts over time in order to give a rounded profile of the student's learning. The use of a framework for collecting observational data can yield considerable information and can complement the results from other kinds of assessment. Observational assessment can be diagnostic, because it is flexible, adaptable and can be used in natural settings with interactive activities. Reid and Given (1999) have developed such a framework – the Interactive Observational Style Identification (IOSI). A summary of this is shown below;

Exemplar of a framework for classroom observation

Motivation
What topics, tasks and activities interest the student?
What kind of prompting and cueing is necessary to increase motivation?
What kind of incentives motivate the student – leadership opportunities, working with others, free time or physical activity.

Persistence
Does the student stick to a task until completion without breaks?
Are frequent breaks necessary when working on difficult tasks?

Responsibility
To what extent does the student take responsibility for his/her own learning?
Does the student attribute success or failure to self or others?

Structure
Are the student's personal effects (desk, clothing, materials) well organized or cluttered?
How does the student respond to someone imposing organizational structure on him/her?

Social interaction
When is the student's best work accomplished – when working alone, with one another or in a small group?
Does the student ask for approval or needs to have work checked frequently?

Communication
Does the student give the main events and gloss over the details?
Does the student interrupt others when they are talking?

Modality preference
What type of instructions does the student most easily understand – written, oral or visual?
Does the student respond more quickly and easily to questions about stories heard or read?

Sequential or simultaneous learning
Does the student begin with one step and proceed in an orderly fashion or have difficulty following sequential information?

Is there a logical sequence to the student's explanations or do her/his thoughts bounce around from one idea to another?

Impulsive/reflective

Are the student's responses rapid and spontaneous or delayed and reflective?

Does the student seem to consider past events before taking action?

Physical mobility

Does the student move around the class frequently or fidget when seated?

Does the student like to stand or walk while learning something new?

Food intake

Does the student snack or chew on a pencil when studying?

Time of day

During which time of day is the student most alert?

Is there a noticeable difference between morning work completed and afternoon work?

Sound

Does the student seek out places that are particularly quiet?

Light

Does the student like to work in dimly lit areas or say that the light is too bright?

Temperature

Does the student leave his/her coat on when others seem warm?

Furniture design

When given a choice does the student sit on the floor, lie down, or sit in a straight chair to read?

Metacognition

Is the student aware of his/her learning style strengths?

Does the student demonstrate self-assessment?

Prediction

Does the student make plans and work towards goals or let things happen?

Feedback

How does the student respond to different types of feedback?

How much external prompting is needed before the student can access previous knowledge?

There are too many manifestations of learning behaviour to observe all at once. One way to begin the observation process is to select one of the learning systems and progress from there. The insights usually become greater as observation progresses.

Criterion referencing: use of exemplars to illustrate work at particular levels

In order to enable teachers to engage in conversations that link back to and promote students' learning outcomes, some schools use authentic examples of students' work that illustrate what the criteria related to the levels described in each of the National

Curriculum statements look like. Using a wide range of authentic examples of students' work, exemplars can illustrate key features of learning, achievement and quality at different stages of student development. They can be used by students and teachers to identify next learning steps and to guide teachers in their interpretation of the descriptive criteria for each curriculum level.

If teachers annotate the students' work samples to highlight important features of the work this can exemplify learning, achievement and quality in relation to the levels described in the National Curriculum documents. Teachers can use the exemplars in a number of different ways to further the learning of students.

Effective use of exemplars

Teachers can compare a student's work sample with the exemplars in order to identify specific strengths and weaknesses, individual teaching and learning needs, and to prioritize new learning goals.

Teachers can use the exemplars collaboratively with the student to review learning outcomes by comparing the progress they have made in relation to the samples of work. In so doing, teachers can exemplify the next learning steps while also raising expectations and collaboratively working towards raising performance and achievement.

Once students are familiar with this process, they may be able to use the exemplars for self and peer review. In this way, they can learn to evaluate their own work and development, and reflect on the next steps in their learning.

Teachers can also use the exemplars as the basis for a discussion about the work of their students with parents and caregivers. By discussing and exemplifying a child's achievement and progress in relation to selected samples of work, parents and caregivers can be better informed about what work at a particular curriculum level looks like and how they too can better support the next learning steps.

Assessing individual behaviours

There are a number of ways of identifying when the challenges presented by an individual student's behaviour require special consideration. One way is to adopt a problem-solving diagnostic approach (Watkins and Wagner 1995).

Assessing individual behaviours: example 1 – a problem-solving approach

The first step is good definition. A useful starting point is to consider the following questions:

What specific behaviour is causing concern?
In what settings/contexts does the behaviour occur, and with which others?
In what settings/contexts situations does the behaviour not occur?
Does anything regularly trigger the behaviour?
Does anything regularly follow the behaviour? Does something maintain it?
What social/communication/learning/classroom skills does the student demonstrate?

What social/communication/learning/classroom skills does the student not demonstrate?
What view does the student have of his/her behaviour? What does the behaviour mean to him/her?
How does the student feel about him/herself?
What view do others have of the student?
Who is most affected/concerned by this behaviour? (Adapted from Watkins and Wagner 1995.)

Another approach to assessing behaviour is the Birmingham (England) Local Education Authority's three-level approach outlined in its strategy document *Behaviour in Schools: Framework for Intervention* (Williams and Birmingham City Council Education Department 1998). In this approach, responses to problematic learning and behaviour begin at Level 1 with an audit of behaviour and of the learning environment. This is followed by reflection on how to alter that environment to make a positive impact on behaviour and learning.

Assessing individual behaviours: example 2 – behaviour in context

The teacher first takes a baseline of behaviour by recording:

- frequency;
- place;
- time;
- social situation;
- setting events;
- description of problem behaviour;
- duration of problem behaviour;
- severity of behaviour (if appropriate);
- consequences to exhibiting child;
- consequences to others (Birmingham City Council and Education Department 2004: 285).

The teacher then audits changeable factors in the general learning environment that may influence the learner's behaviour:

- classroom physical environment, organization and equipment;
- classroom management;
- classroom rules and routines;
- environment, routines and rules outside class;
- whole school policies and support for staff;
- roles of parents and governors (Birmingham City Council and Education Department 2004: 285–6).

Next, s/he considers information relating to the individual student:

- possible sensory difficulty – particularly with hearing;
- significant medical factors affecting the child;

- significant life events which may affect the child (Birmingham City Council and Education Department 2004: 285).

We might add to this list other difficulties in learning, for example in reading, writing and spelling, that might influence behaviour.

The next step is to think about what changes in the environment and teaching approaches might influence behaviour in a positive way, and then implement these changes and monitor the consequences. After this has been done, responses continue if necessary with a greater focus on the individual student within the learning environment. The teacher then goes on to involve external agencies if necessary.

Students' views

As discussed in Chapter 1, we can look at students' learning in a number of ways. If we assume that students are active agents in their own learning we have to try to understand how they feel about difficulties in learning, behaviour, motor skills or any other area in which they experience difficulties, and what they know will support them most effectively, otherwise there is a serious question about how we can know what will best fit what they need. This does not mean, of course, that we have to provide everything a student asks for in a school.

Engaging with students' views in schools

Teachers who try to engage with the perspectives of disaffected young people have to recognize that schools are operating under a number of constraints. In the English national context, for example,

> Recent and current pressures on schools emanating from league tables of absence rates and academic results have made 'disruptive' students less tolerable ... Including students whose behaviour seems threatening to the system is not easy ... Exclusionary pressures resulting from the current competitive climate are very strong.
>
> (Wearmouth 1999: 16–17)

There are a number of philosophical and practical issues surrounding self-advocacy. For example, student self-advocacy may conflict with professionals' values and assumptions, both about themselves with the responsibility for maintaining control and direction in the classroom and the school as a whole, and about students' rights and abilities to express their own views (Garner and Sandow 1995). There are no easy solutions to this issue either. Again, it represents, essentially, conflict between the roles of the participants within the system of the school. If, as in many schools, student self-advocacy, for instance by students whose behaviour may be challenging to schools, is not acceptable, then some professionals may need to take on the role of advocate on behalf of students.

The assessment of students' perceptions of, and feelings about, their own behaviour depends on very finely tuned listening skills as well as suspension of judgemental responses on the part of professionals. In terms of practice it is important to recognize that:

True listening is an art; children will make decisions about people they can talk to and trust, and those they cannot. We know from the counselling literature that good listeners offer time, support, non directive questions, acknowledgement of feelings, reflecting back, and such non-verbal behaviour as eye contact, sitting next to (rather than opposite, behind a desk), and a basically trusting atmosphere which communicates that it is all right to speak honestly.

These are not easy situations to create in school . . .

(Gersch 1995: 48)

An example of a project interview technique: 'Talking Stones'

'Talking Stones' (Wearmouth 2004b) is a powerful strategy that helps students to represent problematic relationships and situations as they see them. During an individual interview, a student is given a pile of stones of varying shapes, sizes, colours and textures. The student is encouraged to project on to them thoughts and feelings about him/herself in relation to school, and about his/her relationships with other students and teachers. The individual selects one stone to represent him/herself as a student in school and discusses his/her choice. Subsequently s/he selects more stones to represent significant others in the school and/or classroom context, describes why they have been chosen, and then places them on a rectangular white cloth or large sheet of paper. The edges of the rectangle form a boundary to the positioning of the stones. Stones, their attributes and their positions and distance in relation to each other can be understood as a student's representation of his/her world of school and his/her place within it.

One way in which a procedure such as 'Talking Stones' can contribute to the process of assessment in schools is in the manner in which it can open up problematic relationships between, typically, teenagers and staff members, and facilitate dialogue between them.

'Talking Stones' is a powerful procedure. Teachers using 'Talking Stones' should be aware of ethical principles associated with techniques of a counselling nature, for example the principle of not doing any harm (McLeod 1998). The use of the technique is ethically questionable unless there is a clear benefit for the student. Asking personal questions may be interpreted as prying into a student's privacy. However, addressing difficult student behaviour can be very difficult if teachers are not aware of major factors driving that behaviour. Reflecting on the ethics of the situation also raises the question of who should decide whether the risks of using a technique such as this outweigh the benefits.

There are many instances in schools where students disclose very sensitive information about themselves to teachers. Before engaging in any activity where this is likely to happen, including using 'Talking Stones', teachers need to familiarize themselves very well with any guidelines that may exist in their own schools about handling information that may emerge from student self-disclosure, for example information relating to sexual abuse.

Engaging with parents' or carers' perspectives

Students have loyalties to communities outside as well as inside the school, most notably to their own families. Schools have a lot of power to affect the lives of children and their families and carers through the kind of assessment and provision that they make. Russell (1997: 79) makes a plea to schools to take this power very seriously:

> Please accept and value our children (and ourselves as families) as we are.
> Please celebrate difference.
> Please try and accept our children as children first. Don't attach labels to them unless you mean to do something.
> Please recognise your power over our lives. We live with the consequences of your opinions and decisions.
> Please understand the stress many families are under. The cancelled appointment, the waiting list no one gets to the top of, all the discussions about resources – it's our lives you're talking about.
> Don't put fashionable fads and treatments on to us unless you are going to be around to see them through. And don't forget families have many members, many responsibilities. Sometimes, we can't please everyone.
> Do recognise that sometimes we are right! Please believe us and listen to what we know that we and our children need.
> Sometimes we are sad, tired and depressed. Please value us as caring and committed families and try to go on working with us.

The planning process: long-, medium- and short-term planning

Curriculum planning for any learner or group needs to incorporate an overall long-term plan based on a global view of the learner and an awareness of the context within which the plan must take effect. A longer-term vision of a range of possibilities for a learner that can be shared between the learner, the parent/carer and the professionals is important to give a sense of direction to the whole planning process. From this long-term plan it is possible to draw up medium- and short-term plans. At the meeting to review the student's progress, a considerable amount of revision and amendment to a pupil's programme might be needed in the light of current achievement and personal development, changes in the learning environment and the stage reached in the National Curriculum.

Framework for planning

This flowchart takes into account some of the principles described in the work of Tod et al. (1998):

Account taken of contextual factors related to the whole-school curriculum:

- national requirements;
- school priorities;
- in-class arrangements for students' learning;
- approaches to diversity and equal opportunities;
- issues of differentiation.

Assessment of the strengths and difficulties experienced by the learner based on:

- teachers' assessments;
- SAT results;
- prior records/ reports, assessment by outside agencies;
- the pupil's views;
- the parents'/carers' views.

Long-term plan for learner based on aspirations and strengths with provision for access to the whole curriculum.

Medium-term plan outlined on the Individual Education Plan document which must:

- reflect strategies appropriate to the context and the individualism of the learner;
- incorporate termly and yearly achievable targets designed to lead to the learner's long-term goal;
- reflect the Key Stage and associated programmes of study;
- offer regular assessment opportunities.

Short-term, day-to-day planning which must:

- incorporate medium-term targets;
- offer opportunities for daily, formative assessment.

(Adapted from Wearmouth 2000.)

The review cycle does not detract from the need to think about possible routes for learners over a much longer period than this. Individuals' needs change over time. It is very important to retain flexibility of thinking so that the planning process is facilitative of learning rather than restrictive.

An example of planning for students with severe motor difficulties

Individual children with severe motor difficulties:

> may have difficulties affecting some or all of their limbs, limited hand function, fine and gross motor difficulties and sometimes difficulties with speech and language. Most, though not all pupils will have a medical diagnosis. A diagnosis may have been given at birth, at about the age of two or a later date, though deteriorating conditions such as muscular dystrophy may not be diagnosed until the child attends school. Some children may have physical difficulties as a result of an accident or illness, which can happen at any age. It must be remembered that, in the same way as other children, they may also have learning difficulties, dyslexia, dyspraxia, asthma, epilepsy, vision and hearing difficulties or hidden handicaps affecting their visual/auditory perception or eye/hand co-ordination etc.
>
> (Pickles 2001: 291)

A long-term plan for these pupils would take into account 'dignity and emotional needs . . . especially in positioning, toileting and transfers . . . to enable pupils to be as independent as possible . . . recognising that teaching methods may need to vary as needs change is all part of inclusion' (Pickles 2001: 292). It would also need to include:

- views of the student as a person, with hopes, expectations and rights, every other student;
- considerations of physical access to the school environment;
- ways in which the needs of the family and the student's place within it can be taken into account by the school;
- in-school factors that support, or militate against, the student's inclusion;
- the role of the support assistant(s) and the kind of relationship that might be established with the student and the family, and any issues this raises;
- the role and function of information and communications technology;
- the role and function of any other appropriate technological aids;
- professional development and awareness raising of teachers and other staff in the school;
- awareness-raising among peers, if appropriate;
- the place of therapy in the student's curriculum.

Medium- and short-term planning should be seen to flow logically from the long-term plan for the learner. For example, as in the case of pupils with severe motor difficulties described by Pickles (2001: 295):

> A life skill, long-term physical target might be for the pupil to stand and walk with a walker. The long term target might be for the pupil to stand and weight bear. The short term target might be for the pupil to use a prone stander in a low angle position, twice daily for 20-minute sessions, in class, taking some weight on the body and raising the angle of the stander by a few degrees with success.

Any specific equipment should also be noted at this point, detailing where, when, how and why it should be used.

Making effective use of individual education plans

In many countries, for example England, Wales, Northern Ireland and New Zealand, the individual education plan, in some form, has become a major tool for planning programmes of study for individual students (DENI 1998; Ministry of Education 1998; DfES 2001). In general terms, these documents are expected to contain details of the nature of the child's learning difficulties, the special educational provision to be made and strategies to be used, specific programmes, activities, materials, and/or equipment, targets to be achieved in a specified time, monitoring and assessment arrangements, and review arrangements and date. The details vary slightly from one country to another. In England, for example, guidance given in the *Special Educational Needs Code of Practice* (DfES 2001: para. 4:27) suggests that the IEP should be 'crisply written' and record 'only that which is *additional to* or *different from* the differentiated curriculum plan that is in place as part of normal provision' (original emphases). It should contain:

- information about the short-term targets, which should be three or four in number;
- 'the teaching strategies and the provision to be put in place';
- 'when the plan is to be reviewed';
- 'the outcome of the action taken'.

In England and Wales the government's 'social inclusion' agenda has led to the issuing of further guidance to schools about ways to reduce student disaffection and truancy. Teachers are expected to identify students who do not respond to actions in school to address disaffection and to design a pastoral support programme (PSP) in liaison with external support services. A PSP should be automatically set up for a student who has several fixed period exclusions that may lead to a permanent exclusion or who has been otherwise identified as being at risk of failure at school through disaffection (www. teachernet.gov.uk/supplyteachers/detail.cfm?&vid=4&cid=17&sid=111&ssid=4030901 &opt=0 accessed 7 May 2008). However it is not intended to replace the assessment and intervention stages of an IEP. Agencies external to the school are involved, as appropriate: social services and housing departments, voluntary organizations and the Youth Service, both statutory and voluntary, careers services and minority ethnic community groups.

Planning a curriculum to meet particular special learning needs of individual students should take place within the context of the same decision-making processes that relate to teaching and learning for all students in a school. In addition it must take account of any formal and informal individual assessment of student learning that has taken place, and this should address any statutory requirements.

Planning to address individuals' learning needs effectively means setting out to work from strengths and interests. Staff attitudes and students' view of themselves as able to learn (or not!) make for potent interactions for good or ill. When planning for students who experience difficulties in learning, we first need to know whether the student or group can, with appropriate access strategies and teaching styles, work on the same learning objectives as the rest of the class. Getting this right will depend on accurate assessment of what the student knows, understands and can do. For some students with communication and interaction needs, for students with sensory or physical impairment, for many dyslexic students and for students with behavioural, emotional and social needs it is highly likely that what is needed is adaptations to teaching styles and the use of access strategies, rather than different learning objectives.

Planning will also need to be informed by the individual priorities for students. Normally it will be appropriate for them to work on objectives that are similar and related to the whole-class topic. However, at other times teachers will also have to consider whether the students have other priority needs that are central to their learning, for example a need to concentrate on some key skills such as communication, problem-solving, working with others, managing their own emotions, and so on. These needs may be detailed in the student's IEP or a Statement of SEN. They can often be met within the whole-class learning; for example relating physiotherapy objectives to the PE curriculum, communication to literacy lessons, problem-solving to mathematics, history or geography. What the teacher wants the student to learn may be distinct and different from the learning objectives for the class, but the activities designed for the class as whole can encompass the student's individual priority need.

Target-setting

In some institutions there may be a difference of opinion over the level of detail required for the targets that are set for students. This might be addressed by considering the purpose of the IEP or individual profile which, as Tod et al. (1998) note, is to facilitate student learning by means of the effective negotiation and planning of learning goals as well as the nature of the assessment it reflects.

Lessons may be planned to facilitate understanding of content, develop concepts or skills, practise problem-solving or encourage students' personal interests. Sometimes it happens that barriers are created to children's learning simply by the way in which material designed to facilitate understanding of a concept is presented. Where students experience difficulty it is essential to tease out whether the problem lies at the level of conceptual understanding or is the result of the mode of communication, especially when this is reliant on written text.

Individual plans, profiles or records can only be as effective as the rigour of the thinking underlying their design. Similar issues arise in relation to target-setting for IEPs and individual profiles as those relating to target-setting within the national context. The strength of targets may be that they provide a focus for the combined efforts of all those concerned to support a learner's progress and highlight the need to link planning and provision. However, there are specific areas of the curriculum where it may be problematic to conceptualize measurable targets. These areas involve behaviour, the emotions and creativity.

Setting measurable targets is closely associated with behavioural approaches. A school and a national curriculum can be seen as a ladder of progression which children are expected to climb, with specific assessment learning goals at each rung. An inherent difficulty in this view, however, is that not all children learn the same way, so setting targets which follow in a similar sequence for all students is not necessarily appropriate. Dockrell and McShane (1993, cited in Open University 2002: 196–7) highlight problems associated with this approach and note that: 'One of the major criticisms of task analysis and learning objectives is the conceptualization of the learning process.' They go on to comment that 'there may be a number of routes by which a child can acquire mastery, rather than a single instructional hierarchy that is common to all children'. They also note that carrying out a task analysis assures that each child will 'learn the task components in the same order, because the task is analysed and not the learning processes or the learning context'. There is also the possibility that an 'over-reliance on task components can lead to a rigid application of prescriptive teaching, which takes no account of the knowledge a child brings to any given task or the specific strategies that a child utilizes' (Dockrell and McShane 1993, in Open University 2002: 196–7). In addition, some areas lend themselves to this approach more easily than others.

In Chapter 5 we discuss the planning process for a dyslexic student 'Sonia' and illustrate what an IEP designed to take account of the learning needs of a dyslexic student such as Sonia might look like.

'Multi-element planning' (MEP) to address behavioural concerns

As noted in Chapter 3, the design and development of effective individual intervention programmes require clear assessment of both student performance and the learning environment. One practical approach currently used in parts of the UK as well as in other areas of the world is that of 'multi-element planning'. This approach takes account of:

- potential causes of difficulties experienced by the child;
- factors that appear to maintain the behaviour seen as challenging or otherwise of concern;
- strategies related to improving the learning environment, the teaching skills that will be useful to the child;
- strategies that will prevent the recurrence of the problematic behaviour or provide a way of safeguarding the child, peers and staff when the behaviour does recur.

One of the issues to be considered in multi-element planning is that of ethics. Where teachers deliberately set out to change students' behaviour there is always a question of how that teacher's power is exercised, what behaviour is seen as preferable and why, and in whose interest it is that the behaviour should be changed in this way. Pitchford poses the following questions that should be considered before any assessment or intervention is devised:

> What gives us the right to manipulate or change someone's behaviour?
> How certain are we that the problem behaviour is not a perfectly reasonable response to unreasonable circumstances?
> If we do intervene, how ethically sound are our techniques and what is their record of effectiveness (Cooper, Heron and Heward, 1987; Grant and Evans, 1994)?
>
> (2004: 311)

In his work Pitchford references the multi-element planning described by LaVigna and Donnellan (1986) which has four main components:

- Strategies that 'examine whether there are mismatches between the child and his/her environment that require a change in the environment not a change in the child (Pitchford 2004: 312). Change strategies should be considered in relation to interpersonal, physical, and instructional contexts in which the behaviour occurs.
- Positive programming which involves 'teaching children skills that will have a positive impact on their lives working on the assumption that learning is empowering, gives dignity to the individual, helps them get their needs met and helps them cope with an imperfect world' (Pitchford 2004: 313). Three areas of skill development are addressed: general, functionally equivalent and coping:
  - general: 'academic or life skills that the child has not mastered that are having a negative impact on his/her quality of life' (Pitchford 2004: 313)
  - functionally equivalent: that is, socially acceptable skills or behaviour that will serve the same purpose for the student as that which is seen as unacceptable. 'No matter how strange, behaviour always has a purpose or a function (LaVigna and Donnellan, 1986). If we understand that purpose or function we are more likely to be able to channel it in a constructive way' (Pitchford 2004: 314). Pitchford offers examples of 'problem behaviours and their functions together with the functionally-equivalent skills that could be included in a multi-element plan to help the child achieve the same end' (see Table 4.1)
  - coping skills designed to help students 'manage and tolerate the frustrations and difficulties in their lives'.
- Preventive strategies, comprising the antecedent control strategy and the use of reward strategies (LaVigna and Donnellan 1986):
  - antecedent control strategies include removing those events that act as a direct trigger to problem behaviours (Glynn 1982);
  - reward strategies only work well when they are used in the context of the types of positive programming and ecological strategies described earlier. Rewards can be artificial. The teacher will not always be there to reward the child and since the aim is to teach the child to be independent, rewards may only be a short-term expedient. From a behavioural perspective, basically there are three ways of rewarding children (LaVigna and Donnellan 1986):
    1 Rewarding children for being 'good'.
    2 Rewarding children for not being 'naughty'.
    3 Rewarding children for being 'naughty' less often than they were before. However, as Pitchford comments, this technique may be inappropriate for behaviour seen as dangerous.
- Reactive strategies which 'are included in the plan in order to safeguard the child, his or her peers and staff when things go wrong ... In particular we should know what safe non-punitive techniques will be used if the problem behaviour occurs and what support will be given to the child. Just as important is consideration of the practical and emotional help or support that should be given to the member of staff' (Pitchford 2004: 321).

Table 4.1   Problem/function/equivalent skill

Problem	Function	Functionally Equivalent Skill
Calling out	Make contact with peers.	Teach student to put his/her hand up and wait quietly, or wait and they say politely: 'Excuse me Sir/Miss I've finished my work.'
Bullying of peers	Take other children's possessions. Make other children share possessions unwillingly.	Teach students to take turns, to play in a co-operative way, and/or to negotiate.
Temper tantrums	Express feeling/anger.	Teach child to express feelings through the medium of writing or art or drama.
Tantrums as a result of failure in classroom tasks	Avoid situations involving repeated failure in class	Teach child the required skills. Teach child how to seek help politely.
Makes disruptive noises	To amuse peers/seek peer's attention	Teach child how to tell jokes, and the appropriate time(s) to do so.

Pitchford notes three practical steps need to be taken before drawing up the plan:

- Identify the frequency, seriousness and the contexts in which the behavioural problems occur.
- Prioritize the problems.
- Collect baseline data against which progress can be assessed. All data collected should be used to support the setting of targets for the MEP, reviewing progress and establishing appropriate criteria for rewards.

Planning for individuals within whole-class activities

Targets for individual education plans need to be embedded in the regular cycle of classroom activity integrated with the learning experience offered to the child through the curriculum. In lesson planning, teachers and classroom assistants need to be aware of which pupils have IEPs and be conversant with their content so that they can take adequate account of individual pupils' needs. As we have seen, interventions designed, for example, to address problematic student behaviour should take account of the student's view of the world, fit in with the curriculum offered to peers, and be compatible with the school's policy towards supporting the personal well-being and development of its students.

An intervention to address behaviour problems related to the emotions

The intervention described below meets the expectation that a plan for a student should be embedded into the school curriculum, be based on an appropriate, sensitive assessment of need, be well focused even if the targets do not lend themselves easily to clear measurement, and should take both student's and parents' views into account. This example is intended as a reflection of one teacher's view of children as learners and of the nature of emotional development. This particular teacher adopted an empathetic, problem-solving approach which attempted to understand what 'Jake's' behaviour meant, took account of his grief and anxieties, and used positive feedback from peers.

Eleven-year-old Jake had recently suffered a family bereavement. His extremely aggressive behaviour towards other pupils had drawn him to everyone's attention (Wearmouth 1999). In her initial assessment of the difficulties Jake appeared to be experiencing his teacher noted that he was resistant to direct help. Further informal assessment was carried out through small-group discussion between Jake and his peers. All the students were encouraged to express their feelings about what was important to them and what they found hardest in school.

Two issues appeared to be causing Jake anxiety and upset: lack of friends and the fact that he hurt peers and did not understand his own actions in doing so.

Jake's assessment was discussed with his parents, with his particular needs in mind. As a result, circle time (Mosley 1996) was introduced as the major part of the personal and social education curriculum. A nine-week programme was designed for the whole class, with three main topic areas: friends, recognition and expression of feelings, and bereavement and grief. These topics lent themselves very appropriately to follow-up discussion and written work in English lessons. The targets set for Jake were not easy to specify in the detail which would be required for exact measurement, as is common in the area of behaviour. They centred around developing and maintaining positive relationships with peers and teachers, and were negotiated between the teacher, Jake and his parents. These targets were also seen as appropriate for other students in the classroom. They included:

* listening carefully to others;
* taking turns;
* being polite;
* concentrating on the work in hand;
* looking out for ways to help other people.

New routines were introduced to support the development of these relationships: a 'magic shell' in circle time which bestowed permission to speak solely on the person holding it, personal confidential notebooks to draw, write about or use symbols to describe thoughts; feelings and 'new' behaviour; and play activities designed to build co-operation and mutual trust between the children.

Records were kept of Jake's behaviour in a number of respects:

* Jake kept a record of his own behaviour in his notebook.
* His teacher kept a record through observation in and out of the classroom.
* His family also agreed to write down a description of any worrying behaviour at home.

All these records showed a significant improvement in the areas which had been causing concern to the teacher and his parents, as well as to Jake himself. During this time there were no major aggressive incidents and only one occasion when he felt the need to storm off after an argument. At the same time he appeared to be responding much more positively to his family.

The teacher herself, reflecting on this intervention, was left wondering whether the improvement in Jake's behaviour was the result of the plan drawn up for him, of the closer, happier relationship within his family, of both of these, or of time and added maturity. One of the issues in the area of behaviour programmes often is that we cannot be sure of the reason for change in behaviour. However, this should not detract from clarity of thinking about what might or might not contribute to pupil behaviour which is causing concern or from attempts to understand a situation from the pupil's perspective.

Planning for differentiation

As Cowne (2000) advises, teachers must have a very clear grasp of eight issues when planning lessons that take IEPs for individual pupils into account:

1   how the principal curriculum objectives and key concepts for the lesson relate to the overall schemes for the school;

2   the way in which the principal objectives and key concepts are to be assessed, the criteria which indicate a satisfactory level of skills and understanding of key concepts, ways in which the assessment process might be differentiated and the means by which the outcome of the assessment is to be recorded as part of the IEP;

3   the prerequisite skills for the principal objectives, and the prior level of knowledge required to understand key concepts;

4   the extent to which all pupils in the classroom, including those identified as having special learning needs, have the prerequisite skills and prior knowledge in order that any 'pre-teaching', or a different resource to assist access to information, might be arranged;

5   relevant skills and knowledge that might be cross-referenced from another curriculum area;

6   ways in which various kinds of group work, with or without additional assistance from adults, might assist learning in the particular lesson;

7   the extent to which those pupils with the greatest needs might be expected to fulfil the principal objectives and grasp all key concepts;

8   whether an alternative set of objectives will be needed for any children.

Cowne's views imply a flexibility of approach which demands a thorough grasp of, and familiarity with, the National Curriculum structure and its underlying principles in addition to the strengths and needs of individual pupils.

Differentiation: the example of English in the Primary National Strategy

Planning lessons suitable for a class of children with a range of needs and strengths can seem quite challenging. Taking the example of English, the Framework for Literacy and English in the Primary National Strategy (PNS) has the status of guidance and is not statutory. The PNS website (www.standards.dfes.gov.uk/primary/, accessed 26 June 2008) lists objectives and ideas across the English National Curriculum and highlights children's learning outcomes, questions, activities and ideas to use to assess understanding.

We might take as an example the area of poetry in Year 4, Unit 1 'Creating images': children reading and responding to a range of poems and prose extracts with similes and other simple images used to create a vivid picture (adapted from Hewitt, unpublished manuscript). Stimulus material for the poems can be drawn from other areas of the curriculum or related to cross-curricular themes.

The objectives for the series of lessons taken from the PNS might be:

1. Speaking: respond appropriately to the contributions of others in light of differing viewpoints.
6. Word structure and spelling: use knowledge of phonics, morphology and etymology to spell new and unfamiliar words.
7. Understanding and interpreting texts: explain how writers use figurative and expressive language to create images and atmosphere.
8. Engaging with and responding to texts. read extensively favourite authors or genres and experiment with other types of text. Interrogate texts to deepen and clarify understanding and response. Explore why and how writers write, including through face-to-face and online contact with authors.
9. Creating and shaping texts: develop and refine ideas in writing using planning and problem-solving strategies. Choose and combine words, images and other features for particular effects.
12. Presentation: write consistently with neat, legible and joined handwriting. Use word processing packages to present written work and continue to increase speed and accuracy in typing.

Phase 1 of this sequence of lessons might be planned to include children reading a number of poems that use similes and other simple images to create a vivid picture. Children might perform poems, individually or in groups, using actions and sound effects where appropriate to heighten awareness of the language and imagery used. They might respond to the poems in a variety of ways, for example through dance, drama and art. They might think what the poems are about, discuss the poet's use of language, and identify distinctive features, such as similes and other devices. Then they might reflect on why poets might have chosen to use language in the way they did.

Phase 2 might be planned to explore examples of similes through various games. The teacher might model planning and writing a new poem based upon those read in previous sessions. Children might then write their own poem, using similes and other devices to create imagery.

In phase 3 children might write a poem based on a different model, using similes and other devices to create imagery. They might share outcomes through discussion and performance, or they might be published as a class book, using presentation software or online as a podcast.

Learning outcomes might be that children can recognize and discuss how poets use language (including similes and other simple images) to create a vivid picture in words.

Differentiation of lesson activities, tasks and resources would need to take account of the full range of learning needs among children in the classroom and any requirements on individual education plans. This includes current reading levels, consideration of possible visual and auditory difficulties, interest level of the poems that are used, considerations of student grouping in the classroom, prior experiences of students, the potential range of applications of ICT that might support learning, and so on. Resources include the human as well as the material. In a primary classroom, discussion and preparation with teaching assistants and any other adults prior to the sequence of lessons is vital.

Integrating targets for students with complex physical difficulties into classroom learning for all

Pickles (2001: 292) discusses how targets for students with complex physical difficulties might be integrated in a practical way into lesson planning for all students:

Children with severe motor difficulties may not have been able to internalise concepts such as direction, shape, size, height and weight, because of their inability to explore the environment and objects. They often require adult facilitation, making them more likely to be passive learners, lacking independence and unable to consolidate learning in the same way as the majority of pupils. Pupils in this situation are likely to switch off.

It is vital for teachers to devise activities to enable consolidation and repetition, using a multi-sensory approach, utilising the pupil's auditory, visual, tactile and sensory skills. These activities will also enable the pupil to internalise a wide range of general concepts such as perception, distance, depth, weight etc. Thinking laterally to plan activities to meet the greatest needs, as well as majority needs, is cost effective in time and energy. Activities or games with learning and therapeutic targets using real objects and utensils, ensure that therapeutic targets are used functionally, included into everyday learning and accessible to all.

Although some games may have therapy targets for specific pupils they remain extremely good to teach all pupils, because the learning targets remain the same. It is how the games are played, which enables different therapeutic targets to be incorporated. Multi-sensory games are particularly useful to teach children with any kind of special need as learning is positively reinforced through the senses.

If we focus on the needs of another group of students, those who experience difficulties in language and cognition, it might seem sensible to use Bruner's three modes of representation – enactive, iconic and symbolic – as a general framework for curriculum differentiation. Some students still need to learn by doing and require concrete objects to work with; others need recognizable representations of reality in the form of, for example, pictures; others still can benefit from using symbolic representations and abstract reasoning. This offers a clear justification for stating that good use of practical resources can make lessons interactive and motivational for children.

In terms of assessment opportunities, following the exploration of a poem the teacher might direct the children's attention to a simile and ask them to think about what pictures the words make them see in their minds. Through use of the think–pair–share technique the children might share with a partner what they see in their mind and how they would feel if they were part of the scene, and share ideas with the class. The teacher might then note ideas on the interactive whiteboard (IWB) alongside the simile.

Children might also choose the most powerful image from a selection of poems shared and explored by the class. They might visualize and draw what they would see if they were standing within this scene, note what they would see and hear and how they would feel if they stood as part of the scene.

Assessment of this series of lessons and activities might be through:

* teacher observation;
* teacher questioning;
* marking and feedback (oral and written).

Evidence of children's learning might be through:

* children's discussions and oral responses;
* children's drawings, notes and writing drafts.

Not all teachers wish to follow the sequences of activities suggested on web pages associated with the formal Literacy Strategy. However, it is probably worth following the outline guidance about how to plan a literacy unit from scratch:

Planning a literacy unit for the whole class

You may not want to use the exemplified teaching sequences and create your own from scratch. But even in that case, you may find them very helpful. They provide you with one set of ideas that model good practice. If there is not a planning exemplification for the unit you can still follow the model used as it helps to structure your planning.

Planning considerations
Outcomes
Components of the teaching sequence
The phases
The detail
The text
The environment

Planning considerations – Outcomes
What will the outcome be?
Will the outcome be written or oral? Might it be a performance of some sort?
Will the outcome be the same for all ability groups?
Who is the audience?
What is the purpose?

Planning considerations – Components of the teaching sequence
With the identified objectives and initial thoughts in mind, you should brainstorm possible components of the teaching sequence and learning teaching strategies. This is the creative bit and you can really let your imagination run away with you. You can also refer to teaching sequences that are available and think about how these might be adapted to meet the needs of your children. Amongst other things, you can consider:

- texts, websites and other resources you know that might be useful
- drama strategies
- speaking and listening strategies
- writing opportunities
- modelled, shared and supported composition
- reading journal entries
- links to the assessment foci
- guided reading and writing
- sentence and word level links
- opportunities for ICT

Planning considerations – The phases

Next you need to flesh out the creative ideas onto the bones of the teaching sequence. The order and length of time for each phase of the teaching sequence are made clear at this stage (particularly writing and the writing process).

Objectives are constantly returned to and the ideas are trimmed to focus on the learning outcomes for each phase. You have to decide which strategies and activities will be kept, and which are not necessary for the learning outcomes. For example: Where drama will come? How will this support the learning objectives?

Throughout this process you should keep in mind practical constraints:

- Access to resources – specially ICT
- TA support
- Timetable constrains

Planning considerations – The detail

Next you can plot discrete teaching of certain aspects, for example:

- Will a spelling convention be taught and investigated in week one?
- Can independent strategies be taught within the writing process?
- Which aspects will require modelling?
- Which aspects will require shared or guided reading and writing?
- You can return to the objectives to clarify your thinking at this point.

Planning considerations – The text

An important part of the planning process is to unpick the text or texts you have identified, think of key questions, scaffolds, etc. You should return again to the objectives:

- What will they really be learning?
- What will my teaching ensure the pupils understand?

You will find that thinking about the learning you want to happen helps you to form key questions and plan plenaries which will allow you to assess learning and the children's understanding.

Planning considerations – The environment

Finally, you should consider the learning environment:

- book boxes
- working wall
- role play areas
- possible educational visits

You may want to give as many opportunities for children to immerse and contextualise their literacy learning in its broadest sense.

(*www.standards.dcsf.gov.uk/primary/teachingresources/*, accessed 6 May 2008)

Differentiation to enable all students to access the curriculum remains of prior importance in any teacher's planning activity. There are many ways of differentiating support offered to students who experience difficulties in written expression, and it is worth outlining how this differentiated support might be integrated into a mainstream lesson. Examples of such structural support strategies during, for example, a sequence of lessons intended to facilitate children's written storytelling skills include:

A story hand
Individuals draw around their hands and represent in key words, simple icons or pictures the key events in the beginning (thumb) middle (middle three fingers) and end (little finger) of the story. The themes of the tale can also be shown as rings on the hand or a bracelet encapsulating the narrative.

A physical story board
Groups of children freeze-frame a key element in the story/chapter so that the whole structure is physically represented by the class in several tableaux. The sequential structure can then be revisited and the story retold by the teacher or a child moving between each of the freeze frames. If titles are given to these tableaux, a summary or resume of the tale/chapter is effectively created.

A problem resolution chart
Applicable only to problem resolution tales, this usefully denotes the sequential paragraphs or chapters, that seek to resolve the key problem, and documents the eventual resolution.

Story maps
These can be varied to suit the narrative, but could include the geographical settings in the story (particularly appropriate for journey tales and circular stories), the main movements of the protagonists and antagonists, the sequence of events and the key phrases from the tale (e.g. repetitive story language or significant speech).

Block graphs
These suit cumulative story structures and enable the accumulating building blocks of the narrative to be recorded simply but effectively. Icons can be drawn in each box to show the repetitive sequential pattern in the tale.

Story mountains

These suit climactic stories and clearly demarcate the climax of the tale at the apex of the mountain range. Made out of sugar paper with small pictures or keywords to denote the sections of the story, mountains are very versatile and can be cut to suit the number of significant episodes in the narrative.

Flow charts

These show the development of the story, scene by scene. They can be used to represent a known tale or as a planning device.

Paragraph/scene charts

These provide a series of boxes in which each scene is drawn or notes are made. They can become flexible if 'post-its' are used, as this means that scenes can be moved around. For instance, instead of beginning a story at the beginning, a writer might start with the dramatic event and then have a flashback to the opening, e.g. 'It had only been two hours ago that Mrs Savage had told the two girls not to play by the canal ...'

Enacting the tale

This is a powerful way to represent stories and also acts as a precursor to writing. If children have just acted out a scene or improvised an event then they will find writing easier because the key sequence of events can be more firmly fixed in the mind.

Telling (or retelling) the tale

With children working in pairs, or as a story circle, stories can be retold or invented. Oral rehearsing of a story means that some refining and revision can take place before the act of writing.

Listing scenes

Many writers use the simple technique of making a list of the key events in the story.

Mind mapping

The more children internalise a range of basic structures, the more they are able to write successfully without rigid plans. This is because they know the direction in which the tale must move. This allows them to be imaginative as they are writing and to allow unexpected events to creep into the tale. When children are confident with story structure they can use mind mapping successfully as a way of generating ideas for stories.

(www.standards.dfes.gov.uk/literacy, accessed 6 May 2008)

An example of a daily lesson plan format designed to incorporate provision for differentiated learning might be as shown in Figure 4.2.

DAILY LESSON PLAN			
Year Group: **Class:** **Set (if appropriate):**	**Time of Session:** **Length of Session:**	**Date:**	**No. of children:**

Target(s)

Students' subject knowledge: *Write in bullet points the essential knowledge students need for this session*

Learning Objectives: *Specific, clear learning objectives including reference to NC where appropriate.*

Key Vocabulary:

Resources and materials required: *What equipment/resources will you need to carry out the activity?*

Organization and Management: *Who introduces the activity? How will the children be organized during lesson (e.g. whole class for the introduction, then work as groups or individuals for the activity)? Who will you work with? How will teaching assistants or other adults be used? How will you manage transitions within the lesson e.g. children moving from one area to the next*

Whole-Class Input

Timing	***Share clear, student-friendly learning objective(s).*** *What is the stimulus? How will you capture the students' attention? Include key questions you will ask. What will the students be doing? How will the activity be differentiated? How will you use other adults? What will be your role in the teaching activity?*
Activity: Independent or Adult-Led (e.g. collaborative groups):	

Students with additional access needs
Students with no additional access needs
Higher Attainers
Extension Activities *What will children who finish the activities do next? How will this develop their learning further?*
Conclusion: *(you may have also had 'mini-reviews' during the main part of the lesson)*

Figure 4.2 Daily Lesson Plan

Conclusion

The view of problematic student learning and behaviour in schools seen as associated both with the context and with the attributes of the individual requires an approach to assessment at multiple levels: the individual student, the classroom, the school, and so on. Assessment should be viewed as a tool that supports learning and not simply as a politically expedient solution to perceived concerns about standards and ways to make schools accountable to parents, families and society as a whole (ATL 1996).

Assessment can therefore serve to either reinforce or undermine the motivation to strive for future achievement. Students' sense of themselves as having the potential to be effective in the community of practice of learners may be constructed and/or constrained by the forms of assessment that are used with them. Assessment therefore must aim to build on students' experiences and identities. Assessment that is ongoing, continuous and formative, and provides teachers with formal and informal opportunities to notice what is happening during learning activities, recognize where the learning of individuals and groups of students is going and how they as the teacher can help take that learning further, is likely to lead to positive learning gains. This process begins by ensuring students receive appropriate learning goals and are engaged in interactive conversations throughout their learning activities. In Chapter 5 we contextualize the assessment and planning process with the area of difficulties in literacy.

5 Addressing the needs of learners who experience literacy difficulties

Questions addressed in this chapter

What is known about the characteristics of effective teachers of students who experience difficulties in literacy acquisition?

What might teachers need to know about different theories of literacy acquisition, in order to understand and take a problem-solving approach to addressing the difficulties in literacy experienced by some students?

What strategies can teachers and other adults and peers in classrooms use to support students to improve their literacy levels?

What kind of family and community support might be appropriate for literacy learning?

Introduction

There are many students whose reading level is consistently assessed as several years below what might be expected and whose writing is poor, given their chronological age or given the length of time they have participated in school literacy programmes. Sometimes, targets for the raising of students' literacy levels are expressed in terms of reading scores referenced against the norm for a particular student cohort. Some countries, such as England, have legally required national literacy curricula with close prescriptions of content, modes of teaching and forms of assessment. However, there is no simple recipe for a one-size-fits-all solution to raising the literacy levels of students who experience difficulties. No single programme is uniquely positioned to address the barriers to literacy development experienced by every child (Bond and Dykstra 1967; Adams 1994).

Questions for reflection

In your opinion or experience:

- How influential is the individual teacher in supporting the success – or otherwise – of teaching programmes?
- How can teachers, as individuals, create the kind of learning environment that can motivate and support students to continue with their efforts to become competent literacy learners, even when they experience considerable difficulties?
- What is 'literacy' all about?
- What do you know about the way children may learn to read and write?

- How do you think our views about the process of reading and writing may impact on our literacy teaching and interpretations of how to implement best research-based practice?
- How do different understandings of what 'literacy' is all about, as well as of the process of reading and writing, impact on literacy teaching and interpretations of how to implement best research-based practice?
- What are the implications of the different literacy practices in students' families and cultures for students' literacy learning?

Attributes of successful teachers of literacy

Among educationalists, there is general agreement about the very grave effects that serious difficulties in literacy development can have on children and their families. As Bruner (1996) notes, one of the prime responsibilities of schools is to support students to see themselves as able to learn and achieve. Particularly where the learner has experienced considerable difficulties in literacy development, it is important that support for literacy learning is offered in ways which are responsive and productive in classrooms. Ten factors that characterize successful literacy teachers were among the findings from an important project researching the effective teaching of literacy more broadly at primary level (Wragg et al 1998):

- A high level of personal enthusiasm for literature, some even supplementing the school's reading resources with their own personal collection of books.
- Good professional knowledge of children's authors and teaching strategies.
- Literacy being made very important, within a rich literacy environment.
- Celebrating progress publicly and increasing children's confidence.
- Being able to individualise and match teaching to pupils, particularly in terms of their reading interests.
- Systematic monitoring and assessment, though the form of it varied.
- Regular and varied reading activities.
- Pupils being encouraged to develop independence and autonomy, attacking unfamiliar words, taking their own reading forward, or backing their own judgement as authors.
- A notably high degree of classroom management skill and good-quality personal relationships with pupils, with some of the highest 'on-task' scores we have recorded.
- High positive expectations, with children striving to reach a high standard, whatever their circumstances.

(Wragg et al. 1998: 265–6)

As Wragg et al. comment (1998: 266), of these ten factors, it is particularly important for teachers to be able to differentiate and match tasks to students who are 'less able and more reluctant readers'. 'Intimate knowledge of available reading materials and individual children themselves' is required, 'taking account not only of varying levels of ability, but also of individual personal interests'. Implied in this is the need for high levels of teacher expertise to support children's literacy acquisition effectively and be responsive to those who experience difficulties. In a similar way, the current Assessment for Learning initiative (Assessment Reform Group 1999) implies, in the context of literacy learning, that tutoring of students' reading or responding to the messages that they write requires feedback that is:

- responsive to the student's current stage of development;
- positive and respectful;
- able to inform the next steps in literacy learning;
- not overpowering or controlling.

An important factor that contributes to low levels of self-confidence in classroom learning is the visibility of assessment information relating to how a child performs relative to peers. Research conducted in mainstream classrooms (Ames and Archer 1988) suggests that, for children who experience difficulty in learning, public comparison with higher-achieving peers can be very damaging. There are many adults who can recall being humiliated by a teacher's public demonstrations of their lack of achievement in literacy in comparison with peers (Open University 2002). However unintentional this may have been on the part of the professional concerned, the fact remains that many adults have had similarly upsetting experiences which they still remember vividly.

Students' views of the 'best' and 'worst' teachers

In a UK study (Riddick 1996: 124) of the personal experiences of 22 students identified as 'dyslexic', and their families, the students reflected on their school experiences of difficulties in literacy. These students had very strong views about which teachers were best able to support them in ways that were positive and productive. They identified the 'best' teachers as those who:

- encourage and praise;
- help students, adapt work and explain clearly;
- understand students and not attempt to humiliate them;
- not shout;
- have a sense of humour;
- know if students are dyslexic;
- treat all students as if they are intelligent.

The worst teachers, on the other hand:

- are cross, impatient and shout;
- criticize and humiliate students;
- are not helpful, and are negative about students' efforts;
- ignore some students and show they consider some students 'useless';
- do not understand the problems faced by students with difficulties in literacy and are insensitive;
- blame students for their problems and call them 'lazy';
- put red lines through students' work.

Similar findings are reflected clearly in a research project in five mainstream New Zealand schools (Bishop et al. 2003) which sought to identify how teacher responsiveness to the experiences and understandings of Māori students at Years 9 and 10 could lead to more effective educational outcomes. Both engaged and non-engaged students identified relationships between teachers and students as key to engagement with curriculum learning. For example, respect from their teachers was extremely important to these students: 'Look pleased to see us. Treat us respectfully. Look like you want to be here. Say "hi" to us when we come in . . . Mark our work often. Tell us when we're doing good. Better still tell our family' (Bishop et al. 2003: 240–1).

Above all they asked to be treated fairly:

> Don't yell at kids . . . If you don't like something we're doing tell us quietly. Talk to us about where we sit. Give us a chance to sit with our mates. If we muck up then warn us and if we are too thick to listen [to the warning] then move us . . . Don't rave on about how you don't want to be here. Don't put us down and don't let us put our friends down. Be fair.
>
> (Bishop et al. 2003: 240–1)

These students wanted their teachers to have expert knowledge in their subject, be well prepared and to focus on high achievement in the classroom: 'Don't start thinking about what you are going to teach us when we walk in the room. Get prepared . . . Be keen about your subject so we want to come . . . Just 'cause we are a "C" class, don't expect us to be dumb' (Bishop et al. 2003: 240–1).

Different views of the process of reading and writing

Teachers' awareness and understanding of the process of literacy learning and, therefore, the barriers to such learning, are particularly important in decisions about which interventions which suit which student and in which circumstances. There are a number of different, and contrasting, views about the act of reading. Traditionally two have dominated: so-called 'bottom-up' and 'top-down' approaches.

'Bottom-up' approaches

From a 'bottom-up' view, reading comprises the process of decoding the abstract and complicated alphabetic code, and reconstructing the author's meaning. Fluent readers look first at the visual features of text such as component letters in the words, and identify symbols with sounds before they move on to consider the meaning of the print (Adams 1994). This view sees reading as a series of small steps to be learned one by one. First children must learn the letters of the alphabet and establish the principle of sound–symbol identification. Then they must learn to apply this in order to decode words. It implies teaching methods which emphasize the mastery of phonics and word recognition. With adequate practice, children will be able to understand written text.

The process of learning about sound–symbol association, that is, the rules about letters and sounds in written language, is usually referred to as phonics.

The phonological system

Components of the phonological system include phonemic awareness and phonological knowledge:

- Phonemic awareness can be demonstrated by a literacy learner's ability to hear and manipulate sounds in speech. It therefore seems to provide a strong foundation for the development of decoding skills. There appears to be a link between the development of phonemic awareness and control over the alphabetical coding system, which in turn provides the basis for fluent word recognition (Stanovich 2000). Children identified as making poor progress in reading are frequently weaker in phonemic awareness than competent readers.
- Phonological awareness usually includes larger segments of speech, for example syllable and rhyme. There is strong experimental evidence that many students who experience difficulty in literacy learning exhibit deficiencies in phonological processing (Stanovich 2000). It is crucial that children develop this knowledge early on in their schooling. Exposure to poems, rhymes, songs, shared books with repeated readings can encourage an interest in language and books and guarantee for most children that phonological training and word reading can effectively be linked together.

Those who see reading essentially as a process of decoding written symbols into sounds are likely to interpret difficulty with visual and auditory factors as important contributors to poor progress in literacy acquisition.

The implication of this view is to highlight the significance of 'synthetic' phonics (see below for explanation), writing and spelling whole words, exercise with frequent blends and digraphs, practice with word families and attention to every letter of the word, in left-to-right order (Adams 1994). It might seem logical to respond to the kind of visual and auditory difficulties listed above with a phonics-based approach. However, there is a strong argument for suggesting great sensitivity here. Focusing on phonics, phonics and more phonics to the exclusion of other techniques may be experienced by students as extremely boring and demoralizing (Wearmouth 2004a). For older students, for example, there have been occasions when, as a teacher, I chose to turn to a 'whole-book' approach (see below) for the sake of re-igniting students' interest in literacy learning, left aside phonics for a while and returned to it at a later date.

'Top-down' approaches

The second approach views reading as the active *construction* of meaning, not simply the decoding of visual symbols into sounds. The reader is assumed to have expectations of what a text might be about, and then to test these expectations and confirm or reject them as s/he proceeds, the so-called 'psycholinguistic guessing game' (Goodman 1996).

Understanding a psycholinguistic approach to the reading process

'[A]s we read, our minds are actively busy making sense of print, just as they are always actively trying to make sense of the world. Our minds have a repertoire of strategies for sense-making. In reading, we can call these psycholinguistic because there's continuous interaction between thought and language' (Goodman 1996: 110–11). Everything readers do is part of their attempt to make sense and construct meaning out of print. According to Goodman, readers do not need to pay attention to every single part of every word to read a text. 'Readers become highly efficient in using just enough of the available information to accomplish their purpose of making sense' (Goodman 1996: 91).

Goodman is highly critical of phonic instruction for children with difficulties in the area of literacy development:

> much misunderstanding still exists about reading and written language in general. I believe that this confusion exists largely because people have started in the wrong place, with letters, letter-sound relationships and words. We must begin instead by looking at reading in the real world, at how readers and writers try to make sense with each other.
>
> (Goodman 1996: 2–3)

This approach has been linked with the whole-book/whole-language approach based on the concept of learning to read through reading, even for students who experience literacy difficulties. There are many examples across the world of reading programmes of this kind which combine emphasis on meaning and interest in text with awareness of the part that others, including peers and parents, can play. In the UK, for example, Waterland, an infant teacher, operated from an assumption that reading may be learned by young children working alongside competent readers through the so-called 'Apprenticeship Approach' (Waterland 1985).

'Interactive' approach

A third, many might say more balanced (McNaughton 2002), view of reading is the 'interactive' model which suggests that readers use information simultaneously from different sources. One set of information, for example identification of sounds with symbols, interacts with another, such as the anticipation of what the word is likely to be from the context of the text. During the development of reading skills, some readers may rely more heavily on visual and auditory cues, others on meaning and context. Readers' weaknesses can be compensated by her/his strengths. Stanovich (2000) calls this process the 'Interactive Compensatory' model because the various processes interact and also because the reader can compensate for weaknesses in one area by relying on strengths on the other aspects. Readers who are good at word recognition have less need to rely on context (Harrison 1994). They can recognize the word because they have mastered the elements of the sound–symbol system. Readers who cannot easily recognize words at a glance need context to aid recognition.

Understanding the interactive view

The interactive view of the process of reading and comprehending text, as McNaughton, (2002) comments, comprises:

- integrating ideas from prior knowledge and experiences with information in texts;
- retrieving information from texts;
- making inferences linked both to the texts that are being read and to prior knowledge;
- evaluating the content, structure and language of texts;
- applying understanding gained from texts;
- integrating readers':
  - phonemic awareness;
  - decoding skills;
  - rapid word recognition of a wide range of vocabulary;
  - knowledge of word meaning in a wide range of contexts;
  - knowledge of text structures and purposes;
  - knowledge of the strategies required to activate prior knowledge, integrate, evaluate and apply knowledge acquired from texts.

Literacy learners may experience difficulties in any one of these areas and, for each student, it is important not to make assumptions but to analyse individual strengths and needs carefully.

Addressing difficulties in reading

As noted already in this chapter, across the world there is a very wide range of teaching programmes and teaching approaches used to support the reading acquisition of those students who experience difficulties. Careful planning is required to address learning needs within a broad, balanced view of literacy and a global understanding of them as individuals as well as in the context of the school and classroom curriculum within which the plan is to be realized. Learning conversations include responsive feedback that connects to students' own experience of difficulties in literacy learning and feed forward to help students identify their next most appropriate learning steps.

As noted already, a balanced view of the reading process is of 'a complex, multi-faceted activity' which requires 'broad-based instruction':

> Children need to learn processing skills, using context and knowledge of syntax to focus on the general meaning of the whole, and also decoding skills focusing on individual letters and words. They need specific teaching of both 'top-down' and 'bottom-up' skills; a certain amount of phonic instruction; careful monitoring in order to give early help to those who make a slow start; interesting meaningful texts; teachers who are enthusiastic about literacy throughout the whole primary range; encouragement from home; and lots of practice.
>
> (Wragg et al. 1998: 32–3)

For the sake of clarity it is useful to separate out ways to address difficulties related to bottom-up and top-down views of what constitutes reading, while accepting the inter-active nature of the process:

- Bottom-up approaches comprise the teaching of phonics and phonological knowledge, word recognition.
- Top-down approaches comprise the teaching of strategies for improving com-prehension; vocabulary knowledge; reading fluency.

Teaching phonics

To teach phonics well teachers have to be knowledgeable. There is no single way that sound–symbol correspondences, blending of sounds together, phonic generalizations and segmentation of sounds for spelling can be taught to every learner. The challenge is always to plan teaching approaches that will help to improve students' literacy skills and understandings. Teacher skill and knowledge about the phonological system is essential, particularly with children experiencing difficulty or 'at risk' of reading failure.

Understanding synthetic and analytic phonics

There are two main approaches to phonics teaching:

- Synthetic phonics where letter-sound correspondences are taught in isolation and students are required to blend individual letters together to form whole words. At the beginning of the reading process, a small number of letter sounds are taught, and children are shown how to blend these sounds to pronounce unfamiliar words. Other groups of letters are taught and then blended. Some writers insist that curriculum guidelines are required for specific exercises attending to letter/sounds and 'subsyllabic sound units'.
- Analytic phonics which involves the analysis of consonants, vowels, blends, diagraphs and diphthongs taught within the context of whole words. Teaching begins at the level of the whole word and involves pointing out patterns in the English spelling system. Typically, children are taught one letter sound per week and shown pictures and words beginning with that sound. Then they are introduced to letter sounds in the middle of words, and so on. At some stage the teacher may show children how to blend con-secutive letters in unfamiliar words, for example 'buh-ah-tuh, bat'. Some writers contend that specific exercises are not necessary as children gather this information incidentally as they are exposed to text-rich environments and programmes.

As the National Institute of Child Health and Human Development (2000) notes, a crucial difference between synthetic and analytic phonics is that, in synthetic phonics, words are pronounced through sounding and blending. In analytic phonics letter sounds are analysed after the word has been identified.

Some popular programmes which can help to develop decoding skills and phonological processing include 'Toe by Toe' (Cowling and Cowling 1993) and 'Sound Linkage' (Hatcher 2000). The last focuses in particular on the sub-skills of reading. For example, in

'Sound Linkage' (Hatcher 2000) there are sections on syllable blending, phoneme blending, identification and discrimination of phonemes and activities on phonological linkage including multi-syllabic words and establishing links between sounds and the written form of words. Hannell (2003: 23) suggests the following sequence of instruction:

1. three letter words in a consonant-vowel-consonant pattern sound *hot ham mud top*
2. four letter words, where two letters slide together to make a sound *flag step best tick*
3. four letter words where two consonants make a new sound *shop thin chat when*
4. four letter words where a vowel and a consonant make a new sound *corn fowl wam quit*
5. four letter words with a final 'e' *mice date kite made*
6. three and four letter words where two vowels make a new sound *rain out loud meat*
7. silent letters *knee gnaw gnat know*
8. five letter words where three letters slide together *strap scrum strip judge squid*
9. five and six letter words where four letters make a new sound *fight dough nation*
10. longer words that combine two or more of the above patterns *jumper beach sprawl tribe*
11. prefixes, suffixes and compound words *predict disagree truthfully household*

Evaluating the effectiveness of phonics teaching

A significant amount of research indicates that explicit teaching of the alphabetical code leads to improved outcomes in reading accuracy (Ehri 2002). However, often the gains are not generalized to reading comprehension (Greaney et al. 1997; Nicholson 2000; Center et al. 2001, cited in de Lemos 2002).

An analysis of research in Australia (de Lemos 2002), has concluded that explicit teaching of phonics is a more effective strategy than little or no systematic instruction in phonics, but such instruction is not effective for all children experiencing difficulties. In a similar way, McNaughton (2002) reports that a programme promoting letter knowledge and letter-sound association, in the first year of schooling for children in economically poorer schools, was not successful in the transference of this knowledge across to word recognition, writing vocabulary and text reading at age 6. Although the children had reached national benchmarks in letter identification and knowledge of sounds after a year at school: 'Their core sight vocabulary was somewhat low, and it was particularly low for a wider, generalised group of words. Their basic writing vocabulary was low too, and they were very different from groups of children in other schools in the level of texts they could read' (McNaughton 2002: 83).

Multi-sensory approaches

One way to reinforce the links between sounds and symbols in order to develop skills in phonics is to take a multi-sensory approach to teaching. Multi-sensory programmes should focus on all modalities – auditory, visual, kinaesthetic and tactile. This means that when teaching the sound of a letter or groups of letters, the teacher might encourage students to say the sound out loud while simultaneously writing the letter(s), perhaps on a textured surface to integrate the memory of the motor movement with the sound and look, that is, the auditory and visual representation, of the letters.

Many reading programmes incorporate the multi-sensory principle and teachers can often develop supplementary materials to ensure that the activities are multi-sensory. This is particularly important when considering the learning needs of dyslexic students for whom the acquisition of phonics skills is often problematic. The 'Hickey Multi-Sensory Language Course' is reviewed on the Department for Children, Schools and Families (DCSF) website (www.dfes.gov.uk/readwriteplus/understandingdyslexia/approaches programmes/structuredcumulative/hickey/, accessed 16 June 2008).

Word recognition

'The 100 most frequently used words account for more than 55% of the words children read and *write*, and the 300 most frequently used words account for 72%' (Eldridge 1995: 165 emphasis added). There is a very strong argument, therefore, for supporting learners to be able to recognize common words on sight. If word recognition is not automatic, then a lot of energy will have to be expended on this and comprehension will be hindered (Stanovich 2000).

Many commonly used words are difficult to learn for some children because they have irregular letter-sound associations, for example 'they', 'what', 'are'. Learning letter sequences is challenging for children who have poor visual perception and retention. Most children learn to recognize commonly used words without any special 'drill' or systematic, sequential teaching through:

- shared and guided and personal reading opportunities which may involve the rereading of familiar texts;
- daily writing;
- word charts of commonly used words;
- word games;
- dictionaries, and so on.

However, others need specially focused multi-sensory teaching very similar to the approaches discussed in the spelling section below.

Vocabulary knowledge

For most children vocabulary is acquired easily and rapidly, without any explicit instruction, a result of engaging in reading or what is sometimes called 'reading mileage' (Graves and Watts-Taffe 2002: 142). Sustained silent reading (SSR) can ensure readers get more opportunity to practise. However,

- the text must be neither too difficult so that it is frustrating, nor too easy so that the text does not provide opportunities to extend and consolidate word recognition and vocabulary knowledge;
- the reading task must be enjoyable.

Sustained silent reading should not be the only type of reading instruction, particularly with students who have not yet developed critical alphabetic and word-reading skills.

Most words are learnt incidentally in the context of normal reading (Stahl 1998; McNaughton 2002). Generally readers work out the meanings of around 15 in every 100 unknown words as they read along. Clay (1979) demonstrated that by the end of their first year at school those children who made good progress had great exposure to numbers, and a wide range, of words, whereas those who were making slow progress had less opportunity to learn new words in context. For some children, vocabulary knowledge that supports literacy development may be limited.

Strategies to support children's vocabulary acquisition

Reading to children provides the opportunity to discuss unknown words (McNaughton 2002). However, just listening to stories may not always lead to vocabulary growth. Some children's attention may need to be engaged specially in discussion of new words and teaching new vocabulary within the context of text may need to be carefully planned (Buikema and Graves 1993):

- Pre-teaching of vocabulary (Nicholson and Tan 1997) before reading can increase children's vocabulary knowledge using flash cards of words likely to cause difficulty, for example.
- Sorting and classifying words prior to reading a text can help students to focus their reading and support their understanding of new concepts (Whitehead 1993). New vocabulary from the text can be used in advance for students to predict the content of the story or article. Questions can be set to clarify understanding of the vocabulary.
- The definitions of words are vitally important but students must be involved in active discussion and use, not just look up, definitions and put them into a sentence.
- Students might clarify new vocabulary by asking questions about:
  - What category does it belong to?
  - What is it like?
  - What are some examples (if it's a group, class or abstract concept)?
- Teachers might support children's memory of new words by thinking aloud about those words and encouraging learners to think aloud about words in ways that are personally meaningful. Teachers might also model ways to work out the meaning of new words from semantic and syntactic cues.
- Important or interesting words might be a special focus in vocabulary selected from books that are read to, read with and read by children. The words should be relevant to the learner at the time.

Developing the skills of reading comprehension

Teachers bear a huge responsibility for inspiring students in classrooms to become competent readers. Probably the most important prerequisite for competence in literacy is the development of oral language.

Responsive oral contexts for literacy

Children need oral language skills to acquire literacy. They will only want to read a text if they can understand what it is that they are reading. To do this they need prior knowledge and experience. Low performance on tests of reading comprehension can also reflect students' limited vocabulary, and/or limited experience in talking about characters and events within stories or concepts of various kinds, and relating these to their own knowledge and experience. Talking is an essential intellectual and social skill that is shaped by how we think, and forms part of how we communicate with others and make sense of the world. The young child's thought development begins through interpersonal negotiation with others, caregivers, teachers and peers at school and this is internalized into personal understanding (Vygotsky 1962). It is clearly very important, therefore, to build up students' oral language skills, by supporting them to talk about what they have been reading and about how what they have been reading connects with what they already know. The potential of a meaningful 'talk to expand literacy' approach that goes beyond studying letters and words is supported by a number of research studies.

From the time a child first begins to understand the world s/he appears to do so by means of story: 'Any understanding we have of reality is in terms of our stories and our story-creating possibilities' (Mair 1988: 128).

Strategies to develop oral skills

There is an important question about how learners can take the step 'from speaking to understanding writing on a page or screen, to realise that knowledge of life and language can help them make sense of words and texts' (Gregory 1996: 95). Orally told stories, rhymes, songs, prayer and routines for meeting and greeting people, all have an important role in literacy acquisition and are promoted within many cultures long before children begin any form of formal education. Sarbin (1986) notes that it is through story that children learn to become functioning members of the society into which they are born:

> It is through hearing stories ... that children learn or mislearn both what a child and what a parent is, what the cast of characters may be in the drama into which they have been born and what the ways of the world are. Deprive children of stories and you leave them unscripted, anxious stutterers in their actions as in their words. Hence there is no way to give us an understanding of any society ... except through the stock of stories which constitute its initial dramatic resources.
>
> (Sarbin 1986: 201)

Gregory advocates addressing the issue of building from the known into new literacy acquisition by explicit scaffolding of children's learning through:

- recognising children's existing linguistic skills and cultural knowledge and building these into both teaching content and teaching strategies;
- limiting the size of the reading task by introducing explicitly common new lexis and language 'chunks';
- modelling chunks of language orally and in an idealised way through puppets and/ or songs and socio-dramatic play;
- devising home-school reading programmes which recognise the role of both parent and child as mediator of different languages and cultures and which families feel comfortable with.

(Gregory 1996: 112)

Gregory (1996: 110) outlines an example of a reading session which draws on children's oral language and makes use of puppets to mediate learning. This should draw on the child's emotions, for example fear, love, sympathy and hate, and aim to tell an adventure or drama.

Explicit strategies for encouraging comprehension skills

Good readers know what they have to do to get meaning from texts (Pressley 2002). However, many readers who experience difficulties in literacy may need explicit teaching about comprehension strategies and guided practice in using them, as well as opportunities to engage with texts.

We know that good comprehenders:

- search for connections between what they know and the new information they encounter in the texts they read.
- monitor the adequacy of their models of text meaning.
- take steps to repair faulty comprehension once they realise they have failed to understand something.
- learn early on to distinguish important from less important ideas in texts they read.
- are adept at synthesising information within and across texts and reading experiences.
- draw inferences during and after reading to achieve a full integrated understanding of what they read.
- sometimes consciously, and almost always unconsciously, ask questions of themselves, the author they encounter and the texts they read.

(Pearson et al. 1992: 154)

Difficulty in comprehension might occur at any of these points. Ways to help readers develop strategies to construct meaning from text include:

- preparing for reading;
- thinking through ways to read and extract information;

- ways to organize and translate the information that has been read.

Preparing for reading

It is essential to make the child aware that they have knowledge that they can bring to bear to make the act of reading meaningful, and that they can comprehend in the light of their past experiences. This is especially important where learners experience difficulties. Teachers might identify and discuss the vocabulary of the text that may be difficult, and/ or overview the topic of the text. Learners might be encouraged to ask:

- What do I know?
- What do I want to know?
- What have I learnt?

Ways to construct meaning

Collaborative reading and writing activities can provide children with the opportunity to support peers' learning through observing, guiding or offering assistance, while the less skilled learner is motivated to respond to and initiate language interactions as well as respond to peer questions and challenges.

Supporting comprehension skills:

1. The example of 'reciprocal teaching'

Palincsar and Brown (1984) report a seminal research study into the successful use of 'reciprocal teaching' to enhance reading comprehension with pupils who experience difficulties in literacy development. Teachers and pupils took turns to lead discussion about the meaning of a section of text that they were jointly trying to understand and memorize. This technique focused on four strategies to assist understanding of the text and joint construction of its meaning: generating questions from the text, summarizing its content, clarifying areas of difficulty and predicting the content of subsequent sections of text based on the content and structure of the current portion. Learners were taught the terminology of reciprocal teaching through direct instruction in each of the four strategies prior to the start of the procedure. This technique emphasized the role of the teacher in modelling expert performance and role of the learner as active participant in his/her learning in addition to the function of social interactions in learning. Assessment of learners' progress was ongoing and judged through their developing contributions to discussion of the texts.

> The basic procedure was that an adult teacher, working individually with a seventh-grade poor reader, assigned a segment of the passage to be read and either indicated that it was her turn to be the teacher or assigned the student to teach that segment. The adult teacher and the student then read the assigned segment silently. After reading the text, the teacher (student or adult) for that segment asked a question that a teacher or test might ask on the segment, summarized the content, discussed and clarified any difficulties, and finally made a prediction about future content. All of these activities were embedded in as natural a dialogue as possible, with the teacher and student giving feedback to each other ...

Gradually, the students became much more capable of assuming their role as dialogue leader and by the end of ten sessions were providing paraphrases of some sophistication.

(Palincsar and Brown 1984: 124–5)

The success of that initial research project has been replicated many times with pairs of tutors and tutees and within small groups.

It is my experience that, where students have severe difficulties understanding text, it is useful to shorten the amount read before questions are asked. This may mean a page by page reading, or even a paragraph by paragraph reading. However, as students pay more attention to the messages conveyed by text the amount of text read before questions are asked can be lengthened.

2. The example of 'Three Level Guides'

So-called 'Three Level Guides' are statements about a text written by teachers to help students become more aware of different levels of deriving meaning from texts. These statements are intended to help students to think about the text, what statements are important and can be verified directly from the text, what statements require them to make inferences from their prior knowledge, and how they can apply information from texts.

The three levels are:

- literal (reading the lines);
- inferential (reading between the lines);
- applied (reading beyond the lines).

The purpose is for students to use their understanding of a passage to decide whether:

- a statement represents what is actually stated in the text or not;
- the statement could be true, or not, dependent on making an inference;
- the statement is something that the author might agree with.

The students should first try to decide by themselves and then discuss and justify their choice with a partner or a small group. The reading activity is intended to be completed collaboratively, so that students learn from each other as they discuss the statements.

Creating a Three Level Guide

In creating a *Three Level Guide* it is important to first determine your content objectives. This gives the guide a clear focus and informs the development of your statements. In this way, the statements will lead the reader to focus on the relevant parts of the text. Your content objectives will determine your applied level statements.

These third level statements should be written first as they influence the development of the statements at the other levels. The third level statements encourage the reader to think beyond the text to its wider implications. These statements reflect the main ideas and concepts you would like the students to explore through the text.

Once you have written the applied level statements, write your literal statements. These statements guide the reader to the information in the text related to the issues explored in the applied level statements. The literal statements support the students by focusing their attention on the relevant information in the text. This teaches the students to be selective in their reading by encouraging them to disregard irrelevant information.

Finally, develop your interpretive level statements which guide the reader to draw inferences from the information in the text. These statements focus on the author's intent behind the words and information selected. Interpretive level statements can also encourage the reader to explore what is omitted in the text.

(www.myread.org/guide_three.htm, accessed 16 June 2008)

There is some very useful information on 'Three Level Guides' to be found on the Internet at www.literacy.org.nz/three-level-guide.php (accessed 15 April 2008).

Fluent reading

Some researchers have noted how repeated reading can assist and develop reading speed and fluency. For example, Chomsky's (1978) tape-assisted reading involved students practising until they can read a passage at the same rate as the tape recording or the story. A similar repeated reading strategy (Samuels 2002) using a mutual peer tutoring approach involved a student and teacher reading together, the student alternating between being the teacher and the learner. Fluency can also be enhanced through opportunities to read silently along with a recording of the text and lead to positive responses to text which can enhance children's reading confidence and attitude to reading. Repeated exposure to text, aurally and visually, can reinforce word recognition, thus freeing up cognitive 'energy' for comprehension.

Gregory (1996: 122) points out that choice of texts for beginning reading should include 'memorable stories and texts from all times and places', perhaps containing 'universal truths, values and morals', which pertain to students of all levels and ages. I remember supporting an 11-year-old non-reader in a secondary school to learn to read through preparing for him audiotapes of *A Hitch Hiker's Guide to the Galaxy*. I taped 30 minutes' worth of text every evening with the agreement that he would follow it through twice the following day. All his friends had read it and he wanted to be able to join in their discussions. Using this approach through a number of texts he progressed from non-reader to reader, able to read the (English) *Daily Mirror* independently at home in six months' time.

If choice of reading material is important, so, too, is listening to children read.

The importance of attentive listening to children's reading

In order that meaningful interactions can take place between reader and listener, classroom conditions must predispose to attentive listening. The adult or peer should be responsive to the learner's understanding of, and interest in, the text and any difficulties that are experienced in reading and understanding. Wragg et al. (1998: 264–5) highlighted research findings which are important in listening to children's reading in the classroom:

we concluded, in the light of observations of what seemed to be successful practice, that there were six ingredients that were needed if teachers were to derive maximum benefit from hearing children read and conversing about the chapter. These were:

- Orderliness – disruptive behaviour by other pupils can be a powerful distractor.
- Focus – a strong focus on reading as the major activity of the moment, so that maths or other problems do not take the teacher away from the principal domain.
- Independence – children reading alone need to be able to make their own decisions, so they are not too dependent on the teacher; equally, those reading with the teacher need independence, so they can guess intelligently at unfamiliar words.
- Priority – the child being heard needs to have top priority, except in emergencies.
- Importance – reading must be made important, so that interruptions are frowned upon.
- Worthwhileness – the chapter needs to be engaging and worth talking about.

Wragg et al. give examples of effective practices of individual teachers whom they observed:

> using the half-hour daily ERIC (everyone reads in class) session when the rest of the class were fully occupied with reading, and by reinforcing her rule that she was not to be interrupted while with a child, she was able to give each one an individualised and focused reading experience. She also ensured that when the classroom assistant or parent helpers read with a child they were seated away from other children and not interrupted.
>
> Infant-age children were likely to read more regularly to the teacher than those in junior schools, where it was generally only the less able readers who did so. Several teachers mentioned that it was better to hear children less often but in a more concentrated fashion, diagnosing their mistakes and discussing their progress with them. Many kept quite detailed records of the child's progress, and these were filled in by whichever adult heard the child. Two teachers had found that they were not hearing the better readers and so arranged to give children a special day when they would guarantee to hear them. Most children knew which chapter to read, or could easily find an appropriate one, but occasionally children in some classes would pick something way beyond them, or others would pick the easiest one they could find.
>
> (1998: 152)

Addressing difficulties in writing

There is less written about writing than reading. However, it is clear that reading is closely linked to writing. Readers and writers use their knowledge and experience in complementary ways: readers to construct meaning from existing texts, and writers to construct meaning in the new texts that they create. As a reader, the learner interacts with words (and letters or letter clusters in words), grammatical structures and other language patterns in texts in order to construct meaning. As a writer, the learner starts with ideas and represents these in grammatical structures and other language patterns in texts in order to construct meaning (Ministry of Education 2006: 123).

In the same way as reading, approaches to writing might sometimes be classified as either:

- a traditional focus on the product, that is, surface features and the mechanics of text, grammar and spelling (Smith and Elley 1997), or

- a focus on the process: that is, for example, processes such as brainstorming, drafting, revising, editing, and publishing content and meaning (Graves 1983).

Focusing on the product

The question of whether or not it is important to learn to spell accurately is one which is fraught with controversy. The English language has an alphabetic writing system in which the symbols bear only some relationship to the sounds of the language: 'It is not a direct relationship ... the symbols (the letters) may best be described as providing a clue to the sounds' (Barton 1995: 97). Some words have clear sound–symbol correspondence – but even then, there is often confusion for speakers whose speech does not conform to Standard English or Received Pronunciation.

English also uses meaning in its spelling system. The similarity of spellings of word parts often indicates meaning: 'sign', 'signature', 'assign' and 'signal' all relate to the Latin word 'signum'. In addition, as Barton (1995) points out, English contains some logographs where one character is a unit of meaning, for example '&' and 'etc'. Many spellings are idiosyncratic and the particular combinations of letters serve as logographs, for example 'right', 'rite' and 'write'. In this case, homophones indistinguishable in speech are differentiated in writing by their spellings, and each has to be learned separately: 'we are never sure of the spelling of a new word we hear until we have seen it written down; we are often unsure of how to pronounce a word we come across in reading until we hear it spoken' (Barton 1995: 100).

Given the complexity of the English spelling system and the difficulty experienced by some students in learning to spell accurately, it is hardly surprising that there is a diversity of approaches both to teaching spelling and to the need for doing so.

Spelling can be approached from a holistic, whole-word approach, or from a partist approach to individual letter-sound identification and combinations of letters into words. Choice of words to be spelt can be made on the basis of what the learner needs and wishes to spell for the purpose of his/her reading. This approach may require students to construct personal spelling lists from the errors they make in their written work. In contrast, choice of words to be learned can be made from word lists. Some spelling approaches group words to be learned in terms of similar letter-sound patterns within words. These may be hierarchical, phonically regular combinations of letters and sounds that the learner is already expected to know. This approach may group words to be learned in terms of similar letter-sound patterns within words. Students may spend a great deal of time learning large lists of words, and getting them correct, but may still show little or no generalization of these patterns into similar words that they may encounter in their writing.

Schools' marking and spelling policies can stimulate a fair amount of controversy. If we take the example of spelling, Bentley (1990) argues that, for the most part, class or group spelling tests are a waste of time since learners will be at different stages in spelling acquisition. However, spelling tests may be a required part of a school's approach to supporting students' literacy development. Teachers may feel that set spelling tests are very important to assess the development in spelling of a whole class or group. On the other hand, they may feel that the degree to which spelling tests are a waste of time may depend on how spellings are chosen for students to learn and how far they are tailored to the needs of the individual child.

Bentley argues that, in addition, schools should have very clear marking policies. On the one hand, it can be argued that, for some students, repeatedly receiving back scripts covered with marks indicating errors is very demoralizing. On the other, there has to be a rational, structured approach to ensuring that students make progress in recognizing mistakes and learning how to correct them. Some teachers may feel it is appropriate to encourage students to proofread their own, or peers', work before handing it in, and/or, perhaps, to correct only words or sentence structure with which they feel students should already be familiar. Whichever strategy schools choose should be supported by reasoned argument. Whatever decisions are made, have both advantages and disadvantages which need to be recognized.

In order to avoid difficulties in spelling later on, children need to be familiar with vowels and syllables at an early stage and to be taught techniques for learning the spelling of words they want or need to use in writing. Students should never simply copy words but should always be encouraged to memorize them and then write them down.

Strategies for learning correct spelling

Example 1: multi-sensory approach 1

For students who find particular difficulty with spelling, Reason and Boote (1994) describe a multi-sensory approach which, while lengthy at first, can, in their view, be slimmed down as students gain confidence and competence in spelling:

- Look at the word, read it, and pronounce it in syllables or other small bits (re-mem-ber; sh-out)
- Try to listen to yourself doing this
- Still looking at it, spell it out in letter-names
- Continue to look, and trace out the letters on the table with your finger as you spell it out again
- Look at the word for any 'tricky bits'; for example, gh in right. (Different students find different parts of a word 'tricky'.)
- Try to get a picture of the word in your mind: take a photograph of it in your head!
- Copy the word, peeping at the end of each syllable or letter-string
- Highlight the tricky bits in colour (or by some other means)
- Visualise the word again
- Now cover it up and try to write it, spelling it out in letter-names
- Does it look right?
- Check with the original
- Are there some tricky bits you didn't spot (i.e. the parts that went wrong)?
- Repeat as much of the procedure as necessary to learn the words thoroughly.

(Reason and Boote 1994: 138)

Example 2: multi-sensory approach 2

I have used a slightly different version of a multi-sensory approach (Bradley 1981) very successfully with students of a range of ages:

The method consists of a series of steps in the following order:

The student proposes the word he (*sic*) wants to learn.

The word is written correctly for him (or made with plastic script letters).

The student names the word.

He then writes the word himself, saying out loud the alphabetic name of each letter of the word as it is written.

He names the word again. He checks to see that the word has been written correctly; this is important, as less able readers are often inaccurate when they copy (Bradley, 1981). Repeat steps 2 to 5 twice more, covering or disregarding the stimulus word as soon as the student feels he can manage without it.

The student practises the word in this way for six consecutive days. The procedure is the same whether or not the student can read or write, and whether or not he is familiar with all the sound/symbol relationships, but it must deteriorate into rote spelling, which is an entirely different thing.

The student learns to generalise from this word to similar words using the plastic script letters.

(Bradley 1981, cited in Bentley 1990: 3)

Many parents or families may not know how most appropriately to help their child to learn new spellings. Guidelines that include a description of Reason and Boote's or Bradley's methods may help to reduce their anxiety levels and may well be very welcome.

Example 3: 'cued spelling' (K. Topping 2001)

Another method of supporting spelling acquisition is what K. Topping (2001) terms 'cued spelling'. This method relies on the principles of praise, modelling, swift error correction and support procedures. Students are encouraged to select target words for themselves and manage their own spelling programme. The steps are set out to represent progression through small incremental stages. When students are familiar with the technique, speed in spelling is emphasized in order to overcome the difficulty with generalization over time and contexts. 'cued spelling' uses words the student wishes to spell and relies on praise, modelling, and swift support procedures to avoid the fear of failure. The technique comprises ten steps (K. Topping 2001): At step 1, the learner chooses words of high interest to him/herself, irrespective of difficulty level. Tutor and learner check the spelling of the word and put a master version in a 'cued spelling diary' (step 2). The pair read the word out loud together, then the learner reads the word aloud alone (step 3). At step 4, the learner chooses cues (reminders) to enable him or her to remember the written structure of the word. These may be sounds, letter names, syllables or other fragments of words, or wholly personal mnemonic (memory) devices. At step 5, the pair repeats the cues aloud simultaneously. As step 6, the learner then repeats the cues aloud while the tutor models writing the word down while it is 'dictated'. Roles then reverse, the tutor saying the cues aloud while the learner writes the word down (step 7). At step 8, the learner repeats the cues and writes the word simultaneously. At step 9, the learner writes the word as fast as possible and decides for him/herself whether to recite the cues out loud. Finally (step 10), the learner reads the word out loud. Each session ends with a 'speed review' where the parent dictates all the target words for that session as quickly as possible. The learner then checks the accuracy of the words against the master copy. Target words which are incorrect are learned again, using the 10 steps, and different memory cues may be chosen. At the end of each week, the parent dictates all the target words for the whole week as quickly as possible. Parent and child together decide what they wish to do about mistakes and whether to include them in the next week's target words.

Spelling approaches such as cued spelling, with their clear breakdown into specific steps would lend themselves to being implemented in either peer-tutoring or co-operative learning contexts. Each pair is encouraged to keep a spelling diary, each page including space to write the master version of up to ten words on all days of the week, with boxes to record daily speed review and weekly mastery review scores and spaces for daily comments from the tutor and weekly comments from the teacher.

Focusing on the process

Sometimes it can help teachers to imagine the human mind as processing information rather like a computer and to see the writing process as driven by a series of goals which are organised in a hierarchy (Flower and Hayes 1980). Those engaged in the writing task achieve their goals through processes of planning, translating and revising what has been written:

- Planning involves generating information to be included in the script, selecting and organizing what is relevant, and deciding on criteria for judging successful completion of the script.
- Translation means converting the plan into the script.
- Revising includes editing for both grammatical errors as well as structural coherence.

Seeing the process of writing like this can be very useful because it enables teachers to focus on the individual processes of writing production. From this point of view, difficulties in writing clearly and effectively can be seen as the result of three factors (Graham and Harris 1993) which can be identified and tackled separately:

- lack of competence in the mechanical skills of producing text, that is, frequent errors in spelling, the use of upper and lower case, and punctuation. Some people consider that the amount of attention some learners have to expend to make sure the mechanics of writing are correct interferes with higher-order skills of planning and the generation of content (MacArthur and Graham 1987);
- lack of knowledge relating to the subject content of the script to be written, and/ or of the conventions and characteristics of different writing genres;
- ineffective strategies in planning or revising text.

An area that has been researched thoroughly in relation to students with difficulties in literacy development is the use of strategies intended to highlight planning processes. Examples of this are self-directed techniques for generating words relevant to the content of the script (Graham and Harris 1993), the use of writing frames to generate and organize ideas (Englert and Raphael 1988; Graves et al. 1990), and articulating 'process goals', that is, the way in which the child intends to achieve the end product (Graham et al.

1989). The theory behind this is that by expressing these thoughts in a visible way we can subsequently rethink, revise and redraft, and we are allowed, indeed forced, to reflect upon our own thinking (Wray 2002). Self-knowledge is important at both the pre-writing and writing stage. The writer's ideas, sequences, starting and finishing points are reflected on, as well as the information to be covered and the ideas the writer wants to incorporate in the writing piece. Students need to reflect on the processes they go through as they write, to reassure themselves that the processes they use are entirely normal and will, in the end, produce the right results. Writers need to anticipate potential difficulties, make judgements and reconciliations between competing ideas as well as show an alertness to the needs of their potential and actual readership. Some strategies to help integrate self-awareness skills in the writing process include thinking aloud while writing, and critically examining and revising writing decisions, for example, asking themselves why did you write this, or why did you explain something in this manner?

Techniques for supporting writing skills

Example 1: writing frames

'Writing frames' (www.warwick.ac.uk/staff/D.J.Wray/Ideas/frames.html, accessed 16 June 2008) are a way of providing learner writers with a support or 'scaffold', that offers, for example, some headings, subheadings and connectives for linking paragraphs when writing an explanatory information text, the layout, greeting, opening sentence and closure when practising a letter; sentence openings for making contrasting points when presenting an argument.

Example 2: 'paired writing'

K.J. Topping (1995; 2001) has piloted a 'paired writing' technique which he suggests should be used for three sessions of 20 minutes per week for six weeks:

> Paired Writing is a framework for a pair working together to generate . . . a piece of writing – for any purpose they wish . . . Paired Writing usually operates with a more able writer (the Helper) and a less able one (the Writer), but can work with a pair of equal ability so long as they edit carefully and use a dictionary to check spellings . . .
>
> The structure of the system consists of six Steps, 10 Questions (for Ideas), five Stages (for Drafting) and four Levels (for Editing). Further details will be found in Topping (1995).
>
> Step 1 is Ideas Generation. The Helper stimulates ideas by using given Questions and inventing other relevant ones, making one-word notes on the Writer's responses.
>
> Step 2 is Drafting. The notes then form the basis for Drafting, which ignores spelling and punctuation. Lined paper and double spaced writing is recommended. The Writer dictates the text and scribing occurs in whichever of the five Stages of Support has been chosen by the pair. If there is a hitch, the Helper gives more support.
>
> In Step 3 the pair look at the text together while the Helper reads the Draft out loud with expression. The Writer then reads the text out loud, with the Helper correcting any reading errors.
>
> Step 4 is Editing. First the Writer considers where s/he thinks improvements are necessary, marking this with a coloured pen, pencil or highlighter. The most important improvement is where the meaning is unclear. The second most important is to do with

the organization of ideas or the order in which meanings are presented. The next consideration is whether spellings are correct and the last whether punctuation is helpful and correct. The Helper praises the Writer then marks points the Writer has 'missed'. The pair then discuss – and agree improvements.

In Step 5 the Writer (usually) copies out a 'neat' or 'best' version. Sometimes the Helper may write or type or word-process it, however. Making the final copy is the least important step.

Step 6 is Evaluate. The pair should self-assess their own best copy, but peer assessment by another pair is very useful. The criteria in the Edit levels provide a checklist for this.

Example 3: metacognitive strategies

The deliberate conscious control of one's actions and thought is called metacognition. 'Metacognitive' strategies are designed to enable students to think about their own cognitive processes so that those who experience difficulty in particular areas of learning can develop alternative routes to accessing these areas. Children can be taught strategies at an early age to help develop metacognitive skills. For examples, teachers might model how to approach the writing process that children can then copy. A typical example of teacher modelling of writing might comprise four stages: pre-writing; composing/drafting; revising; and editing (Tribble 1996: 39).

'Mind-mapping' is an example of one way to plan a structure for producing extended text. It assumes that the structure and content of the text will be of higher quality if the learner is encouraged first to produce a visual representation of all those areas to be covered in the text before beginning on the written task. Those who experience difficulties in writing are likely to benefit by being able to separate out content from the technical aspects of producing the text by focusing on one before the other. Of course, there is considerable overlap between the first process and the second.

The place of narrative

'We dream, remember, anticipate, hope, despair, love, hate, believe, doubt, plan, construct, gossip and learn in narrative' (Westby 1991). It is important for students to learn to express these feelings in written as well as oral form. Narratives can be seen as an early step towards later expository text since they contain a number of essential elements such as: comparisons, problem-solving, exhortation and persuasion, and so on (Montgomery and Kahn 2003). Some students who experience difficulties in literacy may need support to reproduce story grammar. Montgomery and Kahn note an interactive oral teaching strategy 'scaffolded story writing' that has been used as an interactive group activity to support struggling writers: 'In the scaffolded narrative method, questioning is used to help students build their comprehension, organisation, sequence of ideas, and metacognition. This questioning encourages students to become "meaning makers" ' (2003: 145). The learning support teacher introduces the idea of an author, what s/he does and why students might want to be one. The students are taught five elements of an effective narrative: interesting character(s), context, a credible problem, possible solutions to the problem, and a good ending (Apel and Masterton 1998). The support teacher sets up a series of questions to support the students in thinking about the stories they want to write and the students discuss possible approaches with each other.

Using the 'scaffolded story writing' technique

The approach comprises five steps:

Step 1: Draw a sequence story. The [teacher] divides an 8" x 11" blank sheet of paper into six sections and tells the students to draw their stories on the paper in correct sequence, using as many sheets as are necessary ... The students may use stick figures and simple drawings ... Some students need help in sequencing their stories properly

Step 2: Describe the main characters. Students should list descriptive details for the main characters, including age, height, weight, body build, hair colour and style, eye colour, clothes, family, favourite foods, things they like to do ...

Step 3: Begin writing the narrative. The students begin their narratives with an interesting opening sentence or two to catch the reader's interest. The [teacher] might read opening paragraphs from stories he or she has enjoyed to the students. Students should follow their picture sequence when writing their narratives. They should also incorporate the information they compiled before they started writing the story, including the character descriptions.

The [teacher] uses a questioning technique throughout this intervention. She or he must facilitate the student's ability to come up with creative, independent ideas ...

The dialogue between the student and the [teacher] continues until the student is certain about what he or she wants to write ... The [teacher] needs to ask questions until a coherent story emerges, which sometimes occurs in stages. The [teacher] may get the first part down and then move on to the next part. Some stories change in the process as better ideas occur and the student revises his or her initial thoughts. It is best to get a first draft completed and then rewrite.

Step 4: Write the story. From the beginning, the [teacher] reinforces the idea that the story belongs to the student, and changes are never made without consulting the student ...

Step 5: Rewrite and correct. Some students require corrections and help throughout the writing process. They need words to be spelled for them, or they want to try out a sentence or two orally before they write ... Grammar is often incorrect, and syntax is sometimes awkward. Editing the final draft is the point at which these areas must be addressed.

Many students approach the editing process with trepidation ... suggestions for change must be given diplomatically. When the [teacher] suggests a possibility and the student does not like it, the change should not be made.'

(Montgomery and Kahn 2003: 146–7)

Montgomery and Kahn suggest that punctuation and spelling should be taught within the context of such stories: 'The editing process is an ideal point at which to teach language structure to students who want to learn, because it pertains to their stories. They want to make their stories the best that they can be. It is nice to have a final product of which they can be proud' (2003: 148).

Dyslexia

In the dyslexia debate, there are a number of well rehearsed arguments about whether dyslexia is a term favoured by the middle classes to excuse their children's poor academic performance, or whether it really is a condition that should be treated as a disability, or something else. There are those who lobby for recognition of dyslexia as something that should be recognized as a causal factor in contributing to difficulties in literacy development such that require the allocation of additional or alternative resources. There are also those who feel that dyslexia is used as an excuse for attracting unwarranted additional resources for some students.

A very common current approach is to view 'dyslexia' as a psychological explanation of literacy difficulties that, most commonly, refers to the way in which individuals process information. The information-processing system of 'dyslexic' individuals is seen as different from that of non-dyslexics in ways which have an impact on a number of areas of performance, particularly reading and writing. Co-ordination, personal organization, directionality, balance, patterning and so on may also be affected.

In terms of literacy acquisition, the difficulties experienced by dyslexic students are usually related to a bottom-up approach to understanding the process of reading and writing. Learners are seen as experiencing difficulties in processing either visual or/and auditory information. In relation to visual factors, learners may experience difficulty in any of the following areas:

- recognition of the visual cues of letters and words;
- familiarity with left–right orientation;
- recognition of word patterns;
- recognition of letter and word shapes.

Or they may encounter problems with any of the following auditory factors:

- recognition of letter sounds;
- recognition of sounds and letter groups or patterns;
- sequencing of sounds;
- corresponding sounds to visual stimuli;
- discriminating sounds from other sounds;
- discriminating sounds within words.

Having said this, however, poor decoding skills may have a serious impact on comprehension of text and on written expression.

There are a number of theories that attempt to explain the difficulties experienced by dyslexic learners. For example, as Everatt (2002) explains, there are visual-based theories which propose that dyslexia may be the consequence of an abnormality in the neural pathways of the visual system. There are others suggesting a lower level of activity in the areas of the cortex thought to be responsible for identifying the direction of movement (Eden et al. 1996). There is also a view that visual difficulties may be caused by oversensitivity to certain wavelengths (or colours) of light. This is sometimes referred to as scotopic sensitivity syndrome (Irlen 1991). The significance of this is that coloured filters, overlays or lenses which are said to alleviate reading problems for some learners (Wilkins et al. 1994) have increasingly been incorporated into teachers' practice, with variable results. Since the 1980s, however, the dominant theory used to explain dyslexia has been the phonological deficit hypothesis (Bradley and Bryant 1983; Snowling 2000; Stanovich 2000). Phonological representations may be interpreted as the knowledge about sounds which a reader brings to the task of reading. Phonological processing, therefore, is strongly related to the development of reading. Difficulties experienced at the level of phonological representation and the relationships between symbols and the sounds they represent constrain reading development. Hatcher and Snowling (2002) comment that one of the effects of this is that learners who experience difficulties at the phonological level are less able to generalize knowledge about the phonological properties of sounds and words they are taught. Activities such as non-word reading are problematic because of the difficulties associated with sound–symbol relationships. Hatcher and Snowling feel that this can be viewed as one of the most robust signs of dyslexia.

Hatcher and Snowling suggest that the phonological representations hypothesis is also compatible with differences between the profiles of individual children which are characteristic of dyslexia. They suggest that the most crucial factor in the individual profile of dyslexic children is the actual severity of the lack of development in phonological representations. This can account for the differences and the different presenting characteristics of the dyslexic group. In addition dyslexic children with poorer phonological representations will have fewer compensatory word attack strategies to draw on, which will further undermine their reading performance.

Hatcher and Snowling conclude that assessment of phonological skills is therefore necessary and they provide examples of tasks: rhyme recognition, rhyme production, phonological manipulation such as phoneme deletion and letter knowledge, which can be found in some of the established tests available for this purpose. This view has considerable implications for practice and particularly intervention programmes in the early years. The same kind of approaches to addressing reading and writing difficulties are appropriate for dyslexic learners as for other students. However, multi-sensory approaches are even more important in harnessing all the senses to support students' learning. Hatcher and Snowling outline examples of phonological awareness training such as rhyme activities, identifying words as units within sentences, syllable awareness and blending tasks. Phonemic awareness can develop only when there is good experience of speaking and listening. When children are very young it may be difficult for them to realize that speech can be broken down into individual words. It is a further step to recognize that words can also be broken down into sounds. Phonemic awareness can be encouraged by playing rhyming games, making up nonsense rhymes, repeating rhyming strings, and playing other games which require the manipulation of sounds.

As Hatcher and Snowling comment, however, it is insufficient to train phonological awareness in isolation as it is important to establish the relationship between sounds and written forms of words. Interventions that rely exclusively on training in phonological awareness are less effective than those that combine phonological training with print and meaning in the context of sentences in text. In addition, interventions that address possible difficulties in co-ordination, personal organization, directionality, balance and patterning may also be needed for some students.

An example of a dyslexic student's learning and teaching needs

'Sonia' was identified as experiencing a number of difficulties in learning of a dyslexic nature:

- significant difference between verbal comprehension abilities and reading accuracy;
- significant weakness in the area of short-term memory processing;
- weakness with the sequencing and organization of information;
- difficulties with tasks requiring the integration of fine motor skills, visual tracking, spatial analysis, visual discrimination and speed of information processing.

As a result she suffered from an extreme lack of confidence in her intellectual and academic abilities.

Sonia needed to gain more experience in reading in order to increase her word identification, knowledge of letter–sound combinations and use of contextual information and inference. Her teacher first discussed with her and her parents, and then organized, a 'paired reading' arrangement to enable her to gain more experience in reading and in visual tracking of the text. Sonia was encouraged to choose reading material that was of high interest to her, from school, the library and from home, irrespective of its readability level. She was never forced to finish a book.

Sonia and her reading partner were always given a quiet and comfortable place for their reading activities in school. The teacher made sure that both children knew they needed to be able to see the text properly so that they could read it out aloud simultaneously. Both children read all the words out loud together, with her partner modulating her speed to match Sonia's. When Sonia felt she was ready, she gave her partner a signal and took over the reading on her own for a while. If she said a word wrong, her reading partner gave her a few seconds to put it right and then, if necessary, just told her the correct way to say the word. Sonia repeated it correctly and the pair carried on reading simultaneously again.

Sonia also needed to improve the speed of her reading as well as her ability to track through text quickly. Tracking involves left–right working, orientation, hand–eye co-ordination, sequencing, sound–symbol recognition, and speed and accuracy of scanning. Her parents agreed to look for recordings of books that Sonia really wanted to read in the library and local supermarket. For a while they sat with her in the evenings showing her how to follow the text with her eyes while listening to the recording. Very soon she was doing it for herself. To improve her tracking skill, every week the teaching assistant gave her a printed copy of the alphabet and copies of unwanted magazines or books, and timed her while she tracked through the text from left to right, crossing out letters of the alphabet in the right order as she went.

To support Sonia's spelling acquisition, the teacher used a multi-sensory approach similar to the approaches outlined above.

Writing skills

Sonia's comprehension skills were well in advance of her ability to express herself both verbally and on paper. Allowing her to dictate her stories onto a digital recorder and then transcribing them for her, or allowing her to dictate her stories to the teacher/an older child/ the parent, helped her to get her thoughts and ideas down on paper.

Sonia was provided with writing frames to support her extended writing and encourage logical sequencing. At its simplest level this would be three steps – a beginning, a middle and an ending – moving towards a six-part structure which included for story writing:

- introducing the people;
- describing the setting/place;
- something beginning to happen;
- the exciting part;
- things sorting themselves out;
- the ending.

This structure was gradually differentiated into using the following questions:

- What is the title?
- Who are the main characters?
- Describe the main characters. What did the main characters try to do?
- Who were the other characters in the story?
- What was the story about?
- What was the main part of the story?
- How did the story end?

Research stresses the motivational value of computer assisted learning which increases the time that students are willing to practise academic skills so that mastery learning can take place. A choice of screen colours may also be helpful.

Sonia also benefited from word-processing skills. Research confirms that the editing flexibility of word-processing helps students with specific learning difficulties to overcome their problems with organizing ideas and structuring written work. The appearance of the work improves greatly and the students no longer have to concentrate on the physical skill of handwriting (this is especially important for Sonia). Spelling too seems to improve when students see the image on the screen.

Information technology, including word-processing packages with a spellcheck facility, helped Sonia to be more confident in terms of using more sophisticated vocabulary in her written work. It became easier to identify mistakes on the screen. The text could be changed, moved around and corrected as often as necessary until the work was acceptable. Drafting and correcting became less laborious and the printed copy could be corrected away from the machine by the student or the teacher and improved versions created without difficulty. Everything can be saved and reused easily, allowing work to be done in small amounts. Presentation is improved; when the final version was printed it was legible and well presented.

Spellcheckers removed much of Sonia's inhibition about writing that came from poor spelling.

Memory skills

Sonia's short-term or 'working' memory skills were weak. The teaching assistant regularly encouraged her to increase the span of items that were to be remembered by laying out plastic or wooden letters of the alphabet in an arc in front of her. The TA gave her a sequence of letters verbally, starting with three and aiming to build up to seven. Sonia listened, repeated the sequence, then pulled the letters out from the arc. The length of time between presenting the sequence and asking for recall was gradually increased by 5-second intervals. As her memory span increased, an intervening task was given between presentation and recall.

The TA introduced games such as 'I went to the market and bought . . .' starting with letters in the order of the alphabet – apples, bananas, carrots, and so on. The TA also deliberately gave her a set of verbal instructions to follow every day, starting with one or two only – 'Please pick up the pen and put it on the shelf' – and increasing to longer sequences. At the end of the school day, Sonia's teacher asked her to recall as many activities in which she had been engaged during the day.

The TA also encouraged Sonia to use simple mnemonics to aid her memory, and to think up her own. To maximize the effect of repetition of learning it was important that a multi-sensory mode of learning was used. Repetition of the material to be learned was accomplished through oral, visual, auditory and kinaesthetic modes. Although Sarah's 'working' memory skills were weak, her visual memory skills were stronger than her auditory skills. She was, therefore, encouraged to make use of visual strategies to help her to organize her written work, for example, using mind maps.

When copying from the board, the teacher ensured that Sonia was facing the board and was not forced to turn round. Sonia found copying from the board very difficult as she tended to lose the place and had to resort to rereading and checking her work.

Sonia's dyslexic difficulties caused her to experience difficulties in some areas of mathematics including:

- the learning of number bonds;
- the learning of multiplication tables;
- the understanding of concepts involving spatial awareness;
- orientation through having to process different spatial directionality;
- visual discrimination resulting in confusion of signs;
- mental arithmetic (mental manipulation of number/symbols in short-term sequencing activities).

When teaching mathematics, therefore, the teacher applied the principles of a multi-sensory approach (visual, auditory, tactile-kinaesthetic), for example, introducing new mathematical concepts and processes using concrete materials, diagrams, pictures and verbal explanation and then asking the pupils to explain the process, instructions and so on in their or her own words. The TA monitored Sonia's progress carefully monitored at each stage, checking that a particular concept had been thoroughly mastered and understood.

Visual discrimination/spatial analysis

Sonia experienced particular difficulties in the area of spatial analysis and visual discrimination. The teacher therefore discussed a number of principles with the TA:

- keep all visually presented materials simple in format and uncluttered by excessive stimuli;
- assist the student in planning and organizing assigned tasks written on paper by providing visual cues;

- when giving directions, be specific and use concrete cues;
- teaching techniques should begin with the identification of individual parts, moving to integrated wholes;
- assist the student in planning and organizing assignments by providing step-by-step instructions;
- have the student map out alternate routes to well-known locations in the community; extend to outlining routes for short trips in a twenty-mile range;
- have the student make planned, sequential activities for class projects, family outings;
- have the student make rules for a new game or sequentially list rules for a well-known game.

Examination concessions

The school gave internal examination concessions (extra time, answers in note form, oral test to support written examination, use of a word processor in course work, examinations and so on) and 25 per cent additional time.

Examination papers were duplicated so that Sonia could see both sides of a page at the same time, enlarged or printed on coloured paper, along with the use of highlighting pens to help with the analysis of questions.

Individual education plans for dyslexic students

An individual education plan can only ever reflect a snapshot in time of the provision to be made for students in relation to the long-term plan for their education and progress, their current functioning, learning needs, age, the aspect of the curriculum under consideration, and so on. A small number of targets have to be selected for special attention, together with criteria that clearly indicate whether these targets have been met, the resources and teaching and other strategies that are appropriate, and the timescale in which the learning programme should operate. Figure 5.1 is a sample individual education plan.

Supporting students' literacy acquisition in the family context

Questions for reflection

A sense of belonging and acceptance is a basic human need (Bruner 1996). In your experience:

- How do children feel if their literacy achievements in family, home and community contexts are neither acknowledged nor affirmed in the literacy practices of the school?
- What is the impact on their literacy learning?

Children's learning goals and expectations often stem from the goals and norms of their own community. It is essential, therefore, that when young students enter school,

SAMPLE INDIVIDUAL EDUCATION PLAN

Name: 'Sonia'
Area of concern: dyslexia which is linked to poor literacy skills, poor short-term memory, low self-confidence
Start date: ****
Review date: ****

Targets	Success criteria	Resources	Strategies	Support from teaching assistant
Progress in reading accuracy.	Minimum of 6 months progress on standardized test of reading accuracy.	High interest reading books and CDs.	Paired reading, access to digital recorder.	Organization of paired reading activities, records of books read and progress made.
Measurable improvement in accuracy of spelling in written work.	Minimum of 10 new spellings learned weekly.	Record of personal spellings, spelling books, corrected written work.	Multi-sensory techniques to learn spellings from own written work.	Support to teach technique and keep record of progress.
Improve confidence in producing more extended written work.	Measurable termly increase in quantity of written work produced.	Digital recorder, word processor and printer.	Dictate written work on to digital recorder, transcription provided, access to word processor with spell-checking facility.	Transcription of recorded written work. Monitoring of extent of written work produced.
Improved short-term memory skills.	Remember 5 random items in a list and 5 daily activities.	Pictures, word lists, memory games.	Discuss mnemonics; examples of, and practice in, visualization techniques.	Explain principles of mnemonics and visualization techniques; memory games, monitor progress.
Learn 5x and 6x tables in mathematics.	Accuracy in tables tests.	Tables patterns, auditory recordings, tables cards.	Search for patterns, chant along to recordings, practise with cards, use 'finger' method (see Chapter 6).	TA to give practice in reciting tables, teach multi-sensory strategies.

Figure 5.1 Sample Individual Education Plan

classroom literacy practices can build on their own pre-existing experiences within their own families and communities.

There is no possibility of making sense of what bears no relation to one's own ways of making sense of things. Unfamiliarity with local culture, customs and language on entering school can result in complete bewilderment and an inability to understand the expectations and norms of the literacy curriculum. Gregory (1996: 33) notes, for example, how 'Tony' arrived at school, aged 4 years and 10 months, with an 'eye for detail' and a 'disciplined and structured approach to reading from his Chinese school'. In his Chinese school he had been 'given an exercise book where he had to divide the page into columns and practise ideographs over and over again until they are perfect' (Gregory 1996: 32). The carefully and clearly delineated and constrained tasks set by the previous teacher contrasted sharply with the range of personal choice given to Tony and his classmates in the mainstream classroom in Northampton, England. His aimless wandering around the classroom while peers chose activities for themselves indicated that he appeared unable to cope with the non-realization of his expectations about what school should be about.

An example of the effect of conflict between home and school expectations

The way in which a lack of understanding can feel threatening to oneself and can lead to feelings of anxiety or hostility is illustrated by an inmate of a UK prison who recalls in relation to his own school experiences, 'a cocktail of . . . um . . . conflicts there all the time' as he tried to cope with the expectations of a mainstream London school that conflicted with those of home:

> I was weak in certain subjects, like English mainly, because I tend to write the way I speak. I'm born here my parents are from the West Indies. I am in an English school I had to cope with the different . . . criteria because at home it was like a cross between Caribbean where we tend to speak more Patois or broken English. School was like trying to do it faithfully . . . You get to learn . . . how important language is for you to fit . . . and then, like . . . I might get homework to do and I'll ask my dad and he will say no, it's done this way, which is, their schooling was from the old grammar, and it's always a conflict and I would always believe what my father had said because he was a father figure . . . Yes, and then it was completely wrong, and eventually you get frustrated, and I am not going to do this, and you just sort of throw it out.
>
> (Wearmouth, unpublished interview transcript)

The implications of this discussion, for enabling all children to engage in literacy learning activities in the social context of classroom reading, include:

- the need for teachers to learn of the literacy practices taking place in their pupils' lives outside school;
- the need to find strategies to build on strengths that each of the children in the group bring to school;
- the need to make school interpretations of literacy explicit to children and their families (adapted from Gregory 1996: 45).

Hannon (1999) has identified a number of issues crucial to the discussion of parental willingness to participate in literacy programmes, which all those intending to implement such initiatives might do well to address:

- how families are invited to participate;
- the substance of what they have to do;
- the extent to which the programme can respond to family circumstances. For example, home-based programmes have achieved higher mean take-up and retention rates than centre-based programmes.

Despite often rather negative views on the ability of families with little history of literacy to support their children's literacy development, studies have shown that parents from every ethnic and social group are often very keen to help their children with reading at home (Blackledge 2000).

For students who experience difficulties in literacy it may be particularly important that families and schools can work together to establish home–school links to support the learning of students who experience difficulties in literacy development in ways which take account of:

- a diversity of family and cultural backgrounds;
- broad notions of what constitutes literacy, particularly literacy as a social practice;
- a clear understanding of the models of reading reflected in different approaches.

Family support for children's literacy acquisition

Example 1: 'Paired reading'

There are many examples of initiatives involving parents in the reading development of their children. K. J. Topping (1995; 2001), for example, has set out a number of steps for the 'training' of parents in programmes to support children's literacy development. The 'rules' of his 'paired reading' method are as follows:

> Paired Reading is characterized by the child choosing high interest reading material irrespective of its readability level (provided it is within that of the helper) from any source.
>
> Families commit themselves to an initial trial period in which they agree to do at least five minutes Paired Reading on five days each week for about eight weeks. Grandparents, siblings, friends and neighbours can be encouraged to help, but must all use the same technique – the target child is deliberately asked to quality control the tutoring they receive.
>
> In Paired Reading the child is likely to want to talk about a book they have chosen, and talk is also more necessary given the (probably) greater difficulty of the text, as a check on comprehension.
>
> A very simple and ubiquitously applicable correction procedure is prescribed. After pausing for 4 to 5 seconds to allow self-correction, the tutor just models the correct way to read the word, the child repeats it correctly and the pair carry on.

Much verbal praise and non-verbal approval for specific reading behaviours is incorporated. Undesirable behaviours are engineered out of the system by engineering in incompatible positive behaviours.

Tutors support children through difficult text by Reading Together – both members of the pair read all the words out loud together, the tutor modulating speed to match that of the child, while giving a good model of competent reading.

On an easier section of text, the child may wish to read a little without support. The child signals for the tutor to stop Reading Together, by a knock or a touch. The tutor goes quiet, while continuing to monitor any errors, praise and pause for discussion. Sooner or later while Reading Alone the child will make an error which they cannot self-correct within 4 or 5 seconds. Then the tutor applies the usual correction procedure and joins back in Reading Together.

The pair continue like this, switching from Reading Together to Reading Alone to give the child just as much help as is needed according to the difficulty of the text, how tired the s/he is, and so on. Children should never 'grow out of' Reading Together; but should always be ready to use it as they move on to harder texts.

(Topping 1996: 46)

One of the aspects of planning for a learner's literacy needs that is lacking in an approach such as Topping's is any consideration of family, community and cultural contexts in which learners live and develop.

Example 2: 'Pause prompt praise' (Glynn and McNaughton 1985)

'Pause, prompt, praise', from the outset, was intended to be used with parents of students experiencing difficulties in literacy acquisition. It was designed for use with individual students to facilitate opportunities to self-correct errors and practise strategies for problem-solving. Tutors are taught to:

* pause to allow for self-correction. Pausing has been shown to lead to a greater degree of self correction by the learner and an increase in reading accuracy (McNaughton et al. 1987);
* identify the kind of error made and then offer word meaning or sound–symbol identification cues;
* praise to reinforce the kind of reading behaviour that is desired.

In this technique it is important to supply reading material at a level appropriate to the learner so the learner meets some unfamiliar words but can read enough of the text to make sense of it.

Classroom and school programmes should provide students, who are experiencing difficulties, with access to a wide range of rich literacy texts and activities, including those from their own homes and communities as well as those originating in the classroom. Providing teachers and students with high-quality reading materials, representing a variety of genres, and written and illustrated by writers from students' home communities, can be crucial for engaging students experiencing literacy difficulties.

Students need opportunities to talk about what they are reading, and to talk about what other people understand from reading the same text. Teachers and other adults need to build and deepen their relationships with students through the medium of the literacy tasks they select. Teachers might wish to establish authentic opportunities for students' learning, through the provision of reading texts and writing and speaking tasks that connect with students' own family and community experiences, as well as those of the school and its teachers (Berryman 2000; Au 2002; Glynn 2003). Difficulty or complexity of reading texts should be appropriate to the nature of the task. For example, texts taken home for 'demonstration' reading to one's family or for reading alone for leisure and pleasure may be at an 'easy' level for the reader. However, texts selected for one-to-one tutoring within the context of extra support and scaffolding by a trained and skilful tutor may be at a more demanding or challenging level. Students themselves need to have a real choice of texts to read to ensure that what they read is of high interest to them.

Summary

In schools, becoming literate is often thought of as acquiring basic technical skills in order to be able to read, write and spell competently. Difficulties in literacy that are experienced by students have been seen as the result of deficiency in developing these skills and interventions have been designed to remedy this deficiency. More recently, however, many educators have recognized that it is not just the individual abilities of the learner that matter when students learn to read, write and spell. Particular social features of the learning contexts are important too. The view that failure in literacy learning can result from social and arrangements that fail to support students' engagement with their learning as well as from attributes of individuals (Lave 1993: 10) can lead to a very positive approach to overcoming the difficulties that are experienced. It has the advantage of giving teachers and students more control over learning in two senses. It can take away a feeling of helplessness learned from repeated failure by both teachers and students, and give rise to confidence that students will acquire literacy if appropriate strategies are devised to facilitate children's increasing participation in activities that will support literacy learning.

At the same time, each student with literacy difficulties is an individual. Each situation is unique. Each requires its own solution. There is no easy option. As practitioners, teachers need to bear in mind the wider cultural and social factors, the school and curriculum context, and factors related more specifically to the individual child. The same considerations apply to addressing difficulties commonly experienced by students in the learning of mathematics. It is to this that we turn in the next chapter.

6 Understanding and addressing special difficulties in mathematics

---

Questions addressed in this chapter

What is known about effective teachers of mathematics?

What are the characteristics of learning environments and pedagogy that support effective mathematics teaching?

Are there any specific areas of mathematics learning that are often experienced as problematic by students? If so, what are they?

What is known about ways of addressing barriers to mathematics learning often experienced by students?

Introduction

Many students in schools experience difficulties in learning in the area of mathematics. The challenge for those with an interest in mathematics education is to understand what teachers might do to break this pattern. Many of the problems associated with learning mathematics have little resemblance to those encountered in other curriculum areas. Solving them is not a straightforward matter of importing more general cures. The task of the teacher is 'demanding, uncertain, and not reducible to predictable routines' (Anthony and Walshaw 2007: x). The choices that teachers make about organization, management and the area of the mathematics curriculum on which to focus at any one time, as well as the cognitive demands of mathematics teaching are all part of the complexity of practice in the classroom.

As with other aspects of the school curriculum addressed in this book, the view is taken that the cause of difficulties in mathematical learning is not simply a deficit in the learner's thinking. The learning environment and the teaching approaches that are used are also crucial factors in influencing whether or not a student is likely to experience difficulties greater than those of peers. There are ways of structuring the environment and planning activities in mathematics that are likely to facilitate all students' mathematical learning. Having said this, however, even with the best organized classrooms there are likely to be some students who continue to experience difficulties and may need extra or additional support.

Attributes of effective teachers of mathematics

Questions for reflection

How mathematically knowledgeable does an effective teacher of students who experience difficulties in mathematics have to be, do you think?

Which is more important for that teacher in teaching students who experience difficulties: to be a good mathematician, or to have a positive working relationship with, and understanding of, students who experience difficulties in learning?

Teacher beliefs and attitudes

Those teachers who are effective in teaching mathematics to the whole range of student learners are those who take very seriously, and are committed to, developing students' mathematical thinking (Anthony and Walshaw 2007: 1). This commitment is characterized by a number of principles, among which are:

- an acknowledgement that all students ... have the capacity to become powerful mathematical learners;
- a commitment to maximize access to mathematics;
- empowerment of all to develop mathematical identities and knowledge;
- holistic development for productive citizenship through mathematics;
- relationships and the connectedness of both people and ideas;
- interpersonal respect and sensitivity;
- fairness and consistency.

From these conclusions it appears that teachers' beliefs, expectations and understandings of all students as active agents in their own learning are as important in the area of mathematics as in any other area of the school curriculum.

Teachers who are effective in supporting the mathematical learning of those students who experience difficulties show an interest in what students have to say, listen to their ideas, avoid sarcasm and do not allow students to put each other down. Stipek and colleagues (1998) note that these teachers appear genuinely to like and respect their students and make an effort to make mathematics problems interesting. They give the impression that they value all students' contributions. They might, for example, call on students who often experience difficulties and point out what can be learned from mistakes. In this way they create an environment where students are prepared to take risks because they know that it is safe to do so, that they will not be humiliated by the teacher and that the teacher will stop other students from embarrassing them.

Effective teachers neither embarrass students nor ignore wrong answers. They use mistakes to enhance the teaching. They might, for example comment on the strategies students are using and/or talk about the mathematical concepts that students are learning. They encourage students to monitor their own progress and set their own goals. In a study of effective practice in a Year 10 classroom, Angier and Povey (1999) noted how students' academic and social outcomes were improved by the inclusive ethos that the teacher had established in the mathematics classroom. Some of the students in the class said about her:

> She treats you as though you are … like … not just a kid. If you say look this is wrong she'll listen to you. If you challenge her she will try and see it your way.
>
> (Angier and Povey 1999: 157)

> She doesn't regard herself as higher.
>
> (Angier and Povey 1999: 157)

> She's not bothered about being proven wrong. Most teachers hate being wrong … being proven wrong by students.
>
> (Angier and Povey 1999: 157)

> We all felt like a family in maths. Does that make sense? Even if we weren't always sending out brotherly/sisterly vibes. Well we got used to each other … so we all worked …We all knew how to work with each other … it was a big group … more like a neighbourhood with loads of different houses.
>
> (Angier and Povey 1999: 153)

Constructive feedback

Constructive feedback has a powerful influence on student achievement (Hattie 2002). There is evidence (Wiliam 1999) that feedback that is constructive makes a comparison between where a student is currently at and a standard as interpreted by the teacher. Classroom research at both primary and secondary level (Wiliam 1999; Ruthven 2002) has shown that much of the teacher feedback that students receive is not particularly constructive, however. Ruthven reported that, in the UK, teacher feedback was not assisting students 'to study mathematics and think mathematically' (2002: 189).

There is now a large body of evidence that demonstrates the beneficial effects of students being encouraged to articulate their mathematical thinking (Lampert 1990; O'Connor 1998; Fraivillig et al. 1999). By expressing their ideas, students provide their teachers with information about what they know and what they need to learn. Hiebert and colleagues (1997) have found that teacher talk that is effective in supporting mathematical understanding and competence involves:

- drawing out the specific mathematical ideas that students are using to work out the answers to problems;
- sharing other methods and ways of working through mathematical problems;
- supporting students' understanding of the accepted conventions in mathematics.

Effective mathematics teachers often listen to what students have to say and re-frame student talk in mathematically appropriate language. This provides teachers with the chance to highlight connections between mathematical language and conceptual understanding. Many students who experience difficulty in mathematics lack the confidence to speak out in the classroom; however, I well remember the occasion when teaching mathematics to a bottom set of 14-year-old students in a secondary school I was asked by one boy: ' 'ere, Miss, why do you bother with us when you can teach them clever kids?' As noted already, for students to be prepared to volunteer their answers in mathematics lessons they need to feel safe and know that they will not be humiliated by either the teacher or their peers if they are wrong. The first step for the teacher in all this is probably to ensure this sense of safety for all the students in the classroom.

Teacher knowledge and understanding

Effective mathematics teaching requires teacher knowledge. What teachers do in classrooms is dependent on:

- what they know and believe about mathematics;
- what they understand about the teaching and learning of mathematics.

A teacher who intends to facilitate student understanding will not necessarily achieve this intention. Unless teachers themselves are able to understand the relevant mathematical concepts, they may not be confident enough to expect the best of all students. Nor may they be able to identify points at which they can elaborate on students' current understandings and help them to move towards more complex and sophisticated appreciation of mathematical concepts.

The teacher must make good sense of the mathematics involved or he or she will not be able to help students work with ideas and knowledge (Fraivillig et al. 1999; Schifter 2001). Teachers must have sound content knowledge if they are to recognize the conceptual understandings and misunderstandings that students are using in their methods, and if they are to realize where those (mis)understandings might be leading (Ball and Bass 2000; Kilpatrick et al. 2001; Warfield 2001; Shulman and Shulman 2004; Hill et al. 2005). When teachers demonstrate limited or confused understanding of the subject knowledge relevant to the lesson their students are likely to struggle to make sense of the mathematical concepts (Bliss et al. 1996). Teachers who are unclear in their own minds about mathematical ideas struggle to teach those ideas and often use examples and metaphors that prevent, rather than help, students' mathematical understanding. Where teachers are insecure in their content knowledge, there is often a direct, subsequent student lack of understanding. Limited teacher knowledge of mathematics can lead to misunderstandings of students' solutions and to giving feedback that is inappropriate or unhelpful. In a study of whole-class teaching episodes at three schools, Myhill and Warren (2005) found that many strategies used by teachers worked more as devices to enable students to complete tasks rather than as learning support mechanisms that would help move them towards independence. In the Year 2 and Year 6 lessons observed, teachers often used 'heavy prompts', pointing students to the 'right' answers. Using this strategy, the teachers in the Myhill and Warren study tended to miss critical opportunities for gaining insight into students' prior knowledge or level of understanding. Teachers' fragile subject knowledge prevented them from assessing the current level of mathematical sophistication and put boundaries around the ways in which they could develop students' responses.

Effective teaching is not necessarily related to higher formal qualifications, however. The Effective Teachers of Numeracy Project in the UK (Askew et al. 1997) revealed a slight negative relationship between the level of teachers' formal qualifications in mathematics and the levels of attainment of their students. It was the teachers who were able to make connections between aspects of mathematical knowledge who recorded high academic gains for their students. The Effective Teachers of Numeracy Project indicated that 'highly effective teachers of numeracy themselves had knowledge and awareness of conceptual connections between the areas which they taught in the primary mathematics curriculum' (Askew et al. 1997: 3). Teachers' conceptual understanding and knowledge is critically important at any level.

Learning environments that support mathematics learning

Walshaw (2004) identifies a number of components of the learning environment which help to bring about mathematical learning and the way in which mathematical knowledge is constructed by students:

- how activities are organized and the kind of tasks that are organized to develop mathematical understanding;
- classroom 'discourses' in mathematics, that is, the kind of language that is used and the way that mathematics is talked about and arguments are made and understood;
- the tools and resources that are made available for students to use.

An important recent synthesis of 600 studies of effective mathematical pedagogy (Anthony and Walshaw 2007) confirms the importance of these components and adds a non-threatening classroom atmosphere to this list.

Classroom atmosphere

Effective mathematics teaching for the full range of learners in classrooms means creating a space for both individuals and groups. Small-group work can provide the context for social and cognitive engagement. It is undoubtedly the case also that sometimes students need opportunities and time to work quietly away from the demands of a group.

Opportunities to learn depend to some extent on what is 'normal' in classrooms, what is allowed and disallowed, teacher and peer expectations, and the way that the learning environment is organized. This includes the extent to which there is an expectation that all students have the right to learn and to make mistakes, that they will persevere when they find the work challenging, that they will contribute to discussion and that they will listen to, and support, each other.

Teachers who create effective classroom communities care about student engagement and work hard to find out what helps and what hinders students' learning (Cobb and Hodge 2002). At the same time they make sure that students do not become overly dependent on them and encourage them to ask questions about why the class is expected to do certain things in mathematics lessons, and what is the point (Noddings 1995). There is an implication that, while students have something to learn from teachers, teachers may also have something to learn from their students (Perso 2003).

Examples of the damaging effects of low teacher expectations

Every task or activity in mathematics supports some kinds of thinking and hinders others. In a study of the views and experiences of nearly 1000 students, Boaler et al. (2000) found that, lower-streamed classes had fewer instructional opportunities to learn. Teaching strategies were very narrow, resulting in profound and largely negative learning experiences. Teachers often seemed to ignore students' backgrounds and needs and talked to them in ways that highlighted the difference between these students and those achieving highly in mathematics.

Teachers do not always value students' mathematical contributions equally. Unfairness in the way teachers treat different groups of students can affect students badly (Nash and Harker 2002). Teachers who give less attention to some students than to others tend to offer less encouragement to students that they have labelled as 'not mathematical'. One student in the Nash and Harker study said: 'Like when you ask the teachers you think, you feel like you don't know, you're dumb. So it stops you from asking the teachers, yeah, so you just try to hide back, don't worry about it. Everyday you don't understand, you just don't want to tell the teacher' (2002: 180).

Bartholomew (2003) found that mathematics teachers at a London school valued top-stream students more highly than others. The messages conveyed to students about the way they were valued were clear. With his low-stream class, a teacher behaved in an authoritarian manner, 'insisting that students queue outside the room in absolute silence and eventually counting them in and seating them alphabetically. They had to remain in their seats in silence, were given no opportunities to ask questions, with the result that many students were extremely confused as to what they were meant to be doing' (Bartholomew 2003: 131). In contrast, the teacher's interactions with his top-stream class at the same year level were friendly.

Many studies (Boaler et al. 2000; Sullivan et al. 2003), have shown how low attainers are often presented with a very limited 'diet' of activities in mathematics lessons, where the four rules of number customarily dominate and there is little focus on students constructing their own understandings. This practice may well have a detrimental effect on students' sense of themselves as able to become competent in mathematical thinking. Teacher conceptualizations of students as having the potential to become competent mathematical learners have a strong influence over the achievement of those students. It is very important that negative labelling of students and the difficulties they experience do not overtake any sense that these students might do better.

Learning tasks

Peers can serve as an important resource for developing mathematical thinking and for finding out about the nature of task demands and how those demands could be met. Collaborative activity within a small supportive environment allows students not only to exchange ideas but also to test those ideas critically. Helme and Clarke (2001) found in their secondary school classroom study that peer interactions, rather than teacher–student interactions, provide opportunity for students to engage in high-level cognitive activity. These researchers stress the important role the teacher plays in establishing social rules governing participation in the classroom. These rules can serve to make the engagement in mathematical learning tasks by lower-attaining students possible or impossible. Alton-Lee (2003) reports that the teachers who set aside time to instruct students about the intricacies of effective group processes invariably enhanced students' outcomes. Students who learned to help each other learned that, to make the group work effective, communication and feedback within the group needed to be centred on mathematical explanations and justifications rather than on single answers to problems. Students interacting need to have sufficient competence and experience to allow them to ask appropriate questions of themselves and each other.

There have been successful projects, for example the Improving Attainment in Mathematics (IAMP) project (Watson et al. 2003), that show how focusing on developing students' understanding and introducing them to 'the sorts of practices that distinguish mathematics learners from any others' (Anthony and Walshaw 2007: 18) can lead to improved student achievement and level of interest in the subject. The kinds of practices that Watson et al. are referring to here are:

> choosing appropriate techniques, generating their own enquiry, contributing examples, predicting problems, describing connections with prior knowledge, giving reasons, finding underlying similarities or differences, generalising structure from diagrams or examples, identifying what can be changed, making something more difficult, making comparisons, posing their own questions, giving reasons, working on extended tasks over time, creating and sharing their own methods, using prior knowledge, dealing with unfamiliar problems, changing their minds, and initiating their own mathematics.
>
> (Anthony and Walshaw 2007: 18–19)

Some of the teachers in the project were innovative in their teaching practices, some much more traditional in their approach. What these teachers had in common, however, was a very purposeful approach in setting meaningful activities in lessons, and a deliberate effort to support students to think of themselves as able to become competent mathematicians.

Tools and representations

The opportunity to learn is influenced by what is made available to learners. The activities that teachers plan for their students are crucial to learning. Choice of task, tools and activity significantly influences the development of mathematical thinking. Mathematical tasks should be focused on the solution of genuine mathematical problems. The most productive tasks and activities are those that allow students to access important mathematical concepts and relationships, to investigate mathematical structure, and to use techniques and notations appropriately.

Classroom discourse: the language of mathematics

Effective teaching bridges the gap between students' intuitive understandings and mathematical understandings and conventions in society at large. Language is central to this. Mathematical language is not simply the vocabulary and technical usage of mathematics. It also includes the ways that expert and novice mathematicians use language to explain concepts. 'Teachers who make a difference are focused on shaping the development of novice mathematicians who speak the precise and generalisable language of mathematics' (Anthony and Walshaw 2007: 204).

Sullivan et al. (2003) argue for a very definite, clear approach to teaching mathematics, one where the teacher:

- helps students to 'see through' the language that is wrapped around the mathematical problem to the problem itself;
- offers very clear, intelligible explanations of the mathematics that is required to work out that problem;
- is sensitive to class and cultural differences among the group of students, and between the students and the teacher, and works hard not to alienate students by insensitive trampling on these differences;
- understands that responses to the particular activity might be different from what was anticipated, but nevertheless acceptable mathematically.

Specific difficulties in mathematics learning

Many children who experience difficulties in understanding and using number symbols also experience difficulties in the use of language. As Rogers (2007: 2) comments, most teaching and assessment in the area of mathematics takes place in the context of a symbolic representation of mathematics, that is, through written text and pictures. Learners' ability to understand symbolic representation depends on understanding the first-hand experience to which the symbolic representation refers. In the case of younger learners, this may involve, for example, the handling and counting of everyday items. While activities involving reading and writing numbers may tell us something about children's ability to read and write numbers, they do not necessarily tell us anything about children's conceptual understanding of 'number-ness'. Many children appear to adopt mathematical symbols and algorithms without having grasped the concepts that underpin them (Borthwick and Harcourt-Heath 2007). Rogers (2007: 13) goes on to note that a weak conceptual framework for understanding number in the early years on which to begin formal mathematics teaching:

> makes it both difficult to engage children (Department of Education and Science, 1989) and to correct later (Nunes et al. 1997), It is also well documented that such difficulties soon become compounded, resulting in distress and further delay (Adult Literacy and Basic Skills Unit, 1992). Attention needs to be paid to the negative effects of incomprehension of a prominent part of the mathematics curriculum in which young children are involved on a daily basis. It may be that

such incomprehension prompts the early lack of confidence in mathematics that characterises further failure and poor problem-solving during the later school years. They can often learn to count up and down 'in ones' and can take part in counting games and activities. However, understanding that a number, for example five, is not just the last number in the series 15 (the ordinal principle), but also means the whole set of five (the principle of cardinality) is another matter.

Difficulties in the early years

As Grauberg (2002) notes, there seems to be a preference in the UK and the USA for teaching number in the early years through the use of number sequences. In some other countries in Europe and the Far East, for example Japan, it is different, however, and the preference is for emphasizing cardinal aspects, that is, recognition of small quantities without counting. Recognizing a small number, for example four, as a quantity involves one operation of matching a sound symbol or visual symbol to an amount. This seems, logically, easier than recognizing four from a number sequence. This latter involves remembering that four comes after three and before five, and simultaneously counting up to the total amount. Hughes (1986: 45) exemplifies this point from an interview with a boy named Ram:

> MH: What is three and one more? How many is three and one more?
> Ram: Three and what? One what? Letter? I mean number?
> . . .
> MH: How many is three and one more?
> Ram: One more what?
> MH: Just one more, you know?
> Ram: (Disgruntled) I don't know.

It will take a lot of activities in a variety of different contexts before a child such as Ram:

> . . . will be able to grasp the powerful abstract qualities of a number – which means the concept of 'twoness', 'threeness', 'nness'. Through his experience with many different materials we want him (sic) to see what is common to all (the fact that there are, for instance, 'two' of each) and we want him to learn to ignore what is irrelevant (e.g. size, colour, feel).
>
> (Grauberg 2002: 12)

It might be appropriate to concentrate on establishing the idea of quantity first – a lot, a little, more, less, and so on – and then small numbers as a specific quantity for the child who experiences difficulties in language. As Grauberg (2002) comments, this approach has the potential to establish the concept of 'numberness', before starting on number lines. Often we might consider that it is not a good idea to introduce concepts with clear similarities, but also differences, together, particularly where a child experiences difficulties in the area of language. For example, if we were to introduce a donkey and a pony at the same time and tell the child that the donkey is the one with the big ears, it may be that the child is for ever afterwards confused about which is which. However, when it comes to words that only make sense when they are compared with something else it is a different matter. 'More' and 'less' only make sense in comparison with something else.

The written recording of number work

Children who experience difficulty in language and symbolic representation are also likely to find it problematic to acquire and use written symbols for numbers. Learning to use number symbols is likely to occur simultaneously with acquiring the alphabetic principle and sound–symbol correspondence in literacy acquisition and, as Grauberg (2002) comments, 'Where is the 'f' in 5?' It is possible to use other number systems, for example tally charts, first, where one bundle represents five and clearly made up of five. Or, for some children it might be important to use concrete aids to establish number learning, for example Cuisenaire rods and/or an abacus, for much longer than for other children.

Common problems: the examples of place value and 'zero'

It is my experience that difficulties with the concept of place value and 'zero' can be experienced not just by children with language difficulties. They are very commonly experienced by other students also, to the end of their secondary education. I realized that place value was not properly understood by many of the teenagers who were expected to cope with the concept of hundreds, thousands and millions in other curriculum areas while I was still trying to support them to develop a basic understanding of place value. I thought it was hardly surprising that students found concepts such as population density expressed in thousands per square mile so frustratingly complex and difficult in their geography lessons and their behaviour became disruptive. They could not handle the concepts of thousands and millions competently and confidently, either in an ordinal or cardinal sense, and became very frustrated when expected to apply these concepts.

Zero is another problematic concept, mathematically. I was once asked by 14-year-old students in a mixed comprehensive school: 'How can 44 times nought possibly equal nought? How can something equal nothing when you've started with 44 and made it bigger by multiplying?' (Wearmouth, unpublished). I replied by taking a handful of nothing and putting it down on the desk 44 times to prove the point.

The use of zero as a place holder in a multi-digit line is just as difficult to comprehend – without understanding the whole concept of place value. One way to start to address problems with place value might be to continue to use concrete equipment such as Dienes materials – unit cubes, 'longs' of 10 cm cubes and 'flats' of 100 cm cubes – for much longer than the teacher might have anticipated, providing that this can be done without embarrassing the child(ren). For example, 54 might be written down at first as 50 with the 4 superimposed over the 0, and 504 would be written down as 500 with the 4 superimposed over the last 0. Alternatively, as Grauberg (2002) notes, the numbers may be written on transparencies and then superimposed.

Relational signs: 'plus', 'minus', 'equal(s)'

Adding and subtracting both imply actions. Without an understanding of what the action is there is little point in trying to encourage the use of the symbol. The symbol '='

is often interpreted to children as 'makes', but, as we are all aware, a child's notion of 'makes' is clearly not what '=' means, mathematically. Having said this, primary schools in particular have a lot of equipment that can be used to play games in adding, subtracting and balancing. A major question is how to move from the act of adding, taking away or balancing to competent use of the abstract symbols. One way to do this might be to encourage children to devise their own symbols for the actions first (that is, to spend longer thinking about ways in which children will move into and through the iconic mode of representation where the icon visibly represents their own understandings).

Money
Money is another concept that all students need to acquire, but can be extremely problematic in its acquisition. First, there is the issue of all the difficulties with number that might be experienced by the child. Secondly, there is the question of understanding money as a system of tokens.

One way to approach this might be, again, through the use of Diennes equipment. Rods and cubes can be made up into bundles representing the value of the money in the decimal system first, and used as long as necessary until the transition to toy money and then to the real thing.

Time
As Piaget (1969) noted, time is a complex concept, covering, as it does:

- points in time;
- duration and sequence of events;
- frequency of events, and intervals between them.

Supporting a student to acquire a concept of time is a very different proposition from teaching him/her to tell the time. The point of reference in relation to many indicators of time is not constant. 'Late' could refer to a point in the morning, if a student should have arrived earlier, or to a point at night, for example. Even our sense of the passage of time is very subjective and seems to distort depending on the activity and our engagement with, or enjoyment of, it.

If we attempted to use Bruner's framework of the three modes of representation – enactive, iconic and symbolic – to differentiate activities and approaches for students who experience difficulties in the area of language, it is difficult to see how to do this easily because no concept of time is concrete, as Grauberg (2002) points out. However, using a timer or some sort, perhaps one invented by the students themselves, might help in the initial stages. Students might be asked to see how much of an activity they can complete before a sand timer – or their own timer – runs out. A way to encourage a sense of the duration of time is to focus on the intervals between events – for example, the silence between the sounds emitted after striking a percussion instrument. Concentrating on the sounds themselves might encourage a sense of time as the frequency of events. To encourage the concept of sequence, a teacher might first organize an activity for children to act out a regular sequence of events in their own lives. Then s/he might represent sequence as a series of pictures (Bruner's iconic mode of representation) and ask children to arrange the cards in a logical order and talk about it.

In terms of telling the time, use of a digital clock or watch is a simpler option than a traditional clock face. However, to do this is to lose the context of time itself. The hands of the traditional clock face can be seen to move in the context of the 12-hour cycle, but the numbers on a digital timepiece simply move.

Dyscalculia

Many children identified as dyslexic are often strong in terms of conceptual skills, but, in the area of mathematics, up to around 60 per cent of them (Joffe 1983; Henderson 1998; Miles and Miles 2004) experience difficulty in understanding mathematical concepts and learning computational skills. The term 'dyscalculia' is often used to describe difficulty in grasping computational skills and, despite ability in other areas, difficulty in reasoning and understanding of basic mathematical concepts. Mathematics covers a range of topics – size, time, shape and space – but all these aspects require competence in basic arithmetical skills.

Many of the difficulties experienced by dyslexic students in information processing also affect their progress in mathematics learning:

- the language of mathematics;
- left-right orientation difficulties;
- sequencing problems;
- memory weakness;
- poor spatial awareness and skills of perception;
- slow speed in information processing;
- poor understanding of mathematical concepts.

The language of mathematics

The language of mathematics may prove difficult, with new words, signs and symbols to be learned and considerable ambiguity of meaning with the way words are used outside the context of the subject. As Weavers (2003: 35) notes, there are many terms and expression in mathematics that have the same meaning:

+,   add, sum of, plus, and. altogether, addition, more than, positive
−,   subtract, take away, minus, difference between, less, smaller than, negative
×,   (often confused with +), times, multiply, product of, lots of
÷,   divide, share, how many in, how much each, quotient
=,   equals, becomes, is the same as, makes
>,   greater than, often confused with <, less than.

It is very important that a few words are introduced at a time and learned with their meanings thoroughly understood. It is better to restrict the number of new words to a very few that the student can remember the next day and the next week than to introduce too many so that the student cannot remember any clearly.

Sometimes the same word can denote a completely different calculation. For example, 'What is 10 more than 20?' requires a different operation than 'How many more than 10 is 20?' It can be very helpful to assist students to estimate an answer first by saying whether it should be bigger or smaller than the first number, in order to narrow down the possible calculations. Mathematical problems may need to be read very slowly with an emphasis on each individual word so that the student has an opportunity to think about what the problem means before s/he can consider how to work it out.

Some words have a variety of meanings: 'volume' can refer to quantity or sound, the 'face' or a person is very different from a clock 'face' or the 'face' of a three-dimensional shape.

For many students, the very fact that the teacher is aware of the difficulties that dyslexic students may face may well be a relief. Multi-sensory teaching, that is, emphasizing new concepts, processes and skills by using all the senses simultaneously wherever possible, will help many students. For example, talking students through processes while they are carrying them out, repeating aloud the sequences they should follow and encouraging them to do this also can be very helpful.

Orientation

Children learn to read English from left to right but, in mathematics lessons, are often confronted with working in columns down the page, and from right to left. Differentiating between words indicating direction generally may be problematic: up and down, in and out, and so on. There may be little consistency in writing letters and figures the correct way round. Writing letters and numbers the right way round might be encouraged using multi-sensory strategies, for example by tracing over large letters or numerals or drawing them in sand, with clearly marked beginnings and ends, simultaneously saying the name of the letter or number aloud.

Sequencing problems

Sequencing may prove problematic, for example days of the week, months of the year, and logical progression in setting out work clearly. The current author has experience of teaching a number of secondary-aged pupils who might begin their work anywhere on the page – in the middle, to the right or left – without apparently noticing;

Memory weakness

There may be problems with memory, for example learning and remembering tables, the alphabet, and so on. Memory for unrelated objects, numbers and figures might be encouraged by putting a variety of objects or geometric shapes on a tray, or giving the students sheets with pictures or numbers written on them, showing them the tray or sheet for one minute, and asking them to recall what they saw. Pupils might then discuss with each other what strategies they used for memorizing the objects, shapes or numbers. These strategies (often called mnemonics) might then be practised deliberately.

Students may experience difficulties in making simple calculations without the support of fingers or marks on paper. Lever (2003) offers a way of supporting pupils to work out their tables that she calls 'finger tables'. To use this method, the pupils have to know their tables from 2 times to 5 times. Then the teacher might instruct the pupils to:

- Put their hands, palms up, in front of them. Begin to number the fingers and thumbs – for example with a small white label of felt tipped pen – starting with the thumb on the left-hand side. The left-hand thumb is '10', the forefinger is '9', middle finger '8', ring finger '7' and little finger '6'. On the right hand the thumb is also '10', forefinger '9' and so on (Figure 6.1).

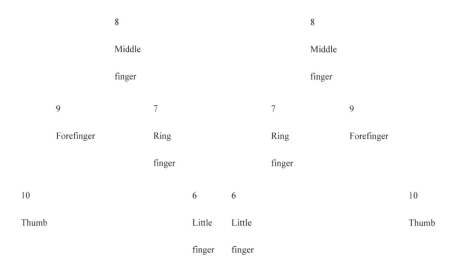

Figure 6.1 Memory: finger tables

- To multiply two numbers, first put the relevant finger tips together, for example 7 × 7. The two fingers touching and the two on the far side of these should be totalled (2 + 2 = 4) and used as the 10s (that is, 40). The nearside fingers on the left hand (that is, 3 of them) should be multiplied with the nearside fingers (that is, 3 of them) on the right hand – 3 × 3 = 9. Then the two numbers 40 + 9 should be added together – 40 + 9 = 49.
- To multiply 7 x 8, put the relevant finger tips together. There are two fingers touching and three on the far side = 5 fingers (50). Multiply the three nearside fingers on the left hand with the two nearside fingers on the right hand: 3 × 2 = 6. Then 50 + 6 = 56.

Weavers (2003) also suggests that children should use a 'table square' rather than a calculator for multiplication of two numbers up to 10. Table squares contain obvious patterns of numbers which students might find interesting and memorable.

Mathematics is an area that relies heavily on previously learned work, so those students with a poor memory can have major problems. Constantly reinforcing and emphasizing understanding can assist students whose memory for rote learning is poor because it gives them a way to start from 'first base' rather than relying on their weak memories. Sometimes students can benefit from working in collaborative groups with peers to ensure that they have all understood the question first.

Poor spatial awareness and organizational skills

Poor spatial awareness and organizational skills may affect the construction and/or interpretation of diagrams and charts, and the copying of data from the board or from a text. In my own experience, dyslexic students might, for example, draw bar charts of any height or width seemingly at random, or might be unable to understand what is meant by a term such as 'right angle' because they cannot easily recognize the shape at sight or when drawn in perspective. Not all dyslexic students have poor visual perception skills, but a considerable number do. Some students find it difficult to interpret maps, outlines, block graphs, the representation of three-dimensional shapes on two-dimensional paper, and so on. Sometimes it helps to use transparent coloured overlays to reduce the overall glare of white paper and black ink. Quite often it helps to enable access to building bricks and blocks of all sizes. I remember teaching a severely dyslexic, but otherwise very intelligent, young man to recognize the shape of a right angle. First, I asked him to look straight down at the sharp-edged corner of his desk and run his hands round the right angle many times until he was used to the shape, feel and sight simultaneously. Then I transferred attention to representing the right-angled corner on paper.

Some students experience difficulty – sometimes extreme – in organizational skills that may manifest themselves in perceiving and, therefore, using structures to organize personal thinking and working. In terms of mathematics, those who experience difficulties of this sort may well experience difficulty in:

- understanding and using the decimal system;
- organizing:
- quantities;
- word problems in mathematics;
- spatial arrangements.

Eleven-year-old Matt, for example, would begin his work at any point on the page, seemingly without noticing. He could not easily 'see' pattern and organizational structure, so it is hardly surprising that he had not grasped the idea of the regular arrangement of base 10 and the decimal system.

Grauberg (2002: 66) suggests that, where students experience this kind of difficulty, it is important to provide them with 'a working model that can illustrate the underlying structure of the decimal system clearly and memorably. They need a tool at their fingertips, a picture in their minds, ready for use'. One way to do this is to support the student to conceptualize 100 as a quantity consisting of a grid with dots marked on it (Figure 6.2).

Students can then see straight away that ten is made of 5 + 5, then, by covering two of the dots in one row, that it can consist of 8 + 2, and so on. Similarly, numbers can be counted in tens and students can see the relationship between 10, 20, 30 and so on to 100. Heavy black lines can be drawn across the grid to separate the dots into 4 blocks, each of 5 x 5 dots, where the teacher sees it as appropriate. Then, by covering the relevant parts of the grid: 'Seven, for instance is seen as five-and-two and is instantly recognised as such; 70 is recognised as five-rows-of-ten-and-two-rows-more. Numbers are thus seen as two-dimensional geometrical shapes, as 'quantity pictures' rather than as points on a

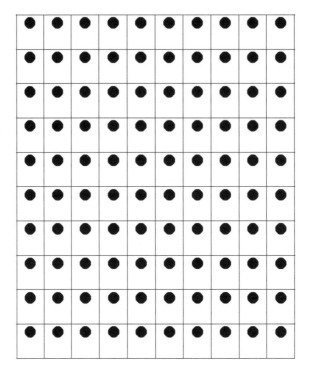

Figure 6.2 100 dots in a grid

number line' (Grauberg 2002: 66). This arrangement of dots is useful for supporting students' understanding of the position on numbers under 100 within this arrangement of dots.

Using Cuisenaire rods is another way to build up a concept of base 10, using groupings of 1, 5, 10 and 50.

Spatial difficulties might manifest themselves to start with by inability to match shapes or line up piles of wooden blocks easily. Eleven-year-old Matt, mentioned above, could never set out work straight on a page, could not discriminate between the left- and right-hand pages of his exercise books, and had terrible problems in drawing and interpreting any kind of graphs. He was also very clumsy. The author saw him once trying to stack tables in a school dining hall and he somehow managed to trap his head in between them in the clumsy way he was working.

A number of studies (Choat 1974; Wheatley and Wheatley 1979; Bishop 1983), together with anecdotal evidence from personal experience lead me to believe that supporting children to work with concrete materials together with a multi-sensory approach of finger tracing of different sorts of geometric shapes while simultaneously verbalizing appropriate terms relating to the activity, can have some very positive results in developing spatial awareness. Later, children can be supported to recognize the significant features of graphs and charts, again by finger tracing over the features that have significance to the meaning and interpretation while verbalizing these.

Slow speed in information processing

Many dyslexic students take a long time to process information thoroughly. Lack of ability to recall information instantly and difficulty in learning number bonds and tables by rote will put them at a considerable disadvantage. Pressure to complete work in a given period of time may cause undue stress, anxiety and further mistakes in the effort to finish on time. During his secondary years, one student known to me said he was 'always exhausted' at the effort it took to do the same work that others coped with easily. It is very important that such students are encouraged to work at their own pace so that they can complete what they start, take pride in their achievements and not become discouraged.

Poor understanding of mathematical concepts

Because a dyslexic student may have spent a long time on repetition and drill, it may be that s/he has little understanding of mathematical concepts or the conventions used in mathematical problem-solving.

Pupils who have little idea of the meaning of numerals or number terms might be supported to develop their understanding through using dice and/or dominoes. Using arrays of dots from 1 to 10 can provide a clear way to comprehend and acquire number bonds.

Mathematical word problems are complex because students need to understand the context in which the problem is set and:

- the logic of the word problem;
- the mathematical procedures that should be used to work out the problem.

Probably the most useful starting point is to ensure that pupils understand the problem in the first place. It might be helpful to encourage them to talk to each other about what they think it means – partly to check understanding of the logic of the problem and partly also to ensure that they have read the text properly. Alternatively, or in addition, students might close their eyes and visualize the problem. Then they might either use concrete objects such as counters or blocks, or draw a picture, to represent the problem before attempting to work out the solution.

Assessment of difficulties in mathematics

Schools are required to collect information about individual students who experience difficulties in learning of any sort from a variety of sources: pupil, parent/carer, teacher, and so on. Assessment must seek to identify what the pupil can do and understand, and also the procedures, concepts and skills where s/he experiences barriers to mathematical learning. For example, knowledge of a word is no guarantor of understanding. The use of practical apparatus may be important for example in assessing spatial concepts such as opposite and between, or the concept of a fraction.

Difficulties might be experienced by students where a mathematical problem is expressed in written form. Many students present their own idiosyncratic layout of mathematical operations, for example column displacement in setting out computations. Coping strategies might include using tally charts or fingers. As (El-Naggar 2001: 11) advises, assessment in the use of written symbols may need to be carried out by checking written examples and by:

- listening to the pupils read symbols aloud;
- presenting a task in written symbols for the pupil to carry out (using apparatus);
- asking the pupil to write down in symbols a problem presented orally;
- observing the way a pupil approaches a problem;
- asking the pupil how s/he reached an answer;
- analysing error patterns.

Understanding, and use, of space and shape may also be problematic for some pupils. Assessment may therefore first begin by asking the pupil to verbalise his/her response to the problem or task. A lot of the assessment of pupils' strengths and weaknesses might be carried out with objects rather than diagrams.

El-Naggar (1996: 20–1) offers some specific examples of children's mathematical errors. 10-year-old Sally:

> was working horizontal additions and producing some very strange answers without discernable patterns.
>
> e.g. $5 + 4 = 8$
>
> When asked to explain how she arrived at her answer Sally verbalised, 'Five add four ... you take the five and then you take six (pencil traced the down stroke of the numeral four), seven (pencil traced the horizontal stroke of the four), eight (pencil traced the horizontal stroke of the four), so the answer is eight.'
>
> Sally was confusing the numeral four with tally marks. What was really alarming was the length of time that the errors ... had gone undetected.

Twelve-year-old Emma found place value difficult when she had to write it down:

6	8	Emma used the algorithm she had been taught. She worked aloud $8 - 5$ and $6 - 5$. When asked to estimate the answer she said she thought it would be about 60.
–	5	

Emma worked several further problems in the same way. She understood the concept but had difficulty positioning the numbers.

Common difficulties in mathematics and techniques to address these

A number of difficulties are common in mathematics:

- Confusion with directionality. This manifests itself in starting computations in different places, confusion with place value, writing numbers the wrong way round, insecurity with right and left, difficulty with the concept of rotation, working with decimal points, and so on. Teachers might consider:

- making calculators available;
- making squared paper available with left and right marked on it;
- writing headings 'HTU' for each computation;
- practising estimating by teaching students to round up and down so that they can check if their answers are approximately correct.

- Problems with vision and perception, particular the recording of symbols, for example numerals and function signs. Teachers might consider:
  - teaching the symbols for numbers in small groups where numerals with similar shapes, for example 6 and 9, are not introduced at the same time;
  - writing the symbols +, –, x and ÷ on different coloured cards;
  - encouraging students to trace over the symbols +, –, x and ÷ while simultaneously saying their names;
  - verbalizing the signs < and > and showing how they can relate to movement on a number line.

- Problems with reading texts. Omissions, errors or reversals of words may mean that a mathematical problem is unintelligible. Teachers might consider:
  - encouraging a reciprocal teaching approach where students work in groups, expect the text to make sense and discuss mathematical problems and possible solutions together;
  - using correct terminology while talking about mathematics;
  - supplying reading lists of mathematical terms essential to the concept being taught and helping students to learn them by the same method that the school uses to teach reading;
  - helping students to highlight the core parts of written questions.

- Problems with remembering terms such as 'circumference', 'radius', 'diameter', 'hexagon', and so on. Teachers might encourage students to develop their own system of mnemonics for these terms.
- Problems with organization that might relate to sequencing and spatial issues. These problems might present themselves in keeping books and files organized in a systematic way, untidy page presentation, loss of pens, pencils and other equipment. Teachers might:
  - give very clear instructions about page layout, and model what is expected;
  - give clear exemplars to individuals, or to all students in the class;
  - insist that lines are drawn with a ruler by all students and that drawings are done in pencil;
  - encourage students to use squared paper and to write one digit per square;
  - allow sufficient time for the work to be completed neatly;
  - ensure that tasks are completed.

- Acute anxiety about mathematics which might show itself as working very slowly, or even work avoidance. Teachers might consider:
  - how to include the students who experience the greatest difficulties in mathematics in whole-class activities such as questions and answers, or practice of tables, without humiliating them publicly;

- – listening to students' worries and concerns and taking account of them;
- – creating opportunities for working in well organized collaborative peer groups.

As a result of general difficulties in information processing, dyslexic students may experience particular difficulties in the area of mathematics. Riddick et al. (2002: 50) offer a number of suggestions about teaching such students:

- Make sure they understand basic symbols: =, +, –, and so on.
- Make sure they understand basic number language, for example, subtract, multiply, and so on.
- Repeat learning and revision of number facts.
- Teach child to estimate a sensible answer.
- Teach child to check their answer against the set question.
- Be alert for reversals which lead to child making a wrong calculation.
- Practise counting forwards and backwards in sequences, for example, in ones, then twos, and so on.
- Use pattern methods to teach number bonds.
- Teach multiplication using table squares.
- Use squared paper to aid correct setting out of calculations.
- Give a sample strip with digits in correct orientation for checking reversals.
- Use multi-sensory teaching; rehearse what has just been learnt with oral revision at the end of the lesson.
- Teach using logic rather than just rules so conceptual ability can be utilized.

Summary

There is evidence that the mathematics curriculum for students known to experience difficulties can be very narrow and restrictive. However, as the Cockroft Report (Cockroft: 1982, para. 243) advocates, certain elements that are required in mathematical teaching to all other pupils should also be apparent in teaching those who experience particular difficulties:

- explanation by the teacher;
- discussion between the pupils and the teacher, and between pupils themselves;
- practical work appropriate to the concept being taught;
- reinforcement and practice of basic skills and routines;
- application of mathematics to everyday situations;
- problem-solving;
- investigations.

The specialized language of mathematics can be problematic for some learners. Particular words, grammar and vocabulary used in school mathematics can hinder access to the meaning sought and the objective for a given lesson. Words, phrases and terms can take on completely different meanings from those that they have in the everyday context. Walkerdine (1988), for example, has reported the difficulties young students encounter in establishing the mathematical meaning of 'less than' and 'more', given their idiosyncratic meanings within specific home practices.

El-Naggar (2001: 9) suggests that teaching in mathematics follows the sequence below:

> Step 1: a clear explanation of what we expect our pupils to do, inviting questions and discussion.
> Step 2: Provision of materials and time for them to understand that explanation in their own way, while working together and discussing (through games, puzzles, problems and role playing).
> Step 3: Recording and reinforcing through the use of work cards, textbooks and recording individual/group results.

Difficulties in learning of the sort described in this and previous chapters that are not recognized or acknowledged by the teacher can be important contributors to poor classroom behaviour by some students. The following chapter picks up on this issue as well as others in outlining approaches to understanding and addressing student behaviour that may be experienced as challenging in schools and classrooms.

7   Behavioural issues in classrooms

Questions addressed in this chapter

Is there a relationship between human learning and behaviour? If so, what are the implications for understanding and addressing problematic student behaviour in schools?

How can we make the link between the basic human need to belong and approaches to supporting positive student behaviour in schools?

What features of classroom management can minimize low level disruption and promote positive behaviour and learning?

How can we address individual extreme behaviour of the sort that hinders students' learning and therefore constitutes a special educational need?

Introduction

Arguments about how to interpret and handle behaviour perceived as challenging in schools often generate a great deal of heated debate. The way in which causes of problematic behaviour are understood and explained really matters. In schools this can have a strong effect on the way teachers deal with students and their parents or carers. We might look, for example, at the way in which use of the term emotional and behavioural difficulties to explain why some students behave badly or inappropriately can influence teachers' confidence in their abilities to respond to students' needs in classrooms. Poulou and Norwich (2002: 112) found from a review of international studies that 'dealing with children with EBD ... can generate feelings of helplessness and incompetence (Lennox, 1991; Bennett, 1992; Leadbetter and Leadbetter, 1993; Chazan et al., 1994; Gray et al., 1996)'. Poulou and Norwich concluded that teachers see themselves as able to deal with students' problematic behaviour if they consider that students' problems are caused by 'factors originating from teachers themselves, like their personality, manners towards the child with EBD, or teaching style'. In other words, if they think they can control the cause of a difficulty they believe 'that they can also sufficiently treat it. In addition, they perceived themselves in such cases as even more responsible for finding an effective solution for the child's problem' (Poulou and Norwich 2002: 112).

These researchers also found that the more teachers think student behaviour stems from problems within the students themselves, such as the 'child wants to attract attention' or the 'child's innate personality' then 'the more they experienced feelings of "stress", "offence" and even "helplessness", especially for conduct and mixed behaviour difficulties' (Poulou and Norwich 2002: 125).

Questions for reflection

In your experience:

- How can teachers put themselves into a strong position to deal with problematic behaviour in classrooms and schools?
- What factors within classrooms and within schools affect the way students behave?
- In addressing difficult student behaviour how can we take account of the way that students make sense of their own worlds? Does this matter?

Classroom management

As Watkins and Wagner (2000) note, student behaviour in schools does not occur in a vacuum. 'Difficult' neighbourhoods tend to produce more 'difficult' students than neighbourhoods in more affluent circumstances (Watkins and Wagner 2000). However, economic impoverishment in the neighbourhood does not necessarily lead to disruptive behaviour in schools (Rutter et al. 1979; OFSTED 2001). Schooling plays a critical part in shaping a student's identity as a learner. Even in areas of disadvantage, good classroom management as well as interventions with individual students, can make a difference to student behaviour, learning and future life chances. 'The collective perception of pupils of what it feels like, in intellectual, motivational and emotional terms, to be a pupil in any particular teacher's classroom' influence 'every pupil's motivation to learn and perform to the best of his or her ability'(Hobby and Smith 2002: 9). A research report on teacher effectiveness in the UK (Hay McBer 2000) concludes that students look towards the teacher for a sense of security and order, an opportunity to participate actively in the class and for the classroom to be an interesting and exciting place. In a similar vein, Visser et al. (2002) have found that in schools that successfully include students with behavioural difficulties the emphasis is on teaching and learning rather than on responding to perceived deficits of the child.

Such conditions are most easily realized where teachers follow what have been characterized as the 'four rules' of classroom management:

- Get them in, by starting lessons smoothly and promptly.
- Get them out, by arranging an orderly conclusion to lessons.
- Get on with it, by selecting suitable content with appropriate methods and materials.
- Get on with them, by awareness of each student as an individual (Smith and Laslett 1993: 3–13).

Applying behavioural principles

Most commonly, understandings and strategies in classroom management are based on principles from behaviourist psychology (Skinner 1938; Baer et al. 1968). Understanding the principles underlying behavioural approaches is therefore very important.

Understanding principles of behaviourism

Almost all the principles of behaviourist approaches were derived from work with laboratory animals, for example Skinner (1938). Early experiments with animals assumed that all behaviour is learned through a process of conditioning. In a famous sequence of trial-and-error learning tasks, rats learned to press levers in order to find food (Skinner 1938). Learning involved the formation of a stimulus–response association, that is, pressing the lever and finding food, in the rats' memory. Reinforcement through a reinforcer, which in this case is food, strengthened the association between stimulus and response. If the association between stimulus and response was broken by removing the reward, the rats' behaviour would gradually cease through 'extinction'. Where something unpleasant occurred as a result of an action it was viewed as 'punishment'. Translating this interpretation of behaviour into human terms in the behaviour of students in schools, behaviour seen as disturbing has been learned through positive reinforcement in some way. One way to address undesirable behaviour is to identify and alter the stimulus context or setting in which that behaviour occurs. Another way is to ensure that whatever is rewarding and reinforcing is removed so that the behaviour will be extinguished. In addition, whenever individuals behave in ways that are seen as more appropriate, they should be rewarded in a way that clearly recognizes the greater acceptability of the new behaviour within contexts and settings where that behaviour is clearly acceptable.

The opposite of positive reinforcement is negative reinforcement. Undesirable behaviour is discouraged and desired behaviour encouraged through putting a stop to something unpleasant. For example, student compliance may be reinforced through avoidance of punishment.

Behavioural methodologies assume that all behaviour is learned and, therefore, can be modified through intervening in the environment. When behavioural principles are applied in classroom or school settings, the reinforcing conditions or consequences of behaviour as well as the physical and social context in which the behaviour occurs may be systematically modified in order to improve students' behaviour.

Underlying behavioural principles is a basic concern with what people say and what they do, and not on assumptions about what they are doing or what their intentions may be. Behaviour statements are based on observed events, not on emotional statements *about* behaviour and its effects.

Applications of behaviourism in schools: ten behavioural principles

Ten principles for understanding and changing students' behaviour within the context of schools are summarized below (Glynn et al. 1997; Berryman and Glynn 2001). Four of these are aimed at changing behaviour through altering the antecedents (contextual or setting events) that precede or accompany it. The remaining six principles are aimed at changing behaviours through altering the contingencies of reinforcement (rewarding or punishing) that follow it.

Changing behaviour by altering the antecedents of the behaviour

1   *Take time to plan ahead*. Careful thinking and planning ahead to foresee possible behaviour difficulties likely to arise in their day, and plan strategies and responses ahead of time, can help avoid having to deal with challenging or undesirable behaviours.

2   *Change the setting*. Altering aspects of the setting or context in which undesirable behaviour occurs can influence that behaviour. For example, changing the arrangement of desks and chairs, or the organization of classroom equipment. This strategy typically requires planning ahead and is usually more powerful than introducing consequences for off-task or non-engaged behaviour in the heat of the moment.

3   *Give clear instructions*. One way to ensure that children and students learn to do as they are told without undue resistance or delay is consistently to give instructions that are polite, clear and concise as an antecedent condition for compliant behaviour. Before an instruction is given, it is important first to gain the child's or student's full attention. This avoids unnecessary repeating of instructions which can undermine their effectiveness.

4   *Model what you want*. Modelling of behaviour is well understood and well used by the advertising industry, and in the teaching of sports and leisure skills. When an adult 'models' or demonstrates specific ways of behaving in particular situations, students observing this behaviour may learn to imitate that behaviour in similar situations. Students may imitate more than the 'model' intended – students imitate teachers' poorest as well as best performances! For example, students observing teachers using abusive or sarcastic language when responding to disruptive behaviour in the classroom may then reproduce this language with each other or with teachers later. Modelling may have even stronger effects if the observer sees the modeller being rewarded.

Changing behaviours by altering the contingencies of reinforcement

5   *Positive consequences*. The behaviour learnt readily and performed most often is behaviour that usually has positive consequences. In classrooms positive consequences can include social attention, praise, recognition, access to favourite activities, and so on. They are most effective when they regularly and reliably accompany or 'reinforce' desirable or preferred behaviour in particular contexts. It is important in classrooms that positive consequences such as extra attention do not follow undesirable behaviour.

6   *Get in early*. The earlier a teacher intervenes to check undesirable behaviour, the easier it is to prevent behaviour from escalating into a major problem.

7   *Accept gradual improvement*. Changing behaviour from undesirable or inappropriate to desirable or appropriate may be gradual. It is important to provide positive consequences for quite small changes in behaviour to begin with. For example, where a student continually interrupts a lesson it may be necessary to acknowledge that s/he is interrupting less often than previously, even if sometimes that behaviour still appears.

8   *A little and often*. The number of opportunities students have to experience the consequences of their behaviour is what is important. For example, frequent praise throughout a lesson for a student who has a low attention span, provided s/he remains actively engaged with a task can be very powerful.

9   *Positive ways to reduce unacceptable behaviour*. One way to reduce undesirable or

unacceptable behaviour is to define and select another behaviour the student can perform that is incompatible with the undesirable or unacceptable behaviour. This alternative behaviour is then reinforced by following it with positive consequences, instead of
providing negative consequences for the original behaviour.

10 *Effective sanctions.* Sanctions must be clearly defined, explained to children, and very
carefully implemented. Implementing these sanctions should not in itself either model or
provoke further physical or verbal abuse and so should never be accompanied by
emotional or angry 'put down' and abusive comments. Sanctions should be imposed for
a specified length of time, and removed when specific behaviour change criteria have
been met. At these times it is most important that children continue to receive positive
attention for any desirable and appropriate behaviours which occur during the time
when unacceptable behaviours are being responded to with sanctions.

'Assertive discipline'

One very well-known framework for classroom management that has been based on
behavioural principles is that of 'Assertive Discipline' (Canter and Canter 1992). 'Assertive teachers' communicate expectations to students clearly and confidently, and reinforce words with actions in order to 'manage' students' behaviour in schools. Canter and
Canter (1992: 12) assert that students need to know 'without doubt' what teachers expect
of them, what will happen if they choose not to comply, and that appropriate behaviour
will be overtly reorganized. They also need to be taught 'how to choose responsible
behavior' (Canter and Canter 1992: 13). In no way, however, does the assertive teacher
violate what is in 'the best interest' of students (Canter and Canter 1992: 14).

Canter and Canter (1992: 17) see teachers' 'own negative expectations about her [or
his] ability to deal with disruptive student behavior' as major factors preventing teachers
from asserting themselves in the classroom. Key to successfully managing classroom
behaviour, therefore, is teachers' positive expectations of their own ability to do this.

Canter and Canter describe three common types of teacher 'response styles' to disruptive behaviour:

- 'wishy-washy', non-assertive, inconsistent responses that
  - convey to students a sense of the teacher's insecurity and lack of confidence;
  - invite a constant testing of wills between the 'powerless' teacher and the
    students;
- 'hostile', rigid authoritarian responses that
  - create a battleground in the classroom;
  - undermine students' self-esteem;
- confident and consistent assertive responses that offer
  - positive expectations and boundary-setting;
  - recognition of students' need for encouragement and learning;
  - 'no room for confusion' about the result of both acceptable and unac-
    ceptable behaviour.

They advocate setting up a classroom discipline plan with three parts: rules, positive recognition and consequences. Rules should be limited in number, focus on observable events, be applicable throughout the time period, apply to behaviour only and may involve students in their compilation. Key to motivating students to choose appropriate behaviour are 'positive reinforcers' which include teacher praise, rewards of various sorts and positive communications with parents. See Figure 7.1 for an example Canter and Canter set out at secondary level.

Sample Discipline Plan for Secondary Students

Classroom Rules

Follow directions.

Be in the classroom and seated when the bell rings.

Do not swear.

Positive Recognition

Praise

Positive notes sent home to parents

Privilege pass

Consequences

First time a student breaks a rule:	Warning
Second time:	Stay in class 1 minute after the bell
Third time:	Stay in class 2 minutes after the bell
Fourth time:	Call parents
Fifth time:	Send to principal
Severe clause:	Send to principal

Figure 7.1 Sample Discipline Plan for Secondary Students (Canter and Canter 1992: 45)

Students should be explicitly taught the classroom discipline plan. Canter and Canter recommend that teachers should take the time to 'identify the academic activities, routine procedures and special procedures for which [he or she needs to determine] specific directions' (1997: 123) at the beginning of every year. By 'specific directions' they mean:

- Don't assume that students know how you want them to behave in all of the situations that occur during a normal school day. These expectations must be taught.
- Identify the classroom situations for which specific directions are needed. Then determine those directions.
- Teach your specific directions immediately prior to the first time the activity takes place.
- Teach the lesson with the same care you would any academic lesson.
- Explain your rationale for teaching the direction.
- Explain the directions.
- Check for understanding.
- Review the specific directions for each activity as long as is necessary.
- Post visual clues (charts, posters, illustrations) around the classroom to help remind students of appropriate behavior during different activities and procedures.

(Canter and Canter 1992: 139)

After implementing the stated consequences of a rule-breaking misdemeanour, teachers should look for every opportunity to recognize appropriate behaviour.

Where students continue to behave inappropriately in class, Canter and Canter (1992: 237) advocate developing an individualized behaviour plan which should very clearly prioritize 'one or two of the difficult student's most critical problem behaviors', establish 'firmer, more meaningful consequences' for the student's behaviour and make provision for positive recognition of improvement.

Classroom practice
Rogers (1994a; 1994b) may also be interpreted as presenting a behavioural approach for encouraging primary school students whom he describes as 'behaviourally-disordered' (BD) to take responsibility for their own behaviour.

> While a school needs to pursue appropriate counselling and welfare provisions for such students, they will often need to *learn* how to behave appropriately. While most students respond to the normal socialisation into rights-respecting behaviour, some will need to be *specifically taught* ... learning targets can be developed as specific *behaviour* plans that involve teacher modelling, student-rehearsal and feedback and encouragement in the natural setting of the class-room.
>
> (Rogers 1994: 166–7, original emphases)

In Rogers's view, a child's background is no 'excuse' for poor behaviour in school. We should not excuse students from 'taking ownership for their disruptive behaviour', or 'facing accountability for such behaviour by facing appropriate consequences' or 'learning that behaviour is not an accident of birth or location, and that 'one can learn to make better and more conscious choices about behaviour' (1994: 167). Effective behaviour management is not simply about increasing and decreasing behaviours, but also about teaching students to discriminate between settings (times and places) where certain behaviours are appropriate and acceptable, and other settings where they are not.

Rogers (1994: 167–9) advocates the use of individualised behaviour management strategies with some students. These strategies should make clear to the student what behaviours are unacceptable but should also provide the student with opportunities for modelling, rehearsing and reinforcement for behaviours that are acceptable. For example, a teacher might explain to the child what his/her current behaviour looks and sounds like, and how it affects the other students in the classroom: 'Do you mind if I show you what you do when …?' It is also important to model the desired behaviour to the student: 'Let me show you how I want you to …' The student might then be encouraged to copy this behaviour. In the classroom the teacher should acknowledge any positive changes in the student's behaviour with positive verbal encouragement. It is important to recognize that this type of intervention involves the skilful manipulation of both antecedents and consequences, and that training takes place in the context where problem behaviour occurs.

Rogers's solution to repeated non-compliance with teachers' expectations of behaviour is time out from the classroom to allow the student 'to regain control and give the class time to regroup' (Rogers 1994: 169–70). In this instance, time out is used as a contingent opportunity for the child to 'escape' from an unsafe or difficult setting. In contexts such as this, there is a serious risk that time out may be functioning as a positive reinforcer for the disruptive or dysfunctional behaviour being engaged in. The effectiveness of time out therefore, depends on the qualities of 'time in'.

The issue of physical handling and restraint of students in schools

Dunckley (1999) refers to physical restraint as a last resort that should only be used to manage a dangerous situation. It should be employed carefully and in accordance with school policies, which should indicate when restraint can be used. It may be necessary to remove a student from a group of peers. This can be achieved 'by asking the other students to leave. It may be more appropriate, and safer, to bring other staff to the place where the student is, rather than the other way around' (Dunkley 1999: 10). It is important for those associated with schools to check school, local area and/or national policies on physical restraint of students in schools.

There are a number of important ethical issues surrounding the restraint of students against their will (Bowers 1996; Cooper 1999; Cornwall 2000). There is a difference between physical restraint, to hold a student still until aggression (hitting, kicking, punching others) subsides, and punitive incarcerations such as locking the student away for extended periods of time, as can occur when the principles of 'time out' are misunderstood, or misapplied, often in the heat of the moment (Cornwall 2004). Writing from a New Zealand perspective, Dunckley comments that students 'in an agitated state require guidance and direction to increase their sense of security … where possible and appropriate give a choice, time for the student to respond, then, after an appropriate time, follow through with consequences' (1999: 16).

It is very important to minimize the risk of physical confrontation in the first instance, rather than having to take action after the event. It seems sensible for teachers to avoid confrontations with students where these can be avoided. However, many of us have experienced situations when they cannot be avoided, for instance, if asked by a colleague to help in some crisis, or where a student's provocative behaviour may have become intolerable. Where this is the case, if

> the student continues to be defiant or provocative, and, if the worst comes to the worst, you have to be sure that you can manage the situation should the student attempt a physical challenge. Once started, confrontations sometimes develop very quickly and unpredictably, so that it is foolish to initiate one and then find that it has gone out of control and escalated into a situation which cannot be managed successfully, becoming demeaning and undignified.
>
> Useful ground rules for both avoiding and managing confrontations are to take care about language, consider whether to respond at all to minor irritations, reflect on non-verbal cues and signals you may be giving, refrain from physical intervention and plan responses which lower rather than raise the temperature of the classroom climate.
>
> (Smith 2004: 261–2)

Managing behaviour of individual students in schools and classrooms

Teachers have a responsibility for maintaining control and direction in the classroom. Good planning of students' learning activities and skilful classroom management minimizes the risk of disruption to students' learning. Most classrooms are well ordered and students well controlled. However, there are occasions when efforts to establish control in the classroom and demands for compliance from unwilling students can provoke disruptive behaviour.

Applying behavioural principles to individual student behaviour

Most work in response to issues of individual students' behaviour that is perceived as disturbing by teachers has been based 'on behavioural management approaches (which employ strategies such as positive reinforcement, response cost, extinction and so on) where the reinforcing conditions or consequences of a behaviour are adjusted in order to moderate its frequency' (Dwivedi and Gupta 2000: 76). Because behavioural methodology is a scientifically based technology, the first requirement is an operational definition of the target behaviour which is of interest. For instance, if a child is thought to be 'hyperactive' Merrett (1985) suggests an operational definition of behaviours such as 'out of seat' will be required. Once the behaviour has been identified and operationally defined, Merrett then discusses the need for systemic observational sampling across times of day, situations, nature of activity, person in charge and so on. Such observations need to be taken over a period of about five days to establish the baseline level of responding. Once the baseline can be clearly seen an analysis detailing the following three stages should be carried out:

> **A** – the antecedent event(s), that is, whatever starts off or prompts
> **B** – the behaviour, which is followed in turn by
> **C** – the consequence(s).
>
> (Merrett 1985: 8)

Merrett discusses different interventions teachers might plan in response to this analysis:

> [Where] a consequence of a behaviour is shown to be maintaining that behaviour at a high level then that consequence is, by definition, and regardless of its nature, reinforcing it positively. Sometimes teachers 'tell children off' for certain behaviours which are temporarily choked off but recur after a very short time, just a few minutes perhaps. This is very frustrating for the teacher but it may be the teacher's chiding which is maintaining the child's behaviour. By definition 'ticking off' is positively reinforcing the child's 'attention-seeking' behaviour. If that positive reinforcement is removed then the rate of occurrence of the behaviour will be reduced. It will eventually become extinguished.
>
> (Merrett 1985: 9)

Strategies to maximize students' learning of new behaviours include 'shaping' which breaks complex tasks down into a series of steps, and ensures that each step is reinforced in a particular sequence. Other procedures include modelling, where students are reinforced for matching the behaviour being displayed for them. Positive reinforcement contingencies rather than aversive (punishment) contingencies are preferable in reducing the rate of acceptable or unacceptable behaviour in educational settings (Merrett 1985: 11).

Critiques of behavioural techniques

It is very important for teachers to be aware of some of the commonly expressed criticisms of behavioural techniques. Behavioural approaches might:

- serve teachers' wishes to manage students rather than encouraging teachers to teach their students through responding to individual needs (Hanko 1994) and engaging students' interests;
- lead children into becoming overly dependent on praise;
- encourage students into unthinking conformity to authority (Milgram 1974). There is an assumption that the school curriculum to which students are expected to comply is appropriate and relevant and that school and teacher processes and practices are equitable and reasonable for all students but we all know that this is not necessarily the case;
- fail to take adequate account of the emotions. As Hanko comments: 'for children with problems, emotional factors affect learning, especially if we see only their provocative or withdrawn facade which usually hides children in constant misery, loneliness, self-loathing and fear ... teachers are frequently baffled by children who "don't respond even to praise", "spoil their work the moment I praise it", "just shrug it off" and "don't seem to care"' (1994: 166);
- tend to ignore the importance of cultural and community contexts, together with the traditional values, in which behaviour is defined and understood (Glynn and Bishop 1995; Macfarlane 1997; 2000a; 2000b). There is an assumption that teachers, from a behavioural view, will necessarily know which types of rewards and sanctions will be 'meaningful' to individual students and will therefore function as positive or negative

reinforcers. However, implementing behavioural management strategies while ignoring norms in the communities in which students are members will seriously limit their effectiveness. Where teachers do not understand the cultural norms of their students, they may 'mis-cue' in their application of behaviour management strategies. Gee (1990) illustrates this point vividly with an example of a small girl who told a story at the class 'sharing time'. The story was full of rhythm, pattern and repetition. In the child's family and local community, where oral performance was prized according to its entertainment value, her storytelling would have been valued highly. Her performance might also have been valued in a high school creative writing class or a literature class. The teacher, however, was anticipating a different (unarticulated) style of oral performance, that of being informative, linear and succinct, and did not appreciate the child's form of storytelling. Subsequently this child was referred to the school psychologist for telling tall tales. The negative effect on the child's identity with this clear devaluing of the worth of her family and community values can only be assumed.

Crucial to an understanding of students' behaviour is an acknowledgement of the students' own perspectives on their behaviour. Teachers need to learn how to help students to evaluate their own efforts, abilities and achievements, and to be their own judge, with the help of the teacher where necessary (Hargreaves 1972). Inappropriate use of praise can be damaging to some students for two reasons. If it is not sincere, students may well see through it. Also, students who have learned from previous experiences that they are likely to find learning activities in school difficult will be very discouraged by teachers' obvious lack of under-standing of their situation. Consequently, 'a praise-refusing student's determination not to be lured into the risks of failing yet again may be further reinforced' (Hanko 1994: 166). In every school I taught, I met students with whom communication has been difficult, who have, seemingly, shut themselves off from teachers. Many have been socially isolated and, to judge by body language, feel appalled at their own loneliness yet just cannot do anything about it. I well remember the case of Paul, undernourished, dirty, smelly and always alone, but hovering as close to the entrance of the school building as he could manage. Deliberation on the situation led me to try to get him involved in a lunchtime mutual-support group of students where we all talked about anything and everything over a hot chocolate and biscuits. No amount of attempts by me to 'shape' his behaviour would have enabled him to socialize more with peers.

Cognitive-behavioural approaches

Cognitive-behavioural approaches have emerged from behavioural psychology and have a number of additional key characteristics, one of which relates to the view of learners as constantly making sense of their own worlds which, as already indicated above is a very important consideration. Cognitive-behavioural approaches can incorporate a wide range of cognitive processes including the use of perception, language, problem-solving, memory, decision-making and imagery. For example in the school situation when stu-dents begin to pay attention to 'the stream of automatic thoughts which accompany and guide their behaviour, they can learn to make choices about the appropriateness of these self-statements, and if necessary introduce new thoughts and ideas' (McLeod 1998: 72).

This can result in behaviour more appropriate to the school context and lead to a higher level of academic achievement.

Techniques to encourage meta-cognitive awareness of behaviour

In the area of student behaviour in schools, a number of researchers have employed the concept of meta-cognitive awareness (that is, awareness of one's own thinking, feelings and emotions) into the area of emotional regulation, or self-management, in order to cope with feelings such as violence, bullying, disaffection or isolation (Meichenbaum and Turk 1976; Shapiro and Cole 1994). A common application of this approach is to the management of feelings of anger (Harris 1976; Wilde 1994; 1995). As Wilde (2001) notes, the first step is to encourage students to recognize bodily sensations that precede displays of anger:

> One of the simplest ways to teach children to identify their internal body cues is to ask them to respond to the query, 'What do you notice in your body just before you get angry?'
> Students often say they:

- feel warm all over
- notice their pulse is racing
- make fists with their hands
- have a clenched jaw and hold their teeth very tight
- start shaking all over and
- feel their muscles get tight, especially in their arms.

(Wilde 2001: 192–3)

The intention is to give them the chance 'to distract themselves or walk away before they react' (Wilde 2001: 192). Distraction involves persuading students to think about something other than the focus of their anger. It can be done through helping them to remember in detail:

> the happiest, funniest, or most relaxing scene they can remember. For example:

- The time they hit a home run to win a game.
- The time they got the perfect present for Christmas.
- Their best birthday party.
- A great day at the beach.

(Wilde 2001: 193)

The assumption behind this is that it is almost impossible, for a student to imagine a happy, funny or relaxing scene and still be angry.

Constructivist approaches

As we have seen already, in recent years there has been an increasing interest in constructivism with its focus on ways in which individuals construct their understanding of the reality in which they live. Learning is interactive between learner and context (Lave and Wenger 1991; 1999; Greeno 1998). In other words, learning is highly dependent on both the context, what the learner makes of the situation in which s/he finds himself and the interaction between them. There is recognition that 'the emotional and behavioural difficulties which people experience in their lives are not caused directly by events but by the way they interpret and make sense of these events' (McLeod 1998: 71–2). If this is the case, then difficulties in learning and behaviour 'problems' in schools are also situated in the interaction between the context and the perceptions of students (Mehan 1996; Lave and Wenger 1999; McDermott 1999). It is important therefore for teachers to understand how children make sense of their own circumstances and what impression is conveyed to students of others' views of them. It appears obvious that taking the young person's view seriously and attempting to understand his/her perspective is essential to any consideration of how we might reduce obstacles to students' learning (Hart 1995). Learning programmes are likely to be more effective when students have some sense of ownership over them. Pragmatically it seems very strange not to involve young people in decision-making about their education when their opinions are sought over so many other things in which they have a strong interest, for example where commercial interests are concerned. As Gardner notes: 'It seems ironical that children's views are taken very seriously by those who wish to produce a new flavour of crisps or a different style of chocolate bar; in other words, where they, as a group, have some economic power to back their choices' (1987: 104).

Developing positive behaviour through engagement with learning

Providing opportunities for students to bring their own experiences and ways of sense-making into class and curriculum activities is one way that teachers can encourage engagement with learning. An example of how students can take the initiative in deciding aspects of their own curriculum comes from my own direct experiences in classrooms. I was teaching a group of secondary-aged students who had experienced considerable difficulties in mathematical learning and suggested that they should make a group decision about the overall aim of their mathematics lessons during the final stages of their compulsory schooling. I asked whether they wished to follow the formal external examination syllabus like all other students, or a less demanding one. I promised that, if they took the more academic option, I would put them at the very top of my list of priorities, and work very hard for them. I said they could ask me for any help they liked, even if it meant asking the same question over and over again. In return, I would expect them to try very hard with their work. Having made their choice, the harder external examination syllabus requirements, their lessons then took the form of a learning co-operative, each member encouraging the other to reach greater depths of mathematical understanding. The difference in their behaviour and engagement with mathematics was outstanding.

'Circle time'

One initiative associated with the resolution of students' disputes at primary school level in schools in the UK that depends on listening to the views of the student community in classrooms is that of 'circle time' (Mosley 1996). As Tew (1998: 20) comments, in many traditional communities the circle is a symbol of 'unity, healing and power' and can be found in the traditions of groups as diverse 'as the North American Indians and Anglo

Saxon monks'. In schools, 'circle time' is a meeting that follows strict protocols of involving all participants in discussion where both teachers and students are bound by rules that stipulate:

- no one may put anyone down
- no one may use any name negatively (creating 'safety' for all individuals including teachers and parents)
- when they speak, everyone must listen
- everyone has a turn and a chance to speak
- all views are taken seriously
- members of the class team suggest ways of solving problems and
- individuals can accept the help or politely refuse it.

(Wearmouth et al. 2005: 184)

To run a 'circle time' session effectively the teacher needs to model behaviour that will demonstrate how participants in the group can show mutual respect and enable individuals to trust peers sufficiently to expose lack of knowledge and skills and open themselves up to new learning. This requires considerable skills:

The ability to listen well
The ability to be honest sometimes about your own feelings and thoughts
The ability to use good eye contact and show emotional warmth and empathy
The ability to recap what pupils have said and reflect it back to them to show you have understood
The ability to notice and thank pupils for the skills focused on in Circle Time: i.e. thinking, looking, listening, speaking and concentrating.

(Mosley 1996: 36)

The rules must be followed strictly. If a student breaks a rule a visual warning is given. If this persists, time away from the circle follows.

'Circle time' is probably best known for its use with younger children and often follows a set structure:

- warm up and fun
- a round where all students have the opportunity to speak
- 'open forum' where individual issues and problems can be raised
- negotiation of group action plan to address the issues raised, if necessary
- celebration of success
- closure, ending on fun.

(Wearmouth et al. 2005: 184)

Recognizing challenges for student self advocacy in schools

It is important for teachers to recognize the challenges implicit in responding to the thoughts and opinions about their experiences of school of students whose behaviour is seen as problematic. On the one hand there is an expectation that students' views will be sought over provision made for him/her and that teachers as well as students will be willing and able to engage in this activity. However, often teacher and student interests may be in conflict. Where students behave in ways that imply rejection of the unspoken values and assumptions on which formal schooling rests, and of the personal beliefs and the 'self' of the teacher, then adults in schools may feel their authority is threatened and may experience particular challenges in engaging with student (Ravenette 1984; McDermott 1999). Traditional school structures and bureaucracy often present barriers to the expression of student opinion (Hargreaves and Hopkins 1991). Teachers are professionals. It is their role to make informed decisions based on their knowledge and experience. In many school staffrooms, attempting to claim the high moral ground by appealing to colleagues to respect the rights of the individual child will not be enough to establish student participation in decision-making processes (Wearmouth 2000). Gersch (2001 lists a number of dilemmas encountered during the development of research initiatives designed to support active student participation in decision-making processes. These include:

- dealing with colleagues who feel that young people should be seen and not heard;
- the questioning of whether some children are mature or capable enough to participate;
- dealing with parent–child dislike;
- the amount of scope children need to negotiate, try things and change their minds;
- ways in which adults can distinguish what a child needs from what he or she wants or prefers;
- the status that should be given to the student's views if the professional responsible for organizing the special or additional provision disagrees with the head teacher over ways of meeting a student's needs.

While international law and current developments within the field of inclusion support student self-advocacy, at the same time 'ascertaining the child's views may not always be easy' (DfE 1994: 3:3). In many schools professionals will have encountered some students with whom communication has been difficult, who have, seemingly, shut themselves off. Some students, like Mark interviewed in a study of adults' recollection of school, may feel that one-to-one discussion on a personal level is unwarranted intrusion into their privacy: 'The first time I saw an educational psychologist she made me so angry that I went away and got hold of some books on child psychology so I could see where she was coming from. She couldn't get through to me at all after that because I put up so many barriers against her' (Wearmouth, unpublished interview transcript).

Clearly there are no easy solutions. Gersch (2001) does not offer a single answer but feels that, if a positive way forward is to be found, then a mutually trusting, listening, open, non-judgemental relationship must be established between teacher and student. The ethos for listening has to be supportive; it will not take place automatically.

An eco-systemic position

The behaviour of individuals can also be viewed as part of an ecosystem. The school and the home are seen as being two separate systems with their own individual ways of operating. The ecosystemic approach understands school behaviour problems in terms of dysfunctions in the family system, in the school system, or in the family-school relationship system (Campion 1985; Dowling and Osbourne 1985).

An example of an eco-systemic approach in practice

Cooper and Upton (1991) illustrate the systemic perspective with the example of John, an 11-year-old boy (Cooper 1990: 29–30, 222–3). John's home background was materially deprived and there was considerable conflict within the family which consisted of John, an older unemployed brother, and his mother, a sole parent. John's mother worked at night in a club and slept during the day. John was a student at a special school for students 'with emotional and behavioural difficulties' where he reported himself to be the victim of bullying. John responded to the bullying by running away from the school. Cooper and Upton (1991) note how John says that when he has done this before he had phoned his mother, who had then shouted at the staff about their failure to care for her son effectively. However, John's mother disliked being woken during the day, and John and his mother began to argue about this. Therefore, when John next absconded, he did not call his mother, but a member of staff did, to inform her of his absence. John, interpreted the teacher's behaviour as malicious, owing to the trouble it caused at home, and assaulted the teacher at school with a chair. Eventually John was moved to a residential school some distance from his mother.

John's family difficulties had an influence on the way he responded to the teacher's behaviour, while the teacher's and John's behaviour influenced the family difficulties. Bullying might be seen as having an important function in the situation. John repeatedly involved his mother in his school life, where she acted as his advocate. It is, therefore, reasonable to assume that John used the excuse of being bullied by staff as a means of bringing out protective behaviour in his mother, even though he never complained to the staff themselves that he was bullied at school. His mother's protection of him in the school situation is a clear contrast to the conflict which characterized their relationship at home. This would begin to explain John's violent response to the teacher, who had stood in the way of John obtaining the positive reaction that he desired from his mother, and elicited the reverse reaction from her. If the suggestion of bullying by staff was eliminated, it is likely that John would find some other way to elicit positive behaviour towards himself by his mother. This analysis of the situation indicates that what is needed is 'an intervention strategy which enables the needs of all participants to be met, and leads to the development of co-operative relationships between the individuals concerned' (Cooper and Upton 1991: 24). Anything else will be resisted in the school–family system.

From an ecosystemic approach, an appropriate intervention would need to aim to involve John and his mother in a collaborative relationship:

> This is usually organised by a consultant family therapist. The purpose of the interview is to observe the pupil–parent–school relationship in action, and to involve all parties in the development of a solution. Such consultations may result in the adjustment of systemic structure (Minuchin 1974), in the form of an adjustment in the roles performed by members of one or other of the systems involved, or in the adjustment of systemic boundaries, whereby weakened boundaries are strengthened, or overstrong boundaries are relaxed (see, for example, Power and Bartholomew 1985). In the present example, for

> instance, it might be suggested that the home-based relationship between John and his mother is lacking in warmth, to the extent that John has to engineer the type of situation described above, in which his mother plays a protective role. A possible remedy for this might be to seek out a situation in which John's mother performs a protective role. The precise nature of this remedy would be dependent upon the outcome of meetings between the family and the therapist.
>
> (Cooper and Upton 1991: 24)

Nurturing young children in schools

One psychological theory of human development that has had considerable influence over educational provision for young children whose behaviour is of concern to teachers is that of attachment theory (Bowlby 1952). Implicit in this theory is the view that:

> children deprived of maternal care ... may be seriously affected in their physical, intellectual, emotional and social development ... Bowlby asserts that 'prolonged separation of a child from his mother (or mother substitute) during the first five years of life stands foremost among the causes of delinquent character development' (Bowlby, 1944; Bowlby, 1952).
>
> (Holmes 1993: 39)

There have been some criticisms of Bowlby's work from psychoanalytic circles and others. However, it is accepted that babies quickly attach themselves emotionally to their adult carers and progress through well-recognized stages of development towards maturity. Successful development depends on needs being adequately met at an earlier stage. Where this is not the case, then: 'Unless there is skilful intervention [children] will persist in inappropriate attachment behaviour, whether over-anxious, or avoidant and aggressive, or will become quite incapable of warm attachment and therefore indifferent to human relationships (Harris-Hendriks and Figueroa, 1995)' (Bennathan 2000: 11).

Attachment theory has influenced education in the early years through the development of 'nurture groups' in some infant schools. Boxall (2002) argues that learning, personality and behaviour difficulties, which are more likely in the young children of families experiencing disadvantage and deprivation, are the result of inadequate early care and support from parents who struggle with poverty, damaged relationships, and harsh and stressful living conditions. The underlying assumption of the nurture group is that children who have fared badly though the learning processes of early childhood need extra support and appropriate experiences, so that they can go on to interact and learn in regular settings. The emphasis within nurture groups is 'on growth' not on a focus on what is wrong inside the child (Bennathan 2000: 11).

Bennathan (2000) argues that nurture groups allow for children with serious social behaviour developmental difficulties to be included in mainstream schooling. These groups accept and work with children who present major challenges to regular class teachers and other students. The critical challenge for nurture groups will be to ensure that their role remains a short-term developmental one and that students will be included in regular classrooms after a relatively short time.

Features of nurture groups

The nurture group attempts to create the features of adequate parenting within school with opportunities to develop trust, security, positive mood and identity through attachment to a reliable attentive and caring adult, as well as autonomy through the provision of controlled and graduated experiences in familiar surroundings. Some features of such groups include: easy physical contact between adult and child; warmth, intimacy and a family atmosphere; good-humoured acceptance of children and their behaviour; familiar regular routines; a focus on tidying up and putting away; the provision of food in structured contexts; opportunities to play and the appropriate participation of the adults; adults talking about, and encouraging reflection by children on, trouble-provoking situations and their own feelings; opportunities for children to develop increasing autonomy. These opportunities incorporate visits outside the nurture group, participation in games, visits to regular classrooms and children's eventual full-time inclusion in a mainstream class.

Biological and medical explanations of behaviour

In the context of school the differences in world views held by different professional groups and their different ways of working may make it difficult for those groups to negotiate effective working partnerships based on reciprocal understandings. These differences may also have a very important influence over students' educational experiences in schools. Biological and medical explanations of behaviour theorize problems as inherent to an individual. From a biological or medical view, behaviour experienced by others as difficult or challenging is the result of an underlying condition, disease or dysfunction which an individual has and which requires treatment.

The use of medication

In some cases, a medical diagnosis of the cause of challenging or inappropriate behaviour in schools, for example AD/HD as discussed in a previous chapter, may result in a prescription for particular kinds of medication. For example, there is evidence that psycho-stimulant medication, while not a cure for AD/HD, can, in conjunction with psychological, social and educational support, facilitate the educational process. The use of psycho-stimulants is based on a theory of biochemical imbalance:

> The medication stimulates areas of the brain regulating arousal and alertness and can result in immediate short-term improvements in concentration and impulse control. The precise mechanism is poorly understood and the specific locus of action within the central nervous system remains speculative.
>
> (BPS 1996: 50–1)

Of the commonly used stimulants, methylphenidate (Ritalin) is most widely prescribed. It is usually administered in the form of tablets to be taken regularly. It is therefore critical to monitor both dosage and time intervals, but it can be quite difficult to manage this properly in the context of school.

One major concern about the use of such psycho-stimulants has been the concern about the effects and side effects of these drugs:

> Since the 1970s the number of American research reports on the various effects of stimulant medication has been voluminous (Hinshaw, 1994; Swanson et al., 1993). Most are concerned with short-term results and very few document long-term consequences. The literature is convincing about immediate short-term benefits as perceived by parents, teachers and others involved ... Psychostimulant medication is seen as a palliative and not sufficient on its own. By temporarily calming children down, it can enable them to take advantage of effective teaching. In addition, because they are able to control their behaviour better, they are better able to interact appropriately in social situations ...
>
> Although children make progress with the assistance of stimulant treatment, a substantial subgroup appear not to benefit and a minority may show adverse responses (Rapport et al., 1994) ...
>
> (BPS 1996: 51–2)

There is also an ethical issue concerning the lack of adequate monitoring of the day-to-day classroom learning and behavioural outcomes of medication prescribed for many students.

> [E]ducational practitioners are concerned about the so-called 'zombie' effect (Sharron, 1995) which may be the result of inappropriate doses and poor monitoring. There is also evidence of 'behavioural rebound' in the afternoons when the medication wears off. These concerns illustrate the practical issues of managing medication at home and at school [as well as the ethical risks in relying on medication alone, without providing appropriate learning tasks and activities that attract positive reinforcement, to bring about behaviour change at school] ...
>
> (BPS 1996: 51–2)

Few studies provide evidence of positive learning outcomes to accompany evidence of reductions in frequency or intensity of specific challenging behaviours in the classroom. There are problems with defining AD/HD as a mental disorder:

> We have evidence that children given the diagnosis ADHD don't attend, don't wait and don't sit still. But just because they don't do all these things does not mean that they cannot do them. The pattern of AD/HD type behaviour might be maladaptive to environmental requirements, but it is not necessarily the result of psychological dysfunction.
>
> The adoption of a disease model may of course have advantages in helping those with severe, persistent and pervasive hyperkinetic problems conceptualise

their difficulties in a way that aids therapy (Taylor, personal communication). But when it comes to the large and heterogeneous group of children subsumed under the heading ADHD, advantages may be outweighed by:

- A lack of evidence that ADHD is the result of a fixed psychological dysfunction;
- The potentially limiting effect of the language of mental disorder in developing environmental approaches to intervention; and
- The possibility of stigmatisation.

(BPS 1996: 23)

There is also some evidence that a few students experience intolerance to particular foods and there is the suggestion of a link between this and difficult behaviour. 'Common allergens included additives, chocolate, dairy products, wheat, oranges and other fruit. These particular substances are found in many commercially produced foods and medicines' (BPS 1996: 52). The area of the influence of diet over behaviour is largely under-researched and controversial:

> There is evidence to suggest that diet may influence difficulties with attention and overactivity. For some students reducing access to certain substances appears to result in increased attention span, reductions in levels of motor activity and other behavioural changes. However, for other students dietary manipulation effects no change. Controlled diet, under the advice of a nutritionist, should not be dismissed if it is part of a multimodal intervention programme. Neither should we assume it is an appropriate intervention for all students with ADHD-type behaviour.
>
> (BPS 1996: 53)

Although the prescription of a chemical psycho-stimulant is fairly common, as noted by the British Psychological Society (1996), apart from all the ethical considerations, prescribing a drug provides an insufficient response. 'Medication must not become the first, and definitely not the only, line of treatment' (BPS 1996: 2). Also needed are appropriate social support mechanisms in school and outside, including ways to address barriers to learning within the classroom or school context. Focusing on the medical and/or biological bases alone to explain behaviour is likely to provide an insufficient remedy because it ignores the holistic nature of well-being and, therefore, all those other elements which contribute to it. Students' core values associated with self-identity, self-esteem and a sense of purpose as a functioning member of a social and cultural group must also be considered in addressing overall well-being. There is a great deal of room for exploring ways in which more inclusive pedagogies within classrooms and schools might improve the learning and behaviour of students who are diagnosed as having AD/HD.

Whatever label might be given to difficult behaviour, for a teacher, dealing with severe behaviour incidents is far more challenging and stressful than dealing with mildly disruptive incidents. However, an appropriate response is often the same.

Practical responses to extreme aggressive behaviour

On occasions, students may be aggressive, out of control and a danger to themselves and others. Dunckley's advice to teachers in this situation is to:

- assist the student to regain control. Safety is a priority and the goal is to defuse the situation . . .
- Staff members will need to follow the school policy. Where the aggressive act has been completed and it is unlikely that further aggression will follow, there is no need to intervene, the violence has stopped. Certainly the matter needs to be dealt with, for example the victim is attended to, and there are consequences for the perpetrator.
- Where the perpetrator is in a highly anxious, or agitated state, have another staff member attend to the victim and get the perpetrator to sit quietly until they are calm enough to talk about what has happened. When they do talk it is important to be non-judgemental and not to lecture, remind the student of the rules and follow through with consequences.
- If the behaviour continues to be threatening and disruptive, isolate the student from the others. Ask for their cooperation in doing this: *Come outside for a minute just until things have settled* . . .
- The purpose is to assist rather than to punish the student. Irrational and abusive language should not be taken personally. If they are being physically aggressive then it may be necessary to restrain them, in accordance with safe practice.

(Dunckley 1999: 17)

Addressing bullying behaviour in schools

Question for reflection

Do you have any experience of bullying?
Was it experience of being bullied, or being the bully?
In your view, do you feel that bullying is better understood as:

- an antisocial act which needs to be reduced through various types of punishment contingencies,
- a dysfunctional imbalance of power in a relationship that requires the (re)establishment of respectful behaviour between people so as to minimize bullying through the abuse of power (Rigby 2002),

or something else?

When bullying is seen as an antisocial act, 'we can best proceed by identifying and punishing behaviour we wish to stop' (Rigby 2002: 463). Typically any violation of rules is treated similarly whether major or minor. Policies may rely completely on 'rules and sanctions and zero tolerance for rule infractions' (Rigby 2002: 238). From the other view, 'positive improvement in behaviour between people can be brought about through instruction, persuasion and modelling of respectful behaviour' (Rigby 2002: 238).

Reponses to bullying behaviour in schools

Example 1: 'bully courts'

One important element in considering how to respond to bullying is the recognition of an imbalance of power between victim and bully. Redressing this imbalance, therefore, may well require the intervention of some kind of authority. An initiative that follows the view of bullying as an antisocial act is the so-called 'bully courts' (Elliott 1991). Here, the victim writes down the details of the incident(s), and victim, bully(ies) and any witnesses are invited to a meeting of the court. Each individual is questioned by a panel consisting of students and teachers. This panel then discusses the case in private, makes its decision about consequences. The head teacher has the right of veto in the case of an appeal. Records are kept for future reference.

Example 2: the 'method of shared concern' (Pikas 1989)

The opposing view, that bullying can be addressed by encouraging and modelling socially acceptable behaviour is reflected in Pikas's (1989) 'method of shared concern' which has been put into practice by schools both in Europe and Australia. This involves working with members of bullying groups individually before involving the victim. In the individual meetings, the teacher expresses concern for the victim, finds out from the bullies what they know about the situation and then invites these individuals to offer a solution. Pikas takes the view that using punishment is often ineffective. Changing group behaviour towards the victim is the most important issue. The victim may not always be totally innocent of drawing the bullying on him/herself. Once the victim is involved, the teacher can then mediate between him/her and the group.

Example 3: the 'no-blame approach' (Maines and Robinson 1991)

Another initiative that assumes the allocation of blame is inappropriate and counter-productive is the so-called 'no-blame approach' (Maines and Robinson 1991). This involves seven steps to be taken by the teacher:

* Take an account from the victim, allowing the victim to express feelings as well as details about the circumstances.
* Hold a meeting of all those involved except the victim. This meeting should include bystanders and those who failed to intervene.
* Explain the distress felt by the victim.
* Inform those present that they can do something to overcome the problem.
* Take suggestions from group members about what they can do to help the situation and put some or all of these suggestions into practice.
* Check the progress of the group one week later.
* Convey to the group a sense of their potential for kindness and support for the victim.

In an evaluation of a project to pilot this approach in an independent boys' school, Demko (1996: 29) concluded that if this approach is to be successful 'the whole school must be committed to it'. In other words, the whole school must share an understanding of what it is all about. 'Before teachers, or anyone else, can understand the effects of bullying, they need first to understand the pain and suffering to enable them to empathise with the victim' (Demko 1996: 30).

Aligning community practices, internal and external

In some schools and local areas, particular programmes have been devised to address issues of problematic behaviour based in general terms on the principles of 'restorative justice'. Restorative justice can employ traditional conflict resolution processes and culturally appropriate mechanisms drawn from the external community to address and resolve tension and make justice visible and more productive in communities inside the school (Anderson et al. 1996). Such initiatives shift the focus on to whole communities and away from the victim or the perpetrator in order to harness the necessary resources to address the problems that have resulted in unacceptable, unsociable behaviours (Schweigert 1999). By incorporating restorative justice principles in their behaviour management strategies, some schools have been able to support the victim(s) of wrongdoing, enable reparation of damage done by individual students and simultaneously maintain their inclusion in the institution, and help to restore the integrity of their communities, inside and outside the school. In order for that restoration to happen, the voices of those affected by the offence need to be heard in the process of seeking redress. (Restorative Practices Development Team 2003: 11)

The aims of restorative practice in schools are to:

- focus on the problem, not the person as problematic;
- encourage understanding of the consequences of the harm that has been done to the school community and to all the individuals involved;
- invite responsibility for the harm done to be taken up (not necessarily all by the offender);
- avoid creating shame and blame;
- promote the healing of hurt;
- open up avenues of redress;
- restore relationships between those involved;
- include everyone (including offenders) in the community internal and external to the school rather than divide people into insider and outsider groups.

A model proposed by Braithwaite (1997) in the UK, which draws from the experience of restorative justice within the criminal justice system to reduce criminal offending, advocates setting up 'family group circles'. Victims and offenders meet with people from the community whom the offender respects and trusts, and who care about the offender, to discuss what needs to be done to help the victim and the offender to right the wrongs and restore their lives. In educational settings, informal social support with education, relationships and employment from people trusted by the young person could be provided by 'youth development circles' where all members of the circles would be chosen by the young person concerned. The circles would remain in place for the whole period of compulsory schooling.

Conclusion

All students' behaviours are situated in a social context and result from interactions between people and their environments or social events. Participation in school activities involves the whole person in its combination of doing, talking, feeling, thinking and belonging. It refers both to taking part in activity and to the connections with others during this process. Personal identity in schools is constituted in the way in which learners participate in activities with others and, therefore, by definition, non-participation. The implication is that the most important concern should be first to establish effective whole-class management and positive classroom learning environments in which individual disruptive behaviour is much less likely to occur. Often, individual students are blamed for their own failure and/or disturbing behaviour in schools rather than looking to explanations at the way society is structured to favour some children, or at the level of school structure, organization, curriculum and classroom management. This has meant that there has been no real pressure to change society's ills or to make schools more responsive to students' needs (Armstrong 1994: 141–2).

Belonging is a fundamental human need.

> Rejecting schooling is nearly always a strongly emotional experience. Even the most hardened pupils will experience intense and often contradictory emotions when they are challenging school. Feelings of anger, fear, frustration, elation and guilt may all be present. In the classroom the peer group may be shown the more positive side when feelings of bravado and elation may be to the fore, while in the privacy of the head teacher's office the same pupils may express guilt and remorse at their actions. The truth is that all of these different feelings are experienced by disruptive and truanting children in contradictory and often confusing ways.
>
> (Furlong 1991: 296)

The human mind actively constructs its own reality and makes its own sense of every situation and context. Student behaviour must therefore relate to the way that students make sense of their worlds. Careful account therefore needs to be taken of students' own sense-making, even if this is experienced as uncomfortable in schools.

In Section III we turn to issues of support for students' learning and behaviour in schools, first by means of information and communication technology, and then through other adults in and around schools.

SECTION III

SUPPORT FOR SPECIAL LEARNING NEEDS

Making provision to address students' special educational needs in the classroom requires a flexibility of approach that may mean becoming familiar with a range of additional and/or unfamiliar resources. Resources that are planned for use with individuals need to be incorporated into the curriculum in ways that enable the student to engage with the same overall curriculum as other students. In this way those individuals can be included in classroom activities with similar intended learning outcomes. This requires a thorough understanding of what resources are available – human, physical and financial – how they are allocated and how they might be re-allocated to improve educational outcomes for students. Section III looks at ways to support the learning and behaviour of those students who experience particular difficulties through the use of information and communications technology, and with the help of other adults both in and around schools and families.

Chapter 8 discusses ICT and its applications. ICT is often:

> used synonymously with terms like information technology, computer technology or simply technology. This, in turn, can include reference to hardware (the machinery), software (the kinds of programs that are available) or networks (communicating with others). Each of these aspects has implications for teaching and learning in general ... [with] specific implications for learners with various types of special educational needs.
>
> (Florian and Hegarty 2004: 8)

It is easy to be impressed by new initiatives such as the development of ICT usage. However, what is as important as the technology itself is the ability of the teacher in applying it appropriately: 'The technology does nothing on its own but rather needs to be made to work in practice by the skill and perseverance of the school team' (Florian and Hegarty 2004: 3).

Chapter 9 concludes Section III and the book as a whole. The chapter is concerned with teachers' relationships with other professionals in two different, but related, areas in schools: support for classroom learning and child protection. It begins by discussing principles and practicalities with regard to the team of adults who may be involved in supporting classroom learning. It continues by outlining and discussing issues related to inter-agency working and the role of the classroom teacher in ensuring children's well-being and safety.

8 Uses of ICT to support students' special learning needs

Questions addressed in this chapter

Are there any principles to guide the effective use of ICT to support individual learning needs? If so, what are they?

In what ways can ICT applications help to address difficulties in accessing the school curriculum that are experienced by some students?

Can the use of ICT help to address any of the emotional concerns often associated with students' experiences of difficulties in learning? If so, how?

What do we need to know about the rationale underlying the design of software applications?

How can the use of ICT be integrated into the whole-school curriculum?

Introduction

Incorporating the use of new resources requires a great deal of careful planning. For the current purpose, the resources under consideration are those related to information and communications technology.

In this chapter we discuss some of the issues relevant to teachers who are interested in the way in which ICT applications can serve to address difficulties in accessing the school curriculum that are experienced by students. As noted above, new technology can seem impressive, of itself. However, the ability of the teacher in making decisions about what form(s) of ICT is appropriate to address individual students' needs, ensuring that everything is in place where and when it is needed, and applying it appropriately is as important as the technology itself.

Principles for effective use of ICT to support individual learning needs

Reflective questions

How can teachers who are not particularly familiar with the use of new technologies become confident enough in the use of ICT to want to experiment with software applications in support of students requiring special access to the curriculum?

How can we justify making (sometimes) expensive technologies available to some students but not to others? What are the implications for issues of equal opportunities?

Developing ways of working with any unfamiliar resource is not easy. Becoming confident with the use of ICT is no different. One head teacher (Open University 2000) has described crucial factors in the development of ICT provision to meet special learning needs as:

- sheer 'bloody-mindedness';
- keeping the development of technology under control;
- stimulating interest among the staff by focusing on authentic, relevant uses of ICT;
- giving staff 'something that will work the first time';
- offering staff training from well informed sources.

Matching ICT resources to the objectives on an IEP

The National Council for Education Technology (NCET 1995: 8–9) has set out a very useful checklist to assist the process of matching IT resources to the educational objectives set out on a student's individual education plan, and on identifying appropriate strategies for support. First, we need to think about the reasons for considering using ICT rather than current available support, and the purpose this will serve for the individual student:

Context
What evidence is there to support the need for IT?
Why isn't the present provision adequate?
Purpose
What does the learner need to achieve?
What else, apart from IT, is needed to meet the learner's needs?
Is the IT provision linked into the learner's Individual Education Plan?

Then we should consider the availability of the technology, how compatible it is with the school's setup, and the training needs of both student and support staff:

Resourcing
Is the IT already available in the school/classroom being fully utilised?
Is the provision appropriate for the learner's age and stage of development?
Is any proposed equipment compatible with the IT already available in the school?
Support
Is the learner familiar with any proposed resources?
Can all adults working with the learner use the equipment appropriately?
Do staff know where to find help?

The tools of technology: word-processing programs, hand-held computers, and assistive devices such as switches and touch screens, specialist keyboards and voice-activated software designed to overcome barriers to learning resulting from sensory or physical impairments all require the acquisition of skills to use that technology to best effect.

Next we should consider how to take account of the views of all concerned, including those relating to management issues:

Expectations
Have the learner's views been taken into account?
Have the parents been involved in the discussion over provision?
What are the class teacher's expectations?

Management
Are all staff committed to supporting a learner with IT provision in the classroom?
Who will take responsibility for ensuring that the equipment is functioning correctly?

Finally we have to work out ways to evaluate the success of the provision and how to plan for the future learning needs of the student:

Monitoring
What criteria will be used to monitor the effectiveness of the provision?
What criteria will be used to monitor the learning targets?

Transition
What planning is in place for considering the changing needs of the learner?
What planning is in place to consider changing needs, both in school and beyond school?
What planning is in place to consider developments in technology?

The principles outlined in this checklist have a generic value in that they can be applied to any other form of resource which might be considered appropriate to meet particular learning needs. There is obviously the question of how far the particular resource can facilitate the individual student's access to the curriculum. There is also the issue of the time required for staff development and, crucially, that of budgetary implications.

Issues of equal opportunities

The kind of special provision which a student is deemed to 'need' or deserve implies a value that is being attributed to that student (Salmon 1995). This issue is clearly important in relation to the cost or availability of particular equipment. It is vital that teachers in classes where students have been allocated additional or special resources are very clear in their procedures and practices which must be open to scrutiny.

Whenever there is a question of allocating additional, alternative or 'special' resources to particular students, inevitably the issue of equality of opportunity arises. On a number of occasions, when running a learning support department in schools I, for example, was asked by both colleagues and students: 'Why should x (student identified as experiencing some kind of difficulty in learning) be given extra time and resources when other students are just as deserving?' There is often no clear dividing line on the continuum of need between those whose requirements for special provision are, indeed, special, and those whose requirements are lesser. There is a view that those who gain most from additional resources are the children of the more literate, persistent and articulate parents (Gross 1996). The Audit Commission (1992) also noted the admission by some local education authorities that factors bearing little relation to the severity of a student's 'need' were highly influential in decisions to maintain a Statement, with its consequent resource implications. Examples of such factors are the 'determination' of the parents and representation by a lawyer. Parent power has to be taken very seriously by schools in a climate of increasing accountability, recourse to litigation and parental choice of schools to which their children will be sent.

How can we justifying additional resources for some?

'Access to the curriculum' is often used as a justification for providing additional or alternative resources for students in schools. The practical implications of putting this principle into practice will vary across schools, depending on:

- the context;
- the particular aspect of the curriculum;
- the severity of an individual student's need.

There are schools where many of the students experience very great difficulty in communication with others, in mobility and in being able to control anything at all in their environment. Hence 'access' may imply:

- ways of being able to express a need, want or choice to someone else;
- means by which to move oneself about or to control aspects of the environment, to turn on a light or stimulate a sound.

For some students with the most profound difficulties in communication it is possible to devise sequences of communication systems from single preset greetings activated by a switch through to email messages associated with voice simulation programmes and/or symbols representing individual words or whole concepts. Curriculum access for other students, for example those who experience specific difficulties in literacy, might be facilitated with the use of laptop computers with talking word processors, spellcheck facilities and use of a printer.

Uses of ICT to support individual learning needs

There are various ways to categorize the application of ICT for use with students who experience difficulties of one sort or another. One useful approach (Means 1994; Florian and Hegarty 2004) is to conceptualize applications of ICT as tutoring, exploration, a tool, communication, assessment and management.

Individualized tutoring

Early programs became popular because they seemed to offer a solution to how to differentiate teaching for individual students who experience difficulties of some sort. In the area of literacy difficulties, for example, often, individual learners worked on programs designed to emphasize drill and practice only, for example ongoing drill in individual letter sounds, or simple number bonds with plenty of repetition and reinforcement. More sophisticated design and so-called 'integrated learning systems' (ILS) have enabled the integration of:

- presentation of curriculum material, often in the area of literacy or mathematics;
- assessment of students' understanding of the material, typically through multiple-choice or single word answers, and immediate feedback;
- management of decision-making about what the next step should be in the learning process. If the student's answer is wrong, the software is often programmed to present similar questions to check the student's understanding more closely. Where the student continues to make errors, the system will present material to fill the gap in the student's knowledge.

Evaluating the use of an integrated learning system

An example of an ILS is 'Successmaker', marketed in the UK by RM. This includes courses in mathematics, writing, spelling and reading for students at all stages. The spelling course, for example, uses a number of approaches: 'Pupils are taught new words of ever-increasing difficulty but are also reassessed on previously learnt vocabulary. Teachers can get a printout of words individual pupils misspelled and the mistakes they made' (Hedley 2004: 67).

A range of courses designed to support reading acquisition include programs aimed at comprehension, vocabulary and skills in thinking. Tasks include cloze activities (that is, filling in a missing word in a sentence), reading a passage from a book and writing about this. Feedback to pupils comprises percentages of correct responses and a visual reward. Printouts can highlight areas of strength and weakness.

Baker (1997) describes a number of considerations regarding the implementation of an ILS such as 'Successmaker' in schools as follows:

The school should have clear curriculum objectives for the ILS, for example to raise the level of basic skills of all Year 7 and Year 8 pupils, prior to starting their GCSE courses.

Careful thought should be given to the staff who will be involved with the ILS. Since proper use of the ILS is likely to have timetable implications, there should be a member of the senior management team who has overall responsibility for the successful implementation of the system. Without such a person, pupils are unlikely to get the number of ILS sessions they need each week and the potential benefits are much reduced.

Subject specialists should be responsible for managing their own classes. An ILS does not have to be managed by an IT specialist. Managing an ILS is not the same as managing a computer network. The former requires technical skills, whereas the latter is curriculum oriented. It may be more appropriate for subject specialists (e.g. the heads of English and mathematics in a secondary school) to lead-manage the ILS.

It is vitally important that the staff who will use the system receive thorough training. Each teacher must understand how to use the system features, in conjunction with their own professional skills, in order to achieve the best results for their classes.

More than one person should be involved in leading the management of the ILS, so that there is always an in-house 'expert' available, regardless of staff absence/turnover. All the staff involved should have some degree of enthusiasm for the new system and it is likely that they will have had some input into the initial planning process.

Pupils should have regular access to the system. Five sessions per week, of about half an hour each (i.e. one per day) have been shown to work best. The session could be divided up so that 10 minutes is spent on mathematics, 10 minutes on reading and 5 minutes on spelling, leaving 5 minutes for classroom management. The optimum session lengths for each course, which are generally between 10 and 20 minutes, may seem short. However, it should be remembered that the pupils are working in a highly concentrated way during this time.

The advantages of such a system are the facility for instant assessment and feedback, and the tailoring of work to fit individual learning attainment. Some of the disadvantages are the constrained ways of presenting and recording information in the system, and the extent to which they might exclude, and marginalize, students in classrooms, rather than include them.

Exploration

Exploratory programs enable students collaboratively to construct knowledge through, for example, simulations and virtual environments, as well as content-free programs. Students who experience complex difficulties in learning and/or require a very high degree of support might benefit from the opportunity to explore simulated or virtual environments in ways that otherwise might not be possible. Since 2003 there has been, for instance, a three-dimensional (3-D) virtual world called 'Second Life' that is created and inhabited by millions of its 'Residents' from around the world. The authors of this site describe the experience of entering this virtual world as follows:

> From the moment you enter the World you'll discover a vast digital continent, teeming with people, entertainment, experiences and opportunity. Once you've explored a bit, perhaps you'll find a perfect parcel of land to build your house or business.
>
> You'll also be surrounded by the Creations of your fellow Residents. Because Residents retain the rights to their digital creations, they can buy, sell and trade with other Residents.
>
> The Marketplace currently supports millions of US dollars in monthly transactions. This commerce is handled with the in-world unit-of-trade, the Linden dollar, which can be converted to US dollars at several thriving online Linden Dollar exchanges.
>
> (http://secondlife.com/whatis/)

Having said this, however, encouraging students to engage in virtual worlds is no substitute for real life. One might think of a number of instances of where using this medium is inappropriate. As an IT co-ordinator in a residential school for students with complex physical disabilities commented, for example, it is patronizing to suppose that a computer simulation of a bus ride will substitute in every respect for students who find independent movement difficult (Open University 2000).

Content-free programs that can be adapted by the teacher can support access to concepts, skills and knowledge by enabling presentation of these in a variety of ways:

The students use a computer to drive a robot round an obstacle course on the floor, directing its movements from the keyboard, by telling the robot how far and in which direction to travel. In this way, they are encouraged to develop an understanding of estimation and direction in a practical setting. On another occasion, exploring a picture of dangers in the home on the overlay keyboard can reinforce messages of health and safety. The students can review their ideas and discuss differing viewpoints by collaborating on the task. By experiencing learning in an active way, they are helped to identify similar situations in the world around them.

(NCET 1995: 4)

ICT as a tool

As a number of researchers have noted, computer-assisted learning has the potential to be used as a tool for reducing barriers to learning in three particular, but overlapping, domains: cognitive, affective and physical (Moseley 1992; Singleton 1994; Florian and Hegarty 2004). These domains largely reflect the areas of need defined by the DfES (2001), as noted previously in Chapter 3.

Cognitive considerations

'Cognition' in general terms refers to information-processing associated with problem-solving, language, perception and memory. As discussed in Chapter 3, where students experience cognitive difficulties, for instance in understanding abstract concepts, teachers might need to build in strategies to classroom teaching which facilitate access to the curriculum in ways that address these difficulties.

Use of symbols in communication

An example of an array of programs that use symbols for communication is that produced by Widgit Software. Widgit describes its symbol system as follows:

Is it important to understand that **symbols are different from pictures**. We use the word **picture** to describe an illustration in a book, or a drawing on the wall. A picture conveys a lot of information at once and its focus may be unclear, while a symbol focuses on a single concept. This means that symbols can be put together to build more precise information.

Symbol-based language and communication has been developed over many years and has a visual structure that supports different parts of speech.

There are different types of symbols . . .

Symbols are grouped in different sets. The most commonly used across the UK are Widgit Literacy Symbols (previously known as Rebus)

Widgit Literacy Symbols © Widgit Software www.widgit.com

PCS Symbols © Mayer Johnson LLC contact Widgit Software www.widgit.com

In total these sets provide a vocabulary of over 12,000 concepts and they are used right across the spectrum of age and ability.

There are other symbolic systems also. For example the Makaton Development Project includes both signs and symbols.

What you use with each person entirely depends on **his or her own needs** and preferences. What is really important to remember is that everyone is different with different abilities in spoken and written language, expression, vocabulary, sight, hearing and other individual factors.

The Widgit Literacy symbols have a much greater vocabulary spanning standard curriculum topics, adult vocabulary and higher literacy levels. They have a schematic structure and include grammatical markers for literacy expression.

(www.widgit.com/index.htm, accessed 31 January 2008)

Widgit claims that symbols can help to support:

- **commmunication** – making a symbol communication book can help people make choices.
- **independence and participation** – symbols aid understanding which can increase involvement, choice and confidence.
- **literacy and learning** – symbol software encourage users to 'write' by selecting symbols from a predetermined set in a grid.
- **creativity and self expression** – writing letters and stories and expressing your own opinions.
- **access to information** – all of us need accessible information and this should be presented in such a way that the reader can understand and use.

(www.widgit.com/index.htm, accessed 31 January 2008)

Among those students for whom Widgit claims to be able to cater with its symbol-based programs are those:

- learning English as an additional language;
- with memory difficulties;
- who are dyslexic, dyspraxic or who experience spatial/time/organizational difficulties;
- who are deaf or hearing impaired;
- who have not yet started to read;
- who have autistic spectrum disorders.

Communication

Many assistive devices are available to enable students to communicate: electronic language boards, voice synthesizers and voice recognition software. For example 'Lunar Screen Magnifier' is intended to support student who experience visual difficulties to access onscreen text, graphics, tool bars, icons through magnification, colour-changing options, speech and Braille output (www.inclusive.co.uk/catalogue/acatalog/Lunar_Screen_Magnifier.html). 'Hal Screen Reader' is another system that provides screen access for visually impaired computer users through speech output and Braille for users with a Braille display. It includes quick navigation keys, full spelling and attribute announcement, column detection, focus tracking and page scrolling (www.inclusive.co.uk/catalogue/acatalog/Hal_Screen_Reader_Standard_Version.html).

Many of the symbol communication systems used by students who experience multiple and profound difficulties in communication are supported by software programs to facilitate writing. A *Clicker Grid* can be adapted for each individual student according to their own interests.

> Clicker is a writing support and multimedia tool for children of all abilities. At the top of the screen is a word processor called 'Clicker Writer'. At the bottom of the screen is the 'Clicker Grid'. This has 'cells' containing letters, words or phrases that you can click on, to send them into Clicker Writer – so children can write sentences without actually writing or using the keyboard.
> (www.cricksoft.com/uk/products/clicker/guide.htm, accessed 29 January 2007)

When both *Clicker* and *Symbols* are loaded and used together, students can then write and have their work read back immediately. There can be a difficulty in the use of voice recognition software to support the writing of text, however, where students' speech is unclear and their words are not sufficiently differentiated, clear or consistent to be encoded into text.

A number of studies (Glynn et al. 1986; 2000) have shown how respondents supplying written feedback in the form of individual personal responses, reactions, or comments focused on the expressive writing of beginning or struggling writers can influence the amount and rate of those children's writing. Typically the respondents shared their own experiences, feelings, thoughts and ideas as stimulated or triggered by each writing sample, but made no reference without referring to the accuracy of spelling, punctuation or grammar. Similarly, a number of studies (Norman 1997; Stanford and Siders 2001) have shown how correspondence by email with penfriends can provide an authentic literacy learning experience. If students who experience difficulties in literacy are paired with those who are more competent in literacy, the latter can support improvement in writing by the former. An example of a program that supports this kind of communication is 'Penfriend XL', a powerful screen reader with multiple onscreen keyboards, which works in nine European languages. It is intended for those with dyslexia or physical/sensory disabilities including visual impairment, adding screen reading with text magnification, word prediction, and onscreen keyboards to almost any other software.

> It predicts and screen reads in Microsoft programs such as Internet Explorer and Word and non Microsoft programs such as Open Office and Firefox. It offers considerable support for users with special needs, helping with spelling, confidence and speed of composing text. It will also read out almost any text, such as web pages or word processed documents.
>
> ... It has an option for automatically putting the screen read text into the clipboard which, with a large font, provides text magnification and highlighting for the visually impaired. Areas that are not read automatically can be highlighted and copied to the clipboard. Right clicking enables the word lists in the thesaurus and spell checker of Word to be spoken.
>
> ... Penfriend works with your word processor and tries to guess the word you are typing when you have entered the first letter, the second letter and so on. One key press then finishes the word for you. You can hear the suggested words spoken too. Penfriend learns the words you use frequently and recently, so it improves as you use it. This information is saved for each user, together with individual settings. For people with disabilities, this saves effort and time. For those with dyslexia, it saves time, improves accuracy and builds confidence in writing.
>
> Penfriend is configurable to suit the preferences and needs of different users and it is easy for teachers to select preferences and add topic specific vocabulary ... edit children's lexicons ...
>
> (www.inclusive.co.uk/catalogue/acatalog/penfriend_xl.html,
> accessed 31 January 2008)

Use of the Internet appears, at face value, to be a very useful medium for supporting the learning of some students who experience difficulty. However, much of it is not accessible without careful consideration of students' special learning needs (Paveley 2002). One aim of the NCET-sponsored research project into the use of Internet curriculum service providers in schools (EISPP) was to investigate the extent to which use of the Internet can help to overcome the special barriers to learning faced by some students. If use of the Internet is to be considered as a means of supporting the learning of those students who experience difficulty of some sort, factors that might need to be taken into account are:

- how far students' access to the Internet is constrained by the nature and severity of the barriers to their learning which might be cognitive and/or physical;
- how far use of the Internet has the potential to enhance all students' learning;

- the kind of pedagogy that would enable students to engage most effectively with their learning.

Findings from the 1998 NCET project indicated that important issues associated with the use of the Internet in relation to meeting students' special learning needs are that:

- 'Real' time access to raw information from the Worldwide Web is unrealistic for many students. This means that teachers will need to find time to save to disk for future use any material that they or students have found interesting or useful.
- The manner in which students are given choice of e-mail and video-conferencing partners is very important. This is the kind of consideration that tends to generate very strongly-held feelings about who, among the students, is allowed to be put into contact with whom.
- Where students are isolated from peers for whatever reason, for example the location of their home, or difficulties with mobility, it may be especially important for students to make contact through e-mail or video-conferencing with peers elsewhere.
- Use of e-mail provides purpose for reading and writing skills and is highly motivating to students. An e-mail system which integrates the use of a concept keyboard, symbols, a talking word processor and text, and which automatically deletes headers when messages are received would be useful.
- The creation of the schools' own website functions to advertise the school, publish students' work and, perhaps most importantly, reduce the isolation of a special school context by promoting e-mail links.
- There appears to be the potential for groups of teachers involved in modifying curriculum materials to share those materials in order to reduce time demands.
- There is a serious concern over the issue of equal opportunities where use of the Internet has a clear contribution to make to the learning of students with a wide range of needs but many schools do not have the necessary prerequisites for its development: a member of staff who is knowledgeable and highly skilled in ICT to act as the catalyst, a computer network, adequate resources, support from senior management, time and resources for staff training.

(Wearmouth 2000: 203–4)

Mapping these potential barriers against the facilities provided by the software described above shows that recent developments have come a long way in making access a reality for many students with special learning needs.

Affective considerations

Motivation
Some schools have developed a highly sophisticated ICT support system. However, any individually devised programme for a student must take into account the student's views

and wishes as well as the purpose for which the programme is designed. Even the most highly developed system will be useless unless the student is motivated enough to engage with it.

There is evidence that some students prefer working with a computer rather than having intensive tuition from a teacher, which they feel is too similar to their primary school experience (Hartas and Moseley 1993). Whether there is a stigma attached to its use may depend on the norms of the particular classroom or school; indeed, it may be seen as a high-status piece of equipment (Brown and Howlett 1994). Information and communication technology can motivate learners to acquire specific skills for reading, spelling and writing, as well as giving more general support in the curriculum (C. Singleton 1991). The use of a word processor can encourage students whose writing or spelling skills do not adequately reflect their higher general level of performance and can produce results which may look as good as those of peers (C. Singleton 1991).

Fear of failure is often thought to prevent some learners from making the effort needed for them to succeed (Lawrence 1971; 1973; 1996). Part of the attraction of computers is their emotional neutrality. The word processor, for example, may avoid the aversion that is often produced by pen and paper: the computer provides a safe environment for students who can take their time, without holding the rest of the class back, and make mistakes in private, without fear of humiliation. The learner with a history of failure is enabled to avoid situations of public failure and consequent damage to self-esteem. The computer can put learners in control of the learning situation and enable them to pace themselves, unlike the usual teaching situation where the teacher has the power and control (Brown and Howlett 1994).

Computer-based activities can allow learners with poor self-esteem to experience the success needed to boost their confidence, allowing written work to be presented to a high standard (C. Singleton 1991; Thomas 1992; Wearmouth 1996). Using a word processor improves the content and presentation of work; students are therefore more likely to experiment with their writing and to express themselves confidently. The student who has failed to learn adequate literacy skills over an extended period can explore ideas in a supportive environment. Anecdotal evidence from secondary classrooms suggests that ICT may be particularly effective in encouraging older students to complete written coursework:

> L. C.: Please can you run me off another copy (a piece of extended coursework in English Literature)?
> Shirley: Why, L.?
> L.C.: Because I want to take it home to show my Mum. (Never been known before!)
> One of the lads, S.: Look at how much I've done. I've never written ten pages before.
>
> (Wearmouth 1996: 124–5)

Enabling physical access

The kinds of physical access supported by ICT can considerably reduce physical barriers to the learning of some students:

A student who cannot use his (*sic*) hands can control the computer by pressing a switch with his head. Through the computer, he can learn to make choices and to select words and images for his own purpose. A youngster who has problems with fine motor control can use a trackerball to move a pointer across the screen. He can select the options in a drawing package to draw a series of geometric shapes, with a confidence that the quality of the results will do justice to his intentions.

(NCET 1995: 4)

Incorporating the use of ICT into IEPs for students with multiple and profound difficulties in learning

Lilley (2004: 82–4) offers a number of examples of an individual programme developed to incorporate the use of ICT for students with multiple and profound difficulties in learning and/or disabilities. For example, 13-year-old Samantha has cerebral palsy and is 'functioning academically at her chronological age but has no expressive language and has poor fine and gross motor control' (Lilley 2004: 82–4). The school has made provision to give her more independent access to the computer:

- An ultra-compact keyboard with guard and a gated joystick allows her to move the cursor on the screen.
- A large 'jelly-bean' switch replaces the left-click function on a normal mouse.
- All the above are linked to a Mouser 3. The Mouser links a normal mouse plus a joystick (or other device). It is a device that connects between the mouse and the computer to allow switches to be used instead of the mouse buttons. It can turn off unwanted mouse buttons to avoid unplanned presses bringing up unwanted menus. It allows any or all of the standard mouse buttons to be turned off. It also allows switch access to these buttons for young disabled users.

(Lilley 2004: 82–4)

Lilley also describes the use of ICT to support curriculum access for 11-year-old Ann who was confined to a wheelchair after a road accident when she lost expressive language. A jelly-bean switch was fixed to a specially adapted tray on her wheelchair, and Ann was encouraged to use a range of software programs designed to help learners understand the principle of cause and effect – a press of the switch causes a reaction on the computer screen. When she had mastered simple switch use she was encouraged to work on 'simple scanning software (Clicker 4 – a widely-used piece of software that allows children to click on pictures and phrases which the computer can speak if desired) that can easily be customized' (Lilley 2004: 84).

ICT can provide:

Access to writing for pupils with poor fine and gross motor control and ease in storing and retrieving work, since the use of ICT aids fine motor control and hand-eye co-ordination.

A means of drafting and re-drafting that is easy, efficient and accessible and so is a great equaliser in presentation. This is particularly important for those pupils following externally accredited qualifications. Pupils are also enabled to create pictures, patterns and designs.

Encouragement for children to work individually, independently and to be an active participant in the classroom, not just a passive observer. Pupils can work more quickly and demonstrate different types of writing exercise and have the opportunity to experiment.

A way to enable pupils to get down in writing their own ideas and not those of adults working with them and thus demonstrate their true ability.

(Lilley 2004: 89)

Connecting the process with the skill

Particularly with software, it is important to understand the rationale underpinning the approach that is taken in a programme to support the development of a particular skill.

ICT support for reading and writing

In the area of difficulties in literacy, for example, as noted in Chapter 5, there are a number of ways, some of them conflicting, in which the reading process has been conceptualized. Software designed to address difficulties in the acquisition of the skill of reading will necessarily reflect a particular conceptual understanding of the reading process. Research on ways in which ICT can support the learning of students experiencing difficulties in acquiring and using literacy skills is sometimes dichotomized between:

- that intended for the remediation of basic skills, for example phonic awareness and spelling; and
- that intended to offer support and access to the curriculum through a holistic approach, for example word recognition software.

Individual programmes to support the development of specific skills have been evaluated in their own terms. The special value of didactic software for dyslexics, for example, has been identified as offering practice in basic skills in a convenient, enjoyable and cost-effective manner (C. H. Singleton 1991).

For most people the 'lower' skills of writing are automatic, and their focus is therefore on the higher level skills involving, for example, the manipulation of ideas. However, for many learners, the lower level skills take over the task and block the ability to produce interesting written work. The use of content-free software such as word-processing packages which provide an environment aimed at facilitating the writing process is increasing in education, particularly as the hardware has become more powerful, enabling the creation of ever more complex software engineering, such as word prediction and speech feedback. The possibility of drafting and re-drafting enables writing to become more closely connected to thought because the writer is able to focus on the content of the text before considering issues of presentation, spelling and punctuation

(NCET 1992). Students can then begin to expand on some of the higher level skills such as considering audience or organizing thoughts coherently. They can perhaps even begin to see themselves as successful writers. In addition, the screen can also provide a distancing effect which increases self-criticism and helps to develop a sense of audience. (NCET 1995).

An example of a word-processing, desktop publishing, multimedia package that can be used in all curriculum subjects for writing and publishing tasks is 'Textease Publisher CT'. Menus and buttons can be configured and customized for pupils with different educational needs. Publisher CT incorporates:

- curriculum mapped resources – thousands of items including clipart, digital photos, videos and sounds all with keyword search for easy location
- natural sounding speech with different voices to choose from
- highlighter and table tool
- toolbars that can flip to the bottom of the screen – great for whiteboard use
- cross-curricular examples
- templates including a birthday card, book review, newspaper, heraldry shield and postcard.

(www.softease.com/textease, accessed 31 January 2008)

Spelling

Some writers have noted how software support such as spellcheckers and word prediction facilitate the growth of the learner's communicative skills (Newell and Beattie 1991; Nellar and Nisbet 1993). The main difficulty for a spellchecker is the writer with faulty auditory perception/articulation who uses bizarre spellings or has inconsistent errors. Many spellcheckers expect the first letter to be typed correctly at least, yet some learners with literacy difficulties do not always do this. Other strategies will be needed by the writer. Even more useful is a spellchecker that will speak the words as well, so that a writer does not have to rely solely on the visual medium to pick out the correct spelling. It is unclear, however, how far a facility of this type can be used by older students. Another useful tool for those with writing difficulties is the spelling predictor which predicts the word based on the first letter(s) typed. An 'intelligent' predictor will also learn the words commonly used, and put them near the top of each list.

Support for reading

The use of symbols on some computer programmes acts as scaffolding for reading. Symbols can be used with one student and gradually withdrawn until those students can read without them. This therefore provides an alternative method of teaching reading. The left–right directionality of reading can be reinforced through the *Clicker* programme (Crick Software). Sound to support reading and writing can be used in many different ways. Word processors with speech synthesis can be very powerful. Learners can hear what they have written, either as they are writing, or hear the whole text after they have finished.

Sound can be introduced to text by dropping it into a standard text to speech utility or talking word processor. The text may also be dropped into a programme such as *Writing with Symbols* (Widgit computing) which gives a symbolic version that can be printed out and spoken aloud. Talking word processors may be particularly useful tools in the future to enable students to decode text downloaded from the Internet.

An example of a program to develop switch-accessible stories and slide shows is 'SwitchIt! Maker 2'. Each activity has a sequence of onscreen pages which can have a picture, video or text-based material, music or recorded speech. Pages can be turned by a simple switch, the computer's spacebar, the mouse buttons or IntelliKeys.

A whole-school approach

Lilley's (2004) work has a number of implications for teachers intending to use ICT in the classroom to address students' special learning needs. Teachers should check that:

- machines/software are working – and available – at the moment they are needed;
- if machines 'crash', there are contingency arrangements for ensuring that students' work is not lost;
- there is enough time, and specialist staff support available, to ensure that machines are set up for every student for whom special ICT resources have been provided, at the time and in the place they are needed. Not to do so is, as noted above, to risk contravening the law;
- computers are updated regularly so that they can accommodate new software as required;
- the school has a licence to enable staff and students access to the relevant software.

Conclusion

Effective use of ICT for students with special educational needs in classrooms requires a clear understanding of a number of issues. Among these are accountability to students, parents, the school and the local authority, the principle of equal opportunities, the nature, availability and function of resources, human, physical and financial, and ways of embedding the use of unfamiliar technology into the curriculum.

Good practice in classrooms of teachers intending to include students who have been identified as experiencing special learning difficulties of some kind might be summarized as:

- Decide whether a computer, or other technological device, is needed to enable effective access to the curriculum by students.
- Determine how students will access the equipment and make the peripherals and furniture that are needed available.
- Ensure the use of ICT is integral to the curriculum as a whole.
- In classrooms where only one computer is available, make sure that tasks are devised so that a number of students have some access.

- Plan lessons to include students who experience difficulties in learning and those who have disabilities.
- Differentiate the classroom tasks to suit the different levels of students' learning needs.
- Ensure that these tasks are achievable, relevant to the particular stage of the curriculum and meaning to students.
- Avoid putting the computer and/or the classroom assistant at the edge of the group or class so that students identified as experiencing special learning needs are not marginalized.
- Encourage and support all the students in the classroom, ensuring that those who are less confident are not marginalized.
- Organize computer clubs as part of the extra curricular activities of the school (adapted from Lilley 2004).

As with some other means of supporting students who experience special learning needs, effective use of ICT in the classroom often involves teaching assistants and other adults broadly associated with the organization of learning support in schools. The final chapter of Section III discusses principles and practicalities with regard to the team of adults who may be involved in supporting classroom learning. It concludes with outlining issues related to inter-agency working and the role of the classroom teacher in ensuring children's well-being and safety.

9   Professional relationships with other people

Questions addressed in this chapter

Are there any principles to guide the effective working of the team of adults who may be involved in supporting classroom learning? If so, what are they?

What are the practical considerations that have to be taken into account when other adults are involved in supporting students who experience special educational needs and their families?

Are there any particular issues related to inter-agency working? If so, what are they?

What is the role of the classroom teacher in ensuring children's well-being and safety, and what part do other adults have in assisting with this role?

Introduction

For teachers, knowing when and how to interact with the vast array of professionals, inside and outside the school, who may become involved with a particular child and family can be confusing and time-consuming, but nevertheless very important to the student's welfare and progress. The type of model encountered or developed within a particular school will depend on such factors as the size of the school and the proximity of other agencies.

In the classroom there may be many reasons why students experience difficulties in learning. In addition, the difficulties experienced by particular students vary and it may be impossible for families or schools to sort out the complex interaction of factors which produce or result in a learning difficulty without the involvement of others. The probability that a student and his or her family will be involved with other agencies in addition to the school depends on the complexity and severity of the difficulty with more complex and severe difficulties (as well as some medical conditions associated with learning problems) generally being identified before school age. In terms of child welfare and protection, the 'Every Child Matters' agenda has a very clear implication for all teachers in being able to listen carefully to what students say and how they behave, working closely with, and under the guidance of, the teacher(s) designated to ensure the safety and well-being of the students, and liaising with outside agencies where appropriate.

The classroom team

One of the major activities in which adults engage in classrooms is talking and discussion with students, thus helping to extend their understanding. The use of support staff in the classroom to assist students who experience some kind of difficulty in learning or physical disability is common practice in many schools these days. The 'core' team in the classroom is usually the class teacher and one or more teaching assistants (who, overwhelmingly, tend to be female). Funding in-class support is an expensive option for schools. It is inevitable that the effectiveness of this kind of provision will come under great scrutiny as demands for accountability in education grow.

There are often occasions when the core team is supplemented by other adults, especially, for example, when students experience difficulties in learning in the classroom, or when their behaviour is disruptive to the progress of other students.

An example of one student's supporting team

It is important to think carefully about the key elements of all adults' roles in contributing to children's learning in the classroom. Probably the most important function of a support teacher is to develop a student's self-esteem by listening to stressed students, helping them complete work which otherwise would have added to the pile of unfinished bits, and often just by getting to know the students as individuals (Lovey 1995).

Steven Lunn (Lunn et al. 2005), employed as a learning support assistant (LSA) to support the learning of 'Matthew', a Year 6 student in a primary school with a Statement of Special Educational Needs, lists the adults with whom Matthew came into contact in the school:

- Matthew's family – his mother and his aunt;
- himself, Stephen, the LSA;
- Matthew's teachers – 'Mr T', the class teacher, and 'Miss J' who taught science and mathematics to the lower-attaining group;
- the school management team – the Deputy Head, the special educational needs co-ordinator (SENCO);
- other school staff – caretaker, librarian, office staff;
- other professionals – educational psychologist, educational social worker, psychiatrist, police.

In the example above, the central relationship was between Matthew and the LSA who worked with him on a one-to-one basis in the classroom and in the quiet room. In the classroom the LSA was able to support Matthew not only with many of the tasks he was expected to carry out, but also in the way he interacted with his peers and the teacher, helping him to develop more positive relationships. It was important for the teacher to be able to discuss with the LSA how he might approach being honest and open with the teaching staff while at the same time retaining Matthew's trust.

The legal position

Teaching assistants and other support staff – 'paraprofessionals' – are part of a growing workforce in schools. Apart from classrooms where responsibility is shared with another teacher, there may be other adults working in the classroom.

Questions for reflection

Are you aware of the differences in teachers' and teaching assistants' legal responsibilities for the learning of students in classrooms?
What guidelines are there about this in your own school?

The teacher of the class has overall responsibility for student learning. The role of another adult in the classroom can be open to some negotiation or quite clearly prescribed – this is particularly true for those who work with statemented students. It is good practice to liaise with the other adults in advance to ensure lesson planning is consistent.

Nursery nurses and qualified classroom assistants

Infant and primary teachers may well have the help of a nursery nurse or qualified classroom assistant, at least for some of the time. Qualified nursery nurses are trained in language and number skills and in social and moral education. They are often employed to support young children identified as experiencing special difficulties in learning.

Unqualified teaching assistants/classroom assistants/bilingual assistants

Most schools employ TAs but their roles vary. They may, or may not, have some formal training, so the range of tasks they can do depends on the individual and on the school's policy. The classroom teacher may be able to negotiate the role of the TA within a range of tasks supporting students' learning.

Special support assistants/special attachment welfare assistants/special individual teachers

Abbreviated to SSAs/SAWAs/SITs, they may be employed in some schools to support children on Statements of SEN arising from the *Special Needs Code of Practice*. Special individual teachers are trained teachers allocated to statemented children.

Special teacher assistants

The STAs are trained to work alongside teachers in classrooms, focusing on key curriculum areas such as mathematics and English.

Governors

In some schools, individual governors are assigned to different classes and make visits to familiarize themselves with classroom life and routines.

Parents

In many schools, parents come in to assist teachers in classrooms. Parental involvement should be a part of accepted practice within agreed policies. Schools should have clear policies for parental involvement and may have a teacher with responsibility for partnership with parents.

There has been a rapid increase in school support staff in recent years. At the same time there has been a shift in the responsibilities of some paraprofessionals in many schools. For example, the rapid expansion in numbers of TAs has shifted the focus of TAs' work from simply preparing resources, general assistance, clearing up, student welfare, and so on, to duties much more clearly focused on student learning and achievement. New TA roles have been introduced: 'learning mentor' in some schools, and 'higher-level teaching assistants' (HLTAs). Funds have been made available through specific government initiatives. One implication of this is that sustaining the roles of paid support staff such as TAs rests on continuation of central government funding.

The responsibility for student–adult interactions in classrooms legally belongs to teachers. There is a legal obligation on teachers to oversee support staff's work with individual students also. Teaching assistants, for example, cannot, legally, be in loco parentis *(in the place of a parent) in the same way as a teacher can.*

Implications of the Education (Specified Work and Registration) (England) Regulations 2003

In 2003, government ministers agreed to contractual changes for teachers to bring about a progressive reduction in teachers' overall hours. This agreement included the reform of support staff roles, and specified circumstances in which certain kinds of school staff – such as support staff – may carry out 'specified work' relating to teaching and learning, including requirements for appropriate supervision by a teacher. Key points covered in the regulations are:

- what 'specified work' is;
- who can undertake 'specified work';
- the conditions that apply to support staff carrying out 'specified work'.

'Specified work' is described in the regulations as:

- planning and preparing lessons;
- delivering lessons to students;
- assessing the development, progress and attainment of students;
- reporting on the development, progress and attainment of students.

'Students' includes individuals as well as groups and whole classes. Omitted are a number of duties that only qualified teachers can do – for example, appraising the work of other teachers.

Persons able to carry out 'specified work' include:

- qualified teachers;
- teachers without qualified teacher status (QTS), for example employment-based trainee teachers, instructors and overseas trained teachers;
- support staff.

A number of conditions apply to support staff carrying out 'specified work':

- They must carry out the specified work in order to assist or support the work of a teacher in the school.
- The headteacher must be satisfied that they have the skills, expertise and experience required to carry out the 'specified work'.
- They must be *subject to the direction and supervision of a teacher* in accordance with arrangements made by the headteacher of the school.

Effective use of support staff in classrooms

The potential for clashes inherent in a situation where, traditionally and conventionally, one professional has been seen to be in control by him/herself is clear. There is the important issue of who is in charge in the classroom. If the adults are not in close agreement, or do not get on, students will play one off against another. Support teachers often lack status and authority in the eyes of staff and students. In this context, even the best qualified, most experienced adult in the support role can be humiliated by a lack of definition of the role, being treated like one of the students and not being able to act in the familiar capacity of authoritative adult.

As in so much of this area of work, implicit in these different aims are contradictions. Arguably, if a support teacher's role is basically seen as managing the behaviour of 'difficult' students there is little incentive to consider a change in pedagogy designed to include all students in the first place. Often, support teachers find themselves propping up the system by helping students through inappropriate lessons, thus, unwittingly, contributing to students' problems in the long run, rather than alleviating them. Cajoling an unmotivated student itself can be both good and bad simultaneously. It certainly can obscure inadequate teaching. On the other hand, some students come to school carrying a lot of personal concerns which the support teacher can help to defuse.

Ideally partnerships between teachers and support staff should be built on a foundation of mutual respect and trust, and a common understanding of how to address the difficulties in learning that some students might face. Having said this, positive relationships are not created automatically. They often develop out of accommodations made by all parties as they negotiate their ways of working and establish their working relationships. An agreed and understood framework of classroom norms and rules underpins the kind of relationships between adults that facilitate learning. Students often have a strong sense of where power and control lies in the classroom, and of fairness. Support staff, teachers and the students themselves can make life easier and more enjoyable, or more difficult, for the others by the way in which they display mutual positive regard, or the opposite. On the whole, students recognize adult authority in schools and expect adults to take charge. However, classroom order is most likely to be maintained where students' voices are listened to and respected. A second adult in the classroom can, as Lorenz (1998) comments:

- increase the child/adult ratio and thus the amount of positive attention available to students;
- be responsible for giving regular praise and encouragement to particular students while the class teacher takes responsibility for the learning programme;
- make time to listen to students and their point of view;
- work with small groups to encourage social skills or raise self-esteem;
- share responsibility for monitoring behaviour;
- intervene early where misbehaviour is developing and nip problems in the bud;
- give individual children space to calm down without disrupting the class.

Concerns about relationships between adults in classrooms

Adults who know that they are respected and valued in a school are much more likely to value and respect the students with whom they work. There is always room for conflict and misunderstanding to arise between the adults in a classroom, and this can be very detrimental to children's learning and behaviour.

Strategies for working effectively with parents in classrooms

Lorenz (1998) notes a number of fears among teachers about involving parents in classroom activities:

- Where parents are not paid for their help in class they may not be reliable.
- Parents may be over-enthusiastic in offering assistance to children
- There may be breaches of confidentiality.
- Children may show off in front of parents.
- There may be complaints from other parents.
- Parents may favour their own children.
- Parents may criticize teachers inside, or outside, the classroom.

Lorenz's solution is to be proactive in negotiating clear roles and boundaries from the start. She advises:

- discussing and agreeing which skills the parents are offering;
- thinking about parents' degree of confidence in assisting with classroom activities and organizing their support in a way that plays to their strengths;
- ensuring parents are fully aware that the teacher is responsible for the group and that the teacher remains in control;
- clarifying what is needed and expected and that the teacher is responsible for the conceptual content of the lesson;
- overtly valuing the help parents offer and not taking parental help for granted;
- limiting the size of the student group working with parents.

Among other factors, the outcome of a potential conflict situation and whether or not it results in an amicable solution depends on individuals':

- sense of self-worth, and the extent to which they feel they have others' respect;
- willingness to listen, share their own views and value differences;
- willingness to look for win–win solutions, or compromises;
- ability to reflect on previous experiences of conflict, and learn from them.

Cremin et al. (2003) comment that having one or more teaching assistants in a classroom does not necessarily lead to improved learning and behaviour for students. Balshaw's (1991) description of LSAs, for example, as potentially being 'overgrown students', 'piggy in the middle', 'spies in the classroom' or 'dogsbodies' illustrates how things can go seriously wrong:

- Situations where LSAs either behave childishly or are treated like children are likely to result in low status for those LSAs among the students.
- Learning support assistants can find themselves in a 'go-between' role if the teacher assumes that responsibility for the learning and behaviour of particular students lies with them. For example, where work expected of the student is far too difficult, easy or otherwise inappropriate, and there is no direct communication or discussion between student and teacher, the LSAs may find themselves shuttling too and fro, overburdened with messages and the task, and unsupported.
- Either students or teachers can feel themselves spied upon if there is little trust in classroom relationships, or where the LSAs do not, or cannot, maintain an appropriate sense of balance in their responsibilities to teachers and individual students.
- Teachers should never treat LSAs as low-paid servants in classrooms. The lack of respect implied in this situation is unhealthy for everyone.

Lessons to be learned from one teaching assistant's experience

Issues similar to those identified by Balshaw (1991) were raised in an interview with 'Susan' (Wearmouth 2000: 172–8), a graduate support assistant employed for 25 hours per week in a secondary comprehensive school to support 'Dean' and five other students, all on Statements, identified as 'slower' to learn than most of the other students and who found difficulty in reading text and in writing coherently:

The 'overgrown student'
> The greatest problem for me in this work is that I feel I'm a nobody. I walk out of the classroom feeling I am more like one of the kids. The kids are my friends. The teachers don't consult me very often. It's up to me to go to the teacher all the time. It is very much down to me to find out what is going on and what have you. I need to go up to the Special Needs area at break time and lunch time just to know what is happening. Quite honestly, to increase the respect and status of the position, the way I feel about it really

when you are going up there at lunch time and talking to staff and talking to kids and helping kids I really ought to be paid for it. I mean, we found out that they are paying sixth formers to stand at the top of the stairs and just stand there, and we aren't paid for helping kids and finding out what we are supposed to be doing at lunchtime. Why could not they offer us that job? I mean, it bloody annoys me that we are another stage up with the ancillary staff.

There are some situations in class where I absolutely can't operate at all, depending where you sit in the classroom. For example, it can be awkward if you think you are interrupting the teacher and what they are doing. The kids will ask you a question, they are in the middle of asking you a question and the teacher will say, 'Right, I want everybody silent,' and I mean how do you get the question out of them? I quite often feel as if I am one of the kids because the teacher will say, 'Now shut up all that talking,' and it's me. It's me explaining to the kids things about what they have got to do, because you know they ask you a question and you are a teacher and you have got to answer it.

'Piggy in the middle'

In a lesson I would say about 60% of my time is given to Dean ... um ... even though there are several other students in the class who are statemented whom I am supposed to be supporting ... The kind of things I do with him are to stand over him quite a lot of the time because he has got great avoidance tactics, he just does not like the idea of being the last to do things, he knows he can't keep up with the pace that everyone else does. Some days he will work really hard and do his best but other days he will think well, I can't do this, I can't do this and you give him a pen and he just pulls it apart and sometimes he refuses to bring a pen because it is just an avoidance tactic ... If he works very hard occasionally he can keep up with the rest of the class. Sometimes he surprises me. He can write things down quite quickly if he wants to. Again, he has not got very good joined up writing or anything but he can work at a pace that he wants to sometimes, depending on the other kids he is with. If he feels pressurized to keep up with them, he will keep up with them. Other times you have to sit by him just to get him started. He is very slow at getting started, 20 minutes to write the title of something and things like this, but once you get him interested he can get involved, but still the writing down is a problem. He would rather talk about it.

He is expected to do pretty much the same level of work as everybody else in the class in some lessons. Sometimes there is some differentiation in the work between him and other students but in general terms he is expected to do exactly the same as everybody else, exactly the same as those who find it very easy to write things down and very easy to understand things quickly. If I had not been there in the last year he would not be turning up at all at school. He just would not be there because he could not cope ... I really think he should have more individual targeted help ... but the English teacher said, 'Well, I would rather he stayed with the class' because they had just started Romeo and Juliet at the time ... 'I really do think that he can cope with it like everybody else in the class because he can understand the story', and in actual fact he has got a lot out of being there with the drama and the acting and all that and he does really well. He has a part and it is good to see him working with the others understanding the story, watching what the others are doing. It probably was better that he was in that class actually with the others.

Now they have got to do an essay on the parents of Romeo and Juliet but it's pointless giving him something like that, but he will still have to do it. That's the writing side and I will just have to dictate in the end what he does because otherwise he can't cope. He just will not be able to do it. He just won't be able to go away and do it on his own.

The teacher never ever asks me for suggestions about what I think he could be doing in the time . . . she is aware of the level that he is at but it is just a case of me making sure that he just does something, she just wants him to produce something whatever it is, however long it is it does not matter. She is very adamant about the fact that it does not matter how much he produces as long as he produces something it is okay.

'Dogsbody'

Another reason why I feel I am a nobody is that they have OFSTED meetings going on with ancillary staff and we were not included, the support staff. When we went to ask we were told: 'Yes, go along,' but the next minute there were other meetings going on with sort of representatives from different areas like the office and what have you but we were not asked. So I felt, well, you know, nobody had ever taken us into account. People seemed to be aware of us wanting to know, but we just were not included in things. I don't know how it works though.

I do get a bit annoyed with some of the teachers because they seem to think my job is to stand over Dean all the time and make him work, but that really is not my job. It is as if it is my fault if he does not do things, and I have got three others in that class. One of them, Paul, is quite childish in his thinking and actually, you know, I got on very well with him at first, but he has become quite abusive to me lately. He will say, 'I don't need help I am fine' when I know very well he can't understand and he can't do it. He would rather copy off other children than accept help from me, and been seen to take help from me. I feel quite honestly that I just can't do enough for the four of them in that lesson. I feel Paul deserves better than I can give him at the moment. He needs more support. He needs someone to discuss things with on his own level.

In some lessons I find myself doing the teacher's job, quite honestly. I mean, the teacher is sitting down marking and I am walking around helping all the kids in the class and I do get annoyed at that sometimes because I don't feel that's my place and it happens with the same teachers over and over again.

'Spy in the classroom'

There is one particular department where every single member of the department is always ten or fifteen minutes late at the beginning of the lesson. You get three classes arriving together and I am the only adult there, and there am I running from one to the other controlling three classes all together and quite honestly that is not my job and then you know I am so angry because I have shouted at the class two or three times . . . So the net result is I just hang around for at least five minutes after the bell before going into the classroom.

One of the important issues here is how far difficulties are created for Susan because she is paid merely as an assistant who, in a highly academic secondary school, is accorded little personal status. It has to be said, however, that in this particular school another support teacher who is a fully qualified teacher and paid as such, reported similar difficulties. Susan's salary was funded from monies coming into the school as a result of provision specified on students' Statements which specified one-to-one input, rather than extra support for all students. However, sometimes the students actively resisted seeking help in front of their peers. She often therefore ended up helping other students and not assisting those for whom this extra resource should have been targeted. Where the students were on Statement but refused her help she was left wondering whom she was there to serve, especially where her aims appeared to be different from the students.

Effective support for classroom learning

The interview with Susan above exemplifies potentially useful functions of a classroom assistant that should be recognized in any evaluation of that role: collection of evidence for an evaluation of student progress, facilitation of learning and close observation of behaviour:

Evidence for evaluating progress

[T]here was a meeting of teachers recently where everybody got together and discussed what they thought ought to happen with Dean and really I was the only one who knew much about him. I was a bit upset because I had not been invited to the meeting originally and I heard about it when other people were talking about it, and I really do think I should have been invited. I think the invitation should have come from the deputy head but nobody seems to have thought about me even though I was the one who seemed to have the most information about him . . . If I had not been there a lot of information about Dean just would not have been there. From that meeting a lot of positive things were worked out for him.

Facilitation of learning

Generally I think the idea of support teaching is very effective, actually. Just having someone there for them is very good for them, but I just feel we could do so much more. The difficulty in History and Geography is the reading side of things. I am always going around the room and they may have two pages there that they have got to read and they don't understand what is on the page anyway. I'll ask them if they want help reading and they say. 'No,' because they don't want to be seen as having help with their English by their friends. A number of students in that class really do value having it read out to them as well. In History in particular I spend so much of my time in class going over what they should be doing. The thing is, I go up to a kid and say, 'Do you want help with the reading?' and it is quite hard and none of them say they want help. But if they can't do the question then I will help them and then they will let me help them. There are a number of students who really are very intelligent, but then there are a large majority of students who really can't or don't . . .

I think there actually is a big place for negotiating more with support teachers appropriate tasks for particular children to do because the support teachers know those children very well, definitely. I feel I know a lot more about the children that I'm with than a lot of the teachers. . . . The trouble is I'm not qualified really to talk, you know, they don't think I'm qualified really to talk about it at all, you know . . .

There was a discussion at the meeting and it was just decided that he was taken out of lessons and because he was doing the reading programme he needed to go home and relax. I never got a chance at that meeting to say what I thought about that, not really. I did not have the status or the position. I felt out of my league there anyway ... A lot of these things you just don't know, do you, until you try it with him really. I would have made him do a certain amount and say to him, 'Look you have got to have a go,' because he just thinks, 'I am Dean Watts and I don't do any homework. Everybody else has to but I don't have to.' That's his label and he has kept that label. 'I'm the one who does not do homework. Everybody else does and I don't' ... The trouble is for me I couldn't monitor his homework and tell him what to do because that is not my role. He does not see me as a teacher. I feel I can't really tell him off about his homework. I mean, I do say to him, 'Well why did not you do your homework Dean?' If it was made clear to him in front of me then possibly it would be different, but I feel that he needs that discipline from the other teachers. The teachers need to reprimand him more. I know it is difficult but he has not got any boundaries in that way. That is the trouble.

Close observation of behaviour

The lesson I enjoy being with kids most is in maths, I think. It is a very small class and you can really get down to sorting them out and helping them and you can see them understanding it and getting on with it at their level. There are only about ten or twelve students in that group. Even so, I spend quite a lot of time with Dean but not as much as I do in other lessons because there are other students there, like John, and they also need help in maths, and there are other students not on statement who also need help. Being a smaller group, I also get on very well with the teacher who does that class. We just get on and work together and she lets me mark their work. I get a lot of responsibility in that class. I walk round she does not leave me just with Dean. She helps him as much as I do, which I think is very good for them, and very good for me, and for my relationships with them and her relationships with them. I wish that a lot more teachers would take more notice of those students that I am supporting and don't just leave it up to the support teacher. You know, it is as if some teachers think, well, there is a support teacher with them I don't need to look at them. I don't need to be with them. Yet it would help them a lot if the main teacher paid them a lot more attention, but teachers just don't bother ... I feel very happy in that lesson. I feel things are a lot better balanced. I feel a lot more valued as a person. I feel like it's a lot more positive, it's like in the other lessons I can't do things that I feel I ought to do. She always discusses beforehand what she is going to do if there is time anyway, and she reflects on the kids' progress with me as well. She does that at the beginning and the end of the lesson and she finds time in the lessons when the kids are working as well and she talks to me about all the kids in the class and what is going on. In a bigger class some teachers try but it is time for them that makes it difficult. Others just don't. That is a different situation because it is a small class anyway, and both of us know them and we both know that we are both there very much to help the class, make things possible for them ...

I think it would definitely help if kids were allowed to talk to each other more about things and help each other more, and were not just expected sit there and get on silently and independently on their own. I think it is partly to do with the organization of the lesson ... There is so much variation amongst the statemented children. I mean John is very intelligent and able to work things out for himself. His basic maths and English aren't very good but his understanding is good and his understanding of what he has got to know is quite good as well. He often puts up his hand and answers questions and things in class. He just needs help with the reading of things and writing it down.

Organizing the classroom team

Effective use of staff and their skills can often depend on how the team is organized. Cremin et al. (2003) describe a number of very structured approaches to organizing teamwork in classrooms, two of the most useful of which are:

- room management, an approach that emphasizes the need for clarity of roles among adults that are defined by looking first at the roles that teachers usually carry out on their own and then determining which of these it is appropriate for others to perform. For example, management of whole-class activities might be differentiated from offering personal support to individuals or groups;
- zoning, that is, dividing the classroom into learning zones where the teacher takes responsibility for the learning and activities of students in one zone, and the TA for the rest. Traditionally the teacher would work with a larger group and, of course, the teacher always retains responsibility for the learning and progress of the whole class. However, there might be a number of different combinations of zoning, depending on the learning needs of the class and the particular expertise of the TA and the teacher.

Clarity in delegating and negotiating responsibilities for students' learning is very important.

Advice on effective deployment of teaching assistants

An experienced SENCO in an upper school in the East Midlands, when first introducing support assistants to classrooms in the school, offered the following advice to staff:

- discuss with the classroom assistant the work you will be expecting in your classrooms;
- set aside specific time to discuss/plan together without interruption where possible;
- a notebook can be useful for jottings/reminders etc when it is not possible to talk;
- classroom assistants should not be expected to work beyond their paid hours;
- remember, you prefer time to prepare before a lesson, so will the classroom assistant;
- plan work for/with the classroom assistant and give clear guidelines;
- make sure the classroom assistant knows exactly what is wanted from the students. The classroom assistant may not have been in the classroom when you were talking with them;
- discuss in advance where, within the class, the classroom assistant is going to work.
(Wearmouth 2000: 179)

Farrell's (1999) report reflects a strong consensus among teachers and LSAs on how effective in-class support should be agreed:

- Learning support assistants must be fully informed about the aims and objectives of a lesson and about the learning needs of students who need assistance.
- Learning support assistants need to be familiar with additional materials and equipment.
- Teachers and LSAs must get on well together, trust each other's judgement and have enough time to plan together.
- Students, teachers and LSAs were in agreement that they wanted support to be given from a distance – that is, they preferred LSAs to 'float around a class' but to be immediately available when needed.
- Teachers' management strategies must provide clear guidance as to how LSAs should work in their classrooms.
- Schools must have policies outlining roles and responsibilities of LSAs.

Child protection

One very important area in which teachers must work closely with other professionals is that of child protection. Children cannot learn effectively in schools, or teachers teach effectively, if those children 'are concerned or frightened about being abused, or being the victims of violence' (DfES 2004b: 3). There are (usually rare) occasions when students' behaviour in classrooms, playgrounds or elsewhere is indicative of a situation requiring investigation by those responsible for child protection policies in the school. Schools are required to 'have procedures in place for child welfare and for protecting children from abuse' (DfES 2004b: 3). The Children Acts (1989, c. 41, and 2004, c. 31) have raised awareness of the responsibilities of schools for the care and protection of children and provide specific guidance on child protection to schools and other institutions. Class teachers as well as head teachers have a responsibility for the care of children inside the school, and outside while on school visits.

The (1989) *United Nations Convention on the Rights of the Child* highlights the rights of children to be listened to and to have their views taken seriously. Children also have needs. Article 19 of the Convention states that children have a right to be protected: 'from all forms of physical or mental violence, injury or abuse, neglect or negligent treatment, maltreatment or exploitation, including sexual abuse, while in the care of parent(s), legal guardian(s) of any other person who has the care of the child' (UNESCO 1989). Further, 'state parties' have a responsibility to take all 'appropriate legislative, administrative, social and educational measures to protect the child' and to ensure the 'identification, reporting, referral, investigation, treatment and follow-up of instances of child maltreatment and, as appropriate, for judicial involvement' (UNESCO 1989). Inevitably this means taking care that students are safe and protected in school.

Child abuse itself is a very emotive topic, and it is essential to be familiar with the procedures in place in schools for addressing child protection issues. Students' experience of abuse is often not easily categorized – neglect, for example, may also be closely associated with feeling of isolation and abandonment; sexual abuse is likely to be linked with lack of self-confidence and low self-respect.

Definition of 'child abuse' (Department of Health, 1999)

The Department of Health outlines four categories of child abuse:

Physical abuse: Hitting, shaking, throwing, poisoning, burning or scalding, drowning, suffocating, or otherwise causing physical harm to a child. Physical harm may be caused when a parent or carer feigns the symptoms of, or deliberately causes ill-health to a child.

Emotional abuse: The persistent emotional ill-treatment of a child such as to cause severe and persistent effects on the child's emotional development. It may involve conveying to children that they are worthless or unloved, inadequate, or valued only insofar as they meet the need of another person. It may feature age or developmentally inappropriate expectations being imposed on children. It may involve causing children frequently to feel frightened or in danger, or the exploitation or corruption of children.

Sexual abuse: Forcing or enticing a child or young person to take part in sexual activities, whether or not the child is aware of what is happening. The activities may involve physical contact, including penetrative (e.g. rape or buggery) or non-penetrative acts. They may include non-contact activities, such as involving children in looking at, or in the production of, pornographic material or watching sexual activities or encouraging children to behave in sexually inappropriate ways.

Neglect: Persistent failure to meet a child's basic physical and/or psychological needs, likely to result in the serious impairment of the child's health and development. It may involve a parent or carer failing to provide adequate food, shelter and clothing, failing to protect a child from physical harm or danger, or the failure to ensure access to appropriate medical care or treatment. It may also include neglect of, or unresponsiveness to a child's basic emotional needs.

(Department of Health 1999: 5–6)

Issues in inter-agency collaboration

In the past it has often been difficult for schools to work closely with outside agencies to protect the welfare of individual students seen by teachers as at risk of injury or abuse. A number of barriers have stood in the way of effective inter-agency working (Roaf and Lloyd 1995). These related to differences between the agencies in priorities for policy, organizational structures, professional practice and financial arrangements. In relation to policy, the three primary care agencies, Education, Health and Social Services tended to have different priorities. Where core values are so different the potential for friction between the various agencies is obvious.

Lack of clear structure to determine responsibilities in inter-agency working could also generate considerable tension, especially when resources were under pressure. The loser is the client and his or her parents or carers. Roaf and Lloyd (1995) quote the frustration of one young person's parents: 'He was offending while truanting from school. A mixture of the two. In the end we felt like tennis balls because Education said it was a social problem and Social Services said it was an education problem, and we were just going backwards and forwards from one to another' (1995, in Wearmouth 2000: 192).

Models of professional practice also varied across agencies. Roaf and Lloyd (1995) found that each agency had its own language and culture, and tended to work on its own with clients, making it difficult to agree joint procedures for taking action.

The 'single most important factor' identified by Wilson and Charlton (1997) underpinning successful inter-agency work was the existence of a clear inter-agency structure where a policy and planning group with members drawn from all the agencies supported a multi-agency, multidisciplinary team. An effective networking system provided feedback about gaps in provision, identified needs and resources, and facilitated the free flow of information among a wide range of practitioners.

The death of Victoria Climbié was very influential in raising awareness of the need for much closer inter-agency working to protect vulnerable children. This young child had been in the care of her aunt, was thought by her school to be at risk and was also known to Social Services. Despite this the child died. Following the report on her death, central government in London developed an initiative 'Every Child Matters' (the Children's Agenda or ECM) (DfES 2004a) in an attempt to ensure that such a tragedy should not be repeated. This initiative has five intended outcomes for children:

- be healthy;
- stay safe;
- enjoy and achieve;
- make a positive contribution;
- achieve economic well-being.

This initiative unified the range of children's services. All local education authorities combined with other services to become local authorities (LAs).

Teachers are not expected to investigate incidents of abuse. Distinguishing accidental injury from abuse can be very difficult. This is the role of other professionals such as social workers, doctors and the police.

Guidance on dealing with suspected abuse cases

The teacher's role is to be aware of signs of abuse and report concerns to appropriate personnel such as the designated person in a school. Department for Education and Skills guidance (2004: 26–7) reads:

> Experience, and consultation with children, shows that they will talk about their concerns and problems to people they feel they can trust and they feel comfortable with. This will not necessarily be a teacher. It is therefore essential that all staff and volunteers in a school or establishment know how to respond sensitively to a child's concerns, who (sic) to approach for advice about them, and the importance of not guaranteeing complete confidentiality.
>
> Children also want to know that they will be listened to and their concerns will be taken seriously, so all education establishments should seek to demonstrate to children that they provide them with a safe environment where it is okay to talk. Displays of helpful information about such things as national children's help lines (Child Line, NSPCC) and peer support schemes for children and young people in easily accessible places (e.g. on

students' year planners) can encourage them to share concerns and help provide assurance about that.

Any member of staff or volunteer who is approached by a child wanting to talk should listen positively and reassure the child. They should record the discussion with the student as soon as possible and take action in accordance with the establishment's child protection procedures.

The available UK evidence on the extent of abuse among disabled children suggests that some may be especially vulnerable to abuse, for example those who have difficulty communicating. Learning support assistants working with children with special educational needs and disabilities provide close support to them and may encounter indications of possible abuse. Whilst extra care may be needed to ensure that signs of abuse and neglect are interpreted correctly, any suspicions should be reported in exactly the same manner as for other children.

The way in which a member of staff talks to a child who discloses abuse could have an effect on the evidence that is put forward if there are subsequent proceedings, and it is important that staff do not jump to conclusions, ask leading questions, or put words in a child's mouth. If a child makes a disclosure to a member of staff, s/he should write a record of the conversation as soon as possible, distinguishing clearly between fact, observation, allegation and opinion, noting any action taken in cases of possible abuse and signing and dating the note.

Anyone who has experience of schools where allegations of inappropriate behaviour have been made against members of staff, or other individuals, will know how difficult and stressful the situation can become for all concerned. Complaints may be well founded, manipulative, malicious or based on a misunderstanding. Whatever the case, it is far preferable to follow agreed school procedures and avoid situations where there is any possibility of a complaint. These days, where more students are included in mainstream schools rather than in special schools, more teachers are likely to come into contact with students with physical difficulties who require intimate care relating for example to managing bodily functions or personal hygiene. In this situation it is very important that those teachers, as well as other adults involved, are very aware of child protection concerns. Teachers should ask for formal guidance if it has not already been offered.

Summary

Work with other professionals is important in two particular areas in schools: classroom learning, and child protection.

Funding in-class support for students is an expensive option for schools. There is research to show that this kind of provision can facilitate the learning of students who experience difficulties, but clear justification must be given and a clear role for the support teacher or assistant must be negotiated and agreed with all concerned. In the classroom there are a number of different ways of conceptualizing the role of support teachers which indicate the need to consider very carefully the aim of this kind of provision. Two useful systems for organizing classrooms so that adults and students are all

Table 9.1 How to use effectively adult support for pupils in the classroom

The role of support staff in your classroom is to help you make sure that each pupil plays a full part and makes progress. In primary schools, paid support staff are often called 'teaching assistants'. Support staff can help to:

- raise the performance of individual pupils
- provide coping strategies for pupils
- assist in the management of pupils' behaviour
- promote pupils' independence
- support the development of differentiated curricular approaches to meet the diversity of pupils' learning needs

Support staff may carry out 'specified work' relating to teaching and learning to include planning, preparing and delivering lessons to groups of pupils, assessing and reporting on pupils progress. *Support staff carrying out 'specified work' must be subject to the direction and supervision of a teacher.* As the teacher of the class, you have overall responsibility for pupil learning.

Support staff can sometimes impede inclusion by working in isolation with individual pupils and too much one-to-one support with a pupil can have a negative impact on participation.

To develop effective classroom practice you should:

- Review the situation frequently to achieve the right balance of individual and group work. Be prepared to make some compromises
- Work together with your support staff to plan and implement programmes of work
- Set aside specific time to discuss/plan together

- Make sure support staff know exactly what is expected of pupils

Ground rules Make sure that you establish at the outset:

- The status to give an adult helper in your class and what they are to be called
- How to organize time to talk about any difficulties
- That the adult helper knows about the classroom rules and the importance of maintaining confidentiality
- How to organize time for the adult helper to find the resources to be used
- Relevant Health and Safety issues

Support in whole-class oral work
Encourage support staff to:

- prompt shy or reticent pupils
- sign or translate core vocabulary or phrases
- help pupils to use specific individual resources
- operate individualized resources as indicated in pupils' IEPs
- observe pupils' responses or behaviour and report back to you

Support for group work
Encourage support staff to:

- ensure that pupils interpret instructions correctly, concentrate and behave responsibly
- remind pupils of teaching points made earlier in the lesson
- question pupils and encourage their participation
- note any difficulties to address in the plenary and/or in future lessons

aware of who has responsibility for what are room management and zoning (Cremin et al. 2003). Even so, adults will need to be very clear about what is expected of them.

Peacey and Wearmouth (2007) summarize important issues related to the effective use of adult support for students' learning in classrooms in Table 9.1.

In terms of child welfare, there is a long history of problems in inter-agency work in the exchange of information between agencies and of disputes over responsibility for offering particular services, sometimes with duplication of interventions by different agencies working on the same case. Different agencies have operated to different legislative frameworks with different priorities and definitions of what constitutes a need. The net result has been that, at times, the system has failed the client, most notably, in recent years, in the case of the tragic death of Victoria Climbié, a child known to be at risk by both educational and social services. This clear failure in the system re-stated the need for closer co-operation between agencies which exist to support children in difficulties and their families or carers. The 'Every Child Matters' agenda has sought to resolve these difficulties by unifying the range of children's services. All local education authorities combined with other services to become local authorities. One important implication for all teachers, particularly classroom teachers, is to listen carefully to what students say and how they behave, and to work closely with, and under the guidance of, the teacher(s) designated to oversee the safety and well-being of the students in the school.

Final word

Including students with special educational needs: moving forward

Education is the opening of students' identities, as learners and as members of the wider society. For many students, identification with, or failure in, marginalization and alienation from, school, will have long-lasting and deep effects throughout their lives. Carrying the identity of marginalization and failure to learn may mean an expectation of marginalization and failure in other institutional contexts. Reflecting on students' learning and finding ways to address the difficulties that may be experienced is challenging and demanding, but also exciting and, at times, very rewarding.

Good, collaborative and supportive teamwork in schools is, of course, very important in all this. So is the kind of school leadership that understands the need to support the learning of everyone within a school, teachers as well as students, and is focused on ways to do this. For the individual teacher the awareness of having contributed to making a difference to a child's learning and, therefore, to future life chances, is priceless. For many of us it makes our working lives worthwhile.

References

Adams, M.J. (1994) *Beginning to Read: Thinking and Learning about Print.* Cambridge, MA: MIT Press.

Adult Literacy and Basic Skills Unit (1992) *The ALBSU Standards for Basic Skills Students and Trainees.* London: Adult Literacy and Basic Skills Unit.

Alton-Lee, A. (2003) *Quality Teaching for Diverse Students in Schooling: Best Evidence Synthesis.* Wellington: Ministry of Education.

Ames, G. and Archer, J. (1988) Achievement goals in the classroom: students' learning strategies and motivation processes, *Journal of Educational Psychology*, 80: 260–7.

Anderson, C., Gendler, G., Riestenberg, N., Anfang, C.C., Ellison, M. and Yates, B. (1996) *Restorative Measures: Respecting Everyone's Ability to Resolve Problems.* St Paul, MN: Minnesota Department of Children, Families and Learning, Office of Community Services.

Angier, C. and Povey, H. (1999) One teacher and a class of school students: their perception of the culture of their mathematics classroom and its construction, *Educational Review*, 51(2): 147–60.

Anthony, G. and Walshaw, M. (2007) *Effective Pedagogy in Mathematics/Pàngarau: Best Evidence Synthesis Iteration.* Wellington: Ministry of Education.

Apel, K. and Masterton, J. (1998) Assessment and treatment of narrative skills: what's the story? in *RTN Learning Book.* Rockville, MD: American Speech-Language-Hearing Association.

Armstrong, D. (1994) *Power and Partnership in Education: Parents, Children and Special Educational Needs.* London: Routledge.

Askew, M., Brown, M., Rhodes, V., Johnson, D. and Wiliam, D. (1997) *Effective Teachers of Numeracy.* London: Kings College.

Asperger, H. (1944) Die 'aunstisehen Psychopathen' im Kindesalter, *Archiv fur psychiatrie und Nervenkrankheiten*, 17: 76–136.

Assessment Reform Group (1999) *Assessment for Learning: Beyond the Black Box.* Cambridge: University of Cambridge School of Education.

Association of Teachers and Lecturers (ATL) (1996) *Bullying at Work: A Guide for Teachers.* London: Association of Teachers and Lecturers.

Au, K.H. (2002) Multicultural factors and the effective instruction of students of diverse backgrounds, in A. Farstrup and S.J. Samuels (eds) *What Research Says about Reading Instruction.* Newark, DE: International Reading Association.

Audit Commission (1992) *Getting in on the Act: Provision for Pupils with Special Educational Needs.* London: HMSO.

Baer, D.M., Wolf, M.M. and Risley, T.R. (1968) Some current dimensions of applied behavior analysis, *Journal of Applied Behavior Analysis* (1): 91–7.

Baker, M. (1997) http://atschool.eduweb.co.uk/mbaker/material/ils.html (accessed 29 January 2007).

Ball, D. and Bass, H. (2000) Interweaving content and pedagogy in teaching and learning to teach: knowing and using mathematics, in J. Boaler (ed.) *Multiple Perspectives on the Teaching and Learning of Mathematics*. Westport, CT: Ablex.

Balshaw, M. (1991) *Help in the Classroom*. London: David Fulton.

Bartholomew, H. (2003) Ability grouping and the construction of different types of learner in mathematics classrooms, in L. Bragg, C. Campbell, G. Herbert and J. Mousley (eds) *Mathematics Education Research: Innovation, Networking, Opportunity* (Proceedings of the 26th annual conference of the Mathematics Education Research Group of Australasia, Vol. 1: 128–35). Sydney: MERGA.

Barton, D. (1995) *Literacy: An Introduction to the Ecology of Written Language*. Oxford: Blackwell.

Bennathan, M. (2000) Children at risk of failure in primary schools, in M. Bennathan and M. Boxall, *Effective Intervention in Primary Schools: Nurture Groups*, 2nd edn. London: David Fulton.

Bennett, R. (1992) Discipline in schools: the report of the Committee of Enquiry chaired by Lord Elton, in K. Wheldall (ed.) *Discipline in Schools: Psychological Perspectives on the Elton Report*. London: Routledge.

Bentley, D. (1990) *Teaching Spelling: Some Questions Answered*. Reading: University of Reading.

Berryman, M. (2000) Whānau-of-interest: a kaupapa Māori response for improving Māori achievement. Paper prepared for presentation at the NZARE conference, University of Waikato, December.

Berryman, M. and Glynn, T. (2001) *Hei Awhina Matua: Strategies for Bicultural Partnership in Overcoming Behavioural and Learning Difficulties*. Wellington: Specialist Education Service.

Birmingham City Council Education Department (2004) A three-level approach to intervention for individual behaviour difficulties, in J. Wearmouth, R.C. Richmond and T. Glynn (eds) *Addressing Pupils' Behaviour: Responses at District, School and Individual levels*. London: Fulton.

Bishop, A.J. (1983) Space and geometry, in R. Lesh and M. Landau (eds) *Acquisition of Mathematical Concepts and Processes*. London: Academic Press.

Bishop, R., Berryman, M., Richardson, C. and Tiakiwai, S. (2003) *Te Kotahitanga: The Experiences of Year 9 and 10 Māori Students in Mainstream Classrooms*. Final report to the Ministry of Education, Wellington.

Black, P. and Wiliam, D. (1998) Assessment and classroom learning, *Assessment in Education*, 5(1): 7–74.

Blackledge, A. (2000) *Literacy, Power and Social Justice*. Stoke-on-Trent: Trentham.

Bliss, J., Askew, M. and Macrae, S. (1996) Effective teaching and learning: scaffolding revisited, *Oxford Review of Education*, 22(1): 37–61.

Boaler, J., Wiliam, D. and Brown, M. (2000) Students' experiences of ability grouping: Disaffection, polarisation and the construction of failure? *British Educational Research Journal*, 26(5): 631–648.

Bond, G.L. and Dykstra, R. (1967) The co-operative research program in first-grade reading instruction, *Reading Research Quarterly*, 2: 5–142.

Borthwick, A. and Harcourt-Heath, M. (2007) Calculation strategies used by Year 5 children, *Proceedings of the British Society for Research into Learning Mathematics*, 27(1): 12–23.

Bowers, T. (1996) Putting back the 'E' in EBD, *Emotional and Behavioural Difficulties*, 1(1): 8–13.

Bowlby, J. (1944) Forty-four juvenile thieves: their characters and home life, *International Journal of Psycho-Analysis*, 25: 19–52.

Bowlby, J. (1952) A two-year-old goes to hospital, *Proceedings of the Royal Society of Medicine*, 46: 425–7.

Boxall, M. (2002) *Nurture Groups in School: Principles and Practice*. London: Paul Chapman.

Bradley, L. (1981) The organisation of motor patterns for spelling: an effective remedial strategy for backward readers, *Developmental Medicine and Child Neurology*, 23: 83–91.

Bradley, L. and Bryant, P.E. (1983) Categorising sounds and learning to read: a causal connection, *Nature*, 301: 419–21.

Braithwaite, J. (1997) *Restorative Justice: Assessing an Immodest Theory and a Pessimistic Theory*. Canberra: Australian Institute of Criminology, Australian National University.

Brandon, S. (1961) An epidemiological study of maladjustment in childhood. Unpublished MD thesis, University of Durham.

British Psychological Society (BPS) (1996) *Attention Deficit Hyperactivity Disorder (ADHD): A Psychological Response to an Evolving Concept*. Leicester: BPS.

Brown, J. and Howlett, F. (1994) *IT Works*. Coventry: NCET.

Bruner, J. (1996) *The Culture of Education*. Boston, MA: Harvard University Press.

Buikema, J.L. and Graves, M.F. (1993) Teaching students to use context cues to infer word meaning, *Journal of Reading*, 33: 504–8.

Campion, J. (1985) *The Child in Context: Family Systems Theory in Educational Psychology*. London: Methuen.

Canter, L. and Canter, M. (1992) *Assertive Discipline: Positive Behaviour Management for Today's Classroom*. Santa Monica, CA: Lee Canter and Associates.

Caygill, R. and Elley, L. (2001) Evidence about the effects of assessment task format on student achievement. Paper presented at the British Educational Research Association, University of Leeds, September.

Center, Y., Freeman, L. and Robertson, G. (2001) A longitudinal evaluation of the Schoolwide Early Language and Literacy Program (SWELL), in R.E. Slavin and N.A. Madden (eds) *Success for All: Research and Reform in Elementary Education*. Mahwah, NJ: Lawrence Erlbaum.

Chazan, M., Laing, A. and Davies, D. (1994) *Emotional and Behavioural Difficulties in Middle Childhood*. London: Falmer Press.

Children Act (1989). London: HMSO.

Children Act (2004). London: HMSO.

Choat, E. (1974) Johnnie is disadvantaged; Johnnie is backward. What hope for Johnnie? *Mathematics Teaching*, 69: 9–13.

Chomsky, C. (1978) When you still can't read in third grade after decoding, what? in S.J. Samuels (ed.) *What Research Has to Say about Reading Instruction*. Newark, DE: International Reading Association.

Clark, C., Dyson, A., Millward, A. and Skidmore, D. (1997) *New Directions in Special Needs*. London: Cassell.

Clarke, S., Timperley, H. and Hattie, J. (2003) *Unlocking Formative Assessment: Practical Strategies for Enhancing Students' Learning in the Primary and Intermediate Classroom*. Auckland: Hodder Moa Beckett.

Clay, M.M. (1979) *Reading: The Patterning of Complex Behaviour*. Auckland: Heinemann.

Cobb, P. and Hodge, L.L. (2002) A relational perspective on issues of cultural diversity and equity as they play out in the mathematics classroom, *Mathematical Thinking and Learning*, 4(2&3): 249–84.

Cockroft, W.H (1982) *Mathematics Counts. Report of the Committee of Inquiry into the Teaching of Mathematics in Schools* (Cockcroft Report). London: Her Majesty's Stationery Office.

Cooper, J.O., Heron, T.E. and Heward, W.E. (1987) *Applied Behavior Analysis*. Columbus, OH: Merrill.

Cooper, P. (1990) Respite, relationships and re-signification: the effects of residential schooling on pupils with emotional and behavioural difficulties, with particular reference to the pupils' perspective. Unpublished PhD thesis, University of Birmingham.

Cooper, P. (1999) Changing perceptions of EBD: maladjustment, EBD and beyond, *Emotional and Behavioural Difficulties*, 4(1): 3–11.

Cooper, P. and Upton, G. (1991) Controlling the urge to control: an ecosystemic approach to behaviour in schools, *Support for Learning*, 6(1): 22–6.

Corbett, J. (1996) *Bad Mouthing: The Language of Special Needs*. London: Falmer Press.

Cornwall, J. (2000) Might is right? A discussion of the ethics and practicalities of control and restraint in education, *Emotional and Behavioural Difficulties*, 5(4): 19–25.

Cornwall, J. (2004) Pressure, stress and children's behaviour at school, in J. Wearmouth, R.C. Richmond, T. Glynn and M. Berryman (eds) *Understanding Pupil Behaviour in Schools: A Diversity of Approaches*. London: Fulton.

Cornwall, J. and Tod, J. (1998) *IEPS: Emotional and Behavioural Difficulties*. London: David Fulton.

Council of Europe (1966) *European Convention on Human Rights (Rome, 1950) and its Five Protocols*. Strasbourg: Council of Europe.

Cowling, K. and Cowling, H. (1993) *Toe by Toe*. Baildon: Toe by Toe.

Cowne, E. (2000) Inclusive curriculum: access for all – rhetoric or reality? in *E831 Professional Development for Special Educational Needs Co-ordinators*. Milton Keynes: Open University.

Cremin, H., Thomas, G. and Vincett, K. (2003) Learning zones: an evaluation of three models for improving learning through teacher/teaching assistant teamwork, *Support for Learning*, 18(4): 154–61.

De Lemos, M. (2002) *Closing the Gap between Research and Practice: Foundations for the Acquisition of Literacy*. Camberwell, Victoria: Australian Council for Educational Research.

Demko, L. (1996) Bullying at school: the no-blame approach, *Health Education*, 1: 26–30.

Department for Education (DfE) (1994) *The Code of Practice for the Identification and Assessment of Special Educational Needs*. London: DfE.

Department for Education and Employment (DfEE) (1997) *Excellence for All Children*. London: DfEE.

Department for Education and Skills (DfES) (2001) *Special Educational Needs Code of Practice*. London: DES.

Department for Education and Skills (DfES) (2002) *National Statistics*. London: DfES.

Department for Education and Skills (DfES) (2004a) *Every Child Matters: Change for Children*. London: DfES.

Department for Education and Skills (DfES) (2004b) *Safeguarding Children in Education*. London: DfES.

Department of Education and Science (DES) (1989) *Discipline in Schools: Report of the Committee of Enquiry Chaired by Lord Elton* (Elton Report). London: HMSO.

Department of Education, Northern Ireland (DENI) (1998) *The Code of Practice for the Identification and Assessment of Special Educational Needs*. Bangor: DENI.

Department of Health (DOH) (1999) *Working Together to Safeguard Children*. London: HMSO.

Disability Discrimination Act (2005). London: HMSO.

Disability Rights Commission (2002) *Code of Practice for Schools: Disability Discrimination Act 1995, Part 4.* London: HMSO.

Dockrell, J. and McShane, J. (1993) *Children's Learning Difficulties: A Cognitive Approach.* Oxford: Blackwell.

Douglas, J.W.B. (1967) *The Home and the School.* St Albans: Panther.

Dowling, E. and Osbourne, E. (eds) (1985) *The Family and the School.* London: Routledge & Kegan Paul.

Dunckley, I. (1999) *Managing Extreme Behaviour in Schools.* Wellington: Specialist Education Services.

Dunn, L., Whetton, C. and Burley, J. (1997) *The British Picture Vocabulary Scale*, 2nd edn. Slough: NFER-Nelson.

Dwivedi, K. and Gupta, A. (2000) 'Keeping cool': anger management through group work, *Support for Learning*, 15(2): 76–81.

Eden, G.F., Stein, J.F., Wood, H.M. and Wood, F.B. (1995) Temporal and spatial processing in reading disabled and normal children, *Cortex*, 31: 451–68.

Education (Specified Work and Registration) (England) Regulations (2003). London: HMSO.

Education Act (1981). London: HMSO.

Education Act (1996). London: HMSO.

Ehri, L C. (2002) Reading processes, acquisition and instructional implications, in G. Reid and J. Wearmouth (eds) *Dyslexia and Literacy: Research and Practice.* Chichester: Wiley.

Eldridge, Jr, R.G. (1995) The possibility of knowledge and reality without science, in B. Hayes and K. Camperell (eds) *Linking Literacy: The Past, Present and Future*, Logan, UT: American Reading Forum.

El-Naggar, O. (2001) *Specific Learning Difficulties in Mathematics – a Classroom Approach.* Tamworth: NASEN.

Elliott, M. (1991) Bully courts, in M. Elliott (ed.) *Bullying.* London: Longman.

Englert, C. and Raphael, T. (1988) Constructing well-formed prose: process, structure and metacognition in the instruction of expository writing, *Exceptional Children*, 54: 513–20.

Everatt, J. (2002) 'Visual processes', in G. Reid and J. Wearmouth (eds) *Dyslexia and Literacy: Research and Practice.* Chichester: Wiley.

Farrell, P. (1999) *The Management, Support and Training of Learning Support Assistants.* Research Report RR 161. London: DfEE.

Florian, L. and Hegarty, J. (eds) (2004) *ICT and Special Educational Needs. A Tool for Inclusion.* Maidenhead: Open University Press.

Flower, L. and Hayes, J. (1980) The dynamics of composing: making plans and joggling constraints, in L. Gregg and E. Steinberg (eds) *Cognitive Processes in Writing.* Hillsdale, NJ: Erlbaum.

Fraivillig, J., Murphy, L. and Fuson, K. (1999) Advancing children's mathematical thinking in everyday mathematics classrooms, *Journal for Research in Mathematics Education*, 30(2): 148–70.

Furlong, V. (1991) Disaffected pupils: reconstructing the sociological perspective, *British Journal of Sociology of Education*, 12(3): 293–307.

Furlong, V.J. (1985) *The Deviant Pupil: Sociological Perspectives.* Milton Keynes: Open University Press.

Galloway, D.M. and Goodwin, C. (1987) *The Education of Disturbing Children: Pupils with*

Learning and Adjustment Difficulties. London: Longman.

Galloway, D.M., Armstrong, D. and Tomlinson, S. (1994) *The Assessment of Special Educational Needs: Whose Problem?* Harlow: Longman.

Gardner, R. (1987) *Who Says? Choice and Control in Care*. London: National Children's Bureau.

Garner, P. and Sandow, S. (1995) *Advocacy, Self-Advocacy and Special Needs*. London: David Fulton.

Gee, J. (1990) *Social Linguistics and Literacies: Ideology in Discourses*. Basingstoke: Falmer Press.

Gersch, I. (1995) Involving the child, in National Children's Bureau *Schools' Special Educational Needs Policies Pack*. London: National Children's Bureau.

Gersch, I. (2001) Listening to children: an initiative to increase the active involvement of children in their education by an educational psychology service, in J. Wearmouth (ed.) *Special Educational Provision in the Context of Inclusion*. London: Fulton.

Glynn, T. (1982) Antecedent control of behaviour in educational contexts, *Educational Psychology* (2): 215–29.

Glynn, T. (2003) Responding to language diversity: a way forward for New Zealand education, in R. Barnard and T. Glynn (eds) *Cultural Issues in Children's Language and Literacy: Case Studies from Aotearoa/New Zealand*. Clevedon: Multilingual Matters.

Glynn, T. and Bishop, R. (1995) Cultural issues in educational research: a New Zealand perspective, *He Pūkengo Kōrero*, 1(1): 37–43.

Glynn, T. and McNaughton, S. (1985) The Mangere home and school remedial reading procedures: continuing research on their effectiveness, *New Zealand Journal of Psychology*, 15(2): 66–77.

Glynn, T., Berryman, M., Atvars, K. and Harawira, W. (1997) *Hei āwhina mātua: a Home and School Behavioural Programme*. Final report to the Ministry of Education. Wellington: Ministry of Education.

Glynn, T., Berryman, M., O'Brien, K. and Bishop, R. (2000) Responsive written feedback on students' writing in a Māori language revitalisation context, in R. Harlow and R. Barnard (eds) *Proceedings of the Conference, 'Bilingualism at the Ends of the Earth'*. Hamilton: University of Waikato, Department of General and Applied Linguistics.

Glynn, T., Jerram, H. and Tuck, B. (1986) Writing as an interactive social process, *Behavioural Approaches with Children*, 10(4): 116–26.

Goodman, K.S. (1996) *On Reading*. Portsmouth, NJ: Heinemann.

Graham, S. and Harris, K.R. (1993) Teaching writing strategies to students with learning disabilities: Issues and recommendations, in L.J. Meltzer (ed.) *Strategy Assessment and Instruction for Students with Learning Disabilities*. Austin, TX: Pro-Ed.

Graham, S., MacArthur, C., Schwartz, S. and Voth, T. (1989) Improving LD students' compositions using a strategy involving product and process goal-setting. Paper presented at Annual Meeting of the American Educational Research Association, San Francisco, March.

Grant, L. and Evans, A. (1994) *Principles of Applied Behavior Analysis*. New York: HarperCollins College.

Grauberg, E. (2002) *Elementary Mathematics and Language Difficulties*. London: Whurr.

Graves, A., Montague, M. and Wong, Y. (1990) The effects of procedural facilitation on story composition of learning disabled students. Paper presented at Annual Meeting of the American Educational Research Association, San Francisco, March.

Graves, D. (1983) *Writing: Teachers and Children at Work*. Exeter, NH: Heinemann.

Graves, M. and Watts-Taffe, S.M. (2002) The place of word-consciousness in a research-based vocabulary programme, in A. Farstrup and S.J. Samuels (eds) *What Research Has to Say about Reading*. Newark, NJ: International Reading Association.

Gray, P., Miller, A. and Noakes, J. (1996) *Challenging Behaviour in Schools*. London: Routledge.

Greaney, K.T., Tunmer, W.E. and Chapman, J. (1997) The development of onset-rime sensitivity and analogical transfer in normal and poor readers, *Journal of Educational Psychology*, 89: 645–51.

Greeno, J.G. (1998) The situativity of knowing, learning and research, *American Psychologist*, 53(1): 5–17.

Gregory, E. (1996) *Making Sense of a New World*. London: Paul Chapman.

Gross, J. (1996) The weight of the evidence, *Support for Learning*, 11(1): 3–8.

Hanko, G. (1994) Discouraged children: when praise does not help, *British Journal of Special Education*, 21(4): 166–8.

Hannell, G. (2003) *Dyslexia*. London: David Fulton.

Hannon, P. (1999) Rhetoric and research in family literacy, *British Educational Research Journal*, 26(1): 121–38.

Hargreaves, D.H. (1967) *Social Relations in a Secondary School*. London: Routledge.

Hargreaves, D.H. (1972) *Interpersonal Relations and Education*. London: Routledge & Kegan Paul.

Hargreaves, D. and Hopkins, D. (1991) *The Empowered School: The Management and Practice of Development Planning*. London: Cassell.

Harris, S. (1976) Rational-emotive education and the human development program: a guidance study, *Elementary School Guidance and Counselling*, 10: 113–22.

Harris-Hendriks, J. and Figueroa, J. (1995) *Black in White: The Caribbean Child in the UK home*. London: Pitman.

Harrison, C. (1994) *Literature Review: Methods of Teaching Reading*. Edinburgh: SOED.

Hart, S. (1995) Differentiation by task or differentiation by outcome? in National Children's Bureau *Schools' Special Educational Needs Policies Pack*. London: NCB.

Hartas, C. and Moseley, D. (1993) Say-that-again, please: a reading program using a speaking computer, *Support for Learning*, 8(1): 16–21.

Hatcher, P.J. (2000) *Sound Linkage*. London: Pearson.

Hatcher, J. and Snowling, M. (2002) The phonological representations hypothesis of dyslexia: from theory to practice, in G. Reid and J. Wearmouth (eds) *Dyslexia and Literacy: Research and Practice*. London: Wiley.

Hattie, J. (2002) What are the attributes of excellent teachers? in B. Webber (ed.) *Teachers Make a Difference: What Is the Research Evidence?* (Proceedings of the New Zealand Association of Research in Education Conference: 3–26). Wellington: NZARE.

Hay McBer (2000) *A Model of Teacher Effectiveness. Report by **Hay McBer** to the Department for Education and Employment* (DfEE). London: DfEE.

Hedley, I. (2004) Integrated learning systems: effects on learning and self-esteem, in L. Florian and J. Hegarty (eds) *ICT and Special Educational Needs. A Tool for Inclusion*. Maidenhead: Open University Press.

Helme, S. and Clarke, D. (2001) Identifying cognitive engagement in the mathematics classroom, *Mathematics Education Research Journal*, 13(2): 133–53.

Henderson, A. (1998) *Maths for the Dyslexic: A Practical Guide*. London: David Fulton.

Hiebert, J., Carpenter, T., Fennema, E., Fuson, K.C., Wearne, D., Murray, H., Olivier, A. and Human, P. (1997) *Making Sense: Teaching and Learning Mathematics with Understanding*. Portsmouth, NH: Heinemann.

Hill, H., Rowan, B. and Ball, D. (2005) Effects of teachers' mathematical knowledge for teaching on student achievement, *American Educational Research Journal*, 42(2): 371–406.

Hinshaw, S. (1994) *Attention Deficit Disorders and Hyperactivity in Children*. Thousand Oak, CA: Sage.

Hobby, R. and Smith, F. (2002) *A National Development Agenda: What Does It Feel Like to Learn in our Schools?* London: The Hay Group.

Holmes, J. (1993) *John Bowlby and Attachment Theory*. London: Routledge.

Holowenko, H. and Pashute, K. (2000) ADHD in schools: a survey of prevalence and coherence across a local UK population, *Educational Psychology in Practice*, 16(2): 181–91.

Hughes, M. (1986) *Children and Number*. Oxford: Blackwell.

Ireson, J. and Hallam, S. (1999) Raising standards. Is ability grouping the answer? *Oxford Review of Education*, 25(3): 343–58.

Ireson, J., Hallam, S. and Plewis, I. (2001) Ability grouping in secondary school: effects on pupils' self-concepts, *British Journal of Educational Psychology*, 71: 315–26.

Ireson, J., Hallam, S., Hack, S., Clark, H. and Plewis, I. (2002) Ability grouping in English secondary schools: effects on attainment in English, mathematics and science, *Educational Research and Evaluation*, 8(3): 299–318.

Irlen, H. (1991) *Reading by the Colours*. New York: Avery.

Joffe, L.S. (1983) School mathematics and dyslexia: a matter of verbal labelling, generalisation, horses and carts, *Cambridge Journal of Education*, 13: 22–7.

Kanner, L. (1943) Autistic disturbances of affective contact, *Nervous Child*, 2: 217–50.

Kilpatrick, J., Swafford, J. and Findell, B. (eds) (2001) *Adding It Up: Helping Children Learn Mathematics*. Washington, DC: National Academy Press.

Kirchner, D.M. and Klatzky, R.J. (1985) Verbal rehearsal and memory in language-disordered children, *Journal of Speech and Hearing Research*, 28: 556–65.

Lampert, M. (1990) When the problem is not the question and the solution is not the answer: mathematical knowing and teaching, *American Educational Research Journal*, 27(1): 29–63.

Lave, J. (1993) The practice of learning, in S. Chaiklin and J. Lave (eds) *Understanding Practice: Perspectives on Activity and Context*. Cambridge: Cambridge University Press.

Lave, J. and Wenger, E. (1991) *Situated Learning: Legitimate Peripheral Participation*. Cambridge: Cambridge University Press.

Lave, J. and Wenger, E. (1999) Learning and pedagogy in communities of practice, in J. Leach and B. Moon (eds) *Learners and Pedagogy*. London: Paul Chapman.

LaVigna, G.W. and Donnellan, A.M. (1986) *Alternatives to Punishment: Solving Behavior Problems with Non-Aversive Strategies*. New York: Irvington.

Lawrence, D. (1971) The effects of counselling on retarded readers, *Educational Research*, 13(2): 119–24.

Lawrence, D. (1973) *Improving Reading through Counselling*. London: Ward Lock.

Lawrence, D. (1996) *Enhancing Self Esteem in the Classroom*. London: Paul Chapman.

Leadbetter, J. and Leadbetter, P. (1993) *Special Children: Meeting the Challenge in the Primary School*. London: Cassell.

Lennox, D. (1991) *See Me After School*. London: David Fulton.

Lever, M. (2003) *Number Activities for Children with Mathematical Learning Difficulties*. London: David Fulton.

Lewis, A. and Norwich, B. (2000) *Mapping a Pedagogy for Learning Difficulties*. Report submitted to the British Educational Research Association (BERA), February.

Lilley, C. (2004) A whole-school approach to ICT for children with physical disabilities, in L. Florian and J. Hegarty (eds) *ICT and Special Educational Needs. A Tool for Inclusion.* Maidenhead: Open University Press.

Lorenz, S. (1998) *Effective In-class Support.* London: David Fulton.

Lovey, J. (1995) *Support Special Educational Needs in Secondary School Classrooms.* London: Fulton.

Lunn, S., Hancock, R., Wearmouth, J. and Collins, J. (2005) Adults and children working together, Study Topic 5, in S. Lunn, R. Hancock, J. Wearmouth and J. Collins, *E111 Supporting Learning in Primary Schools.* Milton Keynes: Open University.

Lunzer, E.A. and Gardner, W.K. (1979) *The Effective Use of Reading.* London: Heinemann Educational.

MacArthur, C. and Graham, S. (1987) Learning disabled students' composing under three methods of text production: handwriting, word processing, and dictation. *Journal of Special Education,* 21: 22–42.

Macfarlane, A. (1997) The Hikairo rationale: teaching students with emotional and behavioural difficulties; a bicultural approach, *Waikato Journal of Education,* 3: 135–68.

Macfarlane, A. (2000a) Māori perspectives on development, in L. Bird and W. Drewery (eds) *Human Development in Aotearoa: A Journey through Life.* Auckland: McGraw-Hill Book Company.

Macfarlane, A. (2000b) The value of Māori ecologies in special education, in D. Fraser, R. Moltzen and K. Ryba (eds) *Learners with Special Needs in Aotearoa New Zealand,* 2nd edn. Palmerston North: Dunmore Press.

Maines, B. and Robinson, G. (1991) *Stamp Out Bullying.* Bristol: Lame Duck.

Mair, M. (1988) Psychology as storytelling, *International Journal of Personal Construct Psychology,* 1: 125–32.

McDermott, R.P. (1999) On becoming labelled – the story of Adam, in P. Murphy (ed.) *Learners, Learning and Assessment.* London: Paul Chapman.

McLeod, J. (1998) *An Introduction to Counselling,* 2nd edn. Buckingham: Open University Press.

McNaughton, S. (2002) *Meeting of Minds.* Wellington: Learning Media.

McNaughton, S., Glynn, T. and Robinson, V. (1987) *Pause, Prompt and Praise: Effective Tutoring of Remedial Reading.* Birmingham: Positive Products.

Means, B. (ed.) (1994) *Technology and Education Reform: The Reality Behind the Promise.* San Francisco, CA: Jossey-Bass.

Mehan, H. (1996) The politics of representation, in S. Chaiklin and J. Lave (eds) *Understanding Practice: Perspectives on Activity and Context.* Cambridge: Cambridge University Press.

Meichenbaum, D. and Turk, D. (1976) The cognitive-behavioural management of anxiety, anger and pain, in P.O. Davidson (ed.) *The Behavioural Management of Anxiety, Anger and Pain.* New York: Brunner/Mazel.

Merrett, F. (1985) *Encouragement Works Better than Punishment: The Application of Behavioural Methods in Schools.* Birmingham: Positive Products.

Miles, T.R. and Miles, E. (2004) *Dyslexia and Mathematics,* 2nd edn. London: Routledge.

Milgram, S. (1974) *Obedience to Authority: An Experimental View.* New York: Harper & Row.

Ministry of Education (MoE) (1998) *The IEP Guidelines. Planning for Students with Special Educational Needs.* Wellington: Ministry of Education.

Ministry of Education (2005) *Effective Literacy Practice in Years.* Wellington: Learning Media.

Ministry of Education (MoE) (2006) *Effective Literacy Practice in Years 5–8.* Wellington: Learning Media.

Minuchin, S. (1974) *Families and Family Therapy*. Cambridge, MA: Harvard University Press.

Montgomery, J.K. and Kahn, N.L. (2003) You are going to be an author: adolescent narratives as intervention, *Communication Disorders Quarterly*, 24(3): 143–52.

Moseley, D.V. (1992) Visual and linguistic determinants of reading fluency in dyslexics: a classroom study with speaking computers, in R. Groner (ed.) *Reading and Reading Disorders: International Perspectives*. Oxford: Elsevier.

Mosley, J. (1996) *Quality Circle Time in the Primary Classroom: Your Essential Guide to Enhancing Self-esteem, Self-discipline and Positive Relationships*. Cambridge: LDA.

Murphy, S. (2002) Literacy assessment and the politics of identity, in J. Soler, J. Wearmouth and G. Reid (eds) *Contextualising Difficulties in Literacy Development: Exploring Politics, Culture, Ethnicity and Ethics*. London: Routledge.

Myhill, D. and Warren, P. (2005) Scaffolds or straitjackets: critical moments in classroom discourse, *Educational Review*, 57(1): 55–69.

Nash, R. and Harker, R. (2002) How are school composition effects and peer group mechanisms related? A theoretical and methodological discussion from the Progress at School Project, *New Zealand Journal of Educational Studies*, 37(2): 171–90.

National Assembly of Wales (2004) *Special Educational Needs Code of Practice*. Cardiff: NAW.

National Autistic Society (2004) website. www.nas.org.uk/nas/jsp/polopoly.jsp?d=10 (accessed 6 May 2008).

National Council for Educational Technology (NCET (1992) *Competencies in Information Technology*. Coventry: NCET.

National Council for Educational Technology (NCET) (1995) *Access Technology: Making the Right Choice*. Coventry: NCET.

National Institute of Child Health and Human Development (2000) *Report of the National Reading Panel. Teaching Children to Read: An Evidence-based Assessment of the Scientific Research Literature on Reading and its Implications for Reading Instruction*. NIH Publication No. 00–4769. Washington, DC: US Government Printing Office.

Neale, M.D. (1997) *The Neale Analysis of Reading Ability*. Windsor: NFER.

Nellar, S.V. and Nisbet, P.D. (1993) *Accelerated Writing for People with Disabilities*. Edinburgh: CALL Centre, University of Edinburgh.

Newell, A.F. and Beattie, L. (1991) The use of lexical and spelling aids with dyslexics, in C.H. Singleton (ed.) *Computers and Literacy Skills*. Hull: Dyslexia Computer Resource Centre, University of Hull.

Nicholson, T. (2000) *Reading and Writing on the Wall: Debates, Challenges and Opportunities in the Teaching of Reading*. Palmerston North: Dunmore Press.

Nicholson, T. and Tan, A. (1997) Flashcards revisited: training poor readers to read words faster improves their comprehension of text, *Journal of Educational Psychology*, 89: 276–88.

Noddings, N. (1995) *Philosophy of Education*. Oxford: Westview Press.

Norwich, B. (1996) *Special Needs Education, Inclusive Education or Just Education for All?* London: Institute of Education, London University.

Norwich, B., Cooper, P. and Maras, P. (2002) Attentional and activity difficulties: findings from a national study, *Support for Learning*, 17(4): 182–6.

Nunes, T., Bryant, P. and Bindman, M. (1997) Morphological spelling strategies: developmental stages and processes, *Developmental Psychology*, 33: 637–49.

O'Connor, M.C. (1998) Language socialisation in the mathematics classroom: discourse practices and mathematical thinking, in M. Lampert and M. Blunk (eds) *Talking*

Mathematics in School: Studies of Teaching and Learning. Cambridge: Cambridge University Press.

Office for Standards in Education (OFSTED) (2001) *Improving Attendance and Behaviour in Secondary Schools.* London: OFSTED.

Open University (2000) Audio interview, in *E831 Professional Development for Special Educational Needs Co-ordinators.* Milton Keynes: Open University.

Open University (2002) Audio interview, in *E801 Difficulties in Literacy Development.* Milton Keynes: Open University.

Open University (2005) *E111 Supporting Learning in Primary Schools,* Study Topic 7: Needs, rights and opportunities. Milton Keynes: Open University.

Palincsar, A.S. and Brown, A.L. (1984) Reciprocal teaching of comprehension – fostering- and comprehension-monitoring activities, *Cognition and Instruction,* 1(2): 117–75.

Paveley, S (2002) Inclusion and the Web: strategies to improve access, in C. Abbott (ed.) *Special Educational Needs and the Internet: Issues for the Inclusive Classroom.* London: RoutledgeFalmer.

Peacey, N. and Wearmouth, J. (2007) *A Guide to Special Educational Needs For Trainee Teachers. A TDA commissioned guide.* London: TDA.

Pearson, P.D., Roehler, L.R., Doel, J.A. and Duffy, G.G. (1992) Developing expertise in reading comprehension, in S. Samuels and A. Farstrup (eds) *What Research Has to Say about Reading Instruction,* 2nd edn. Newark, DE: International Reading Association.

Perso, T. (2003) School mathematics and its impact on cultural diversity, *Australian Mathematics Teacher,* 59(2): 10–16.

Piaget, J. (1969) *The Child's Conception of Time.* London: RKP.

Pickersgill, M. and Gregory, S. (1998) *Sign Bilingualism: A Model.* London: LASER.

Pickles, P. (2001) Therapeutic provision in mainstream curricula, in J. Wearmouth (ed.) *Special Educational Provision in the Context of Inclusion*: *Policy & Practice in Schools.* London: Fulton.

Pikas, A. (1989) Method of shared concern, *School Psychology International,* 10: 95–104.

Pitchford, M. (2004) An introduction to multi-element planning for primary aged children, in J. Wearmouth, R.C. Richmond and T. Glynn (eds) *Addressing Pupils' Behaviour: Responses at District, School and Individual Levels,* London: Fulton.

Pollard, A. (2002) *Reflective Teaching: Effective and Evidence-Informed Professional Practice.* London: Continuum.

Poulou, M. and Norwich, B. (2002) Cognitive, emotional and behavioural responses to students with emotional and behavioural difficulties: a model of decision-making, *British Educational Research Journal,* 28(1): 111–38.

Power, T. and Bartholomew, K. (1985) Getting uncaught in the middle: a case study in family-school system consultation, *School Psychology Review,* 14(2): 222–9.

Prendergast, M., Taylor, E., Rapaport, J.L., Bartko, J., Donnelly, M., Kametkin, A., Ahearn, M.B., Dunn, G. and Weiselburg, H.M. (1998) The diagnosis of childhood hyperactivity, a US-UK cross national study of DSMIII and ICD9, *Journal of Child Psychology and Psychiatry,* 29: 289–300.

Pressley, M. (2002) *Reading Instruction that Works: The Case for Balanced Teaching.* New York: Guilford Press.

Primary National Strategy (PNS) (2005) *Speaking Listening Learning: Working with Children Who Have Special Educational Needs.* Ref 1235/2005. London: QCA.

Qualifications and Curriculum Authority (QCA) (2000) *Curriculum 2000.* London: QCA.

Rapport, M.D., Denney, C., DuPaul, G.J. and Gardner, M.J. (1994) Attention deficit disorder and methylphenidate: normalization rates, clinical effectiveness and response prediction in 76 children, *Journal of the American Academy of Child's Adolescent Psychiatry*, 32: 333–42.

Raven, J., Raven, J.C. and Court, J.H. (1998) *Raven's Progressive Matrices*. Oxford: Psychologists Press.

Ravenette, A.T. (1984) The recycling of maladjustment, *AEP Journal*, 6(3): 18–27.

Reason, R. and Boote, R. (1994) *Helping Children with Reading and Spelling*. London: Routledge.

Rees, D. and the Education Department of Western Australia (2001) *Spelling Development Continuum*. Melbourne: Rigby Heinemann.

Reid, G. and Given, B.K. (1999) The interactive observation style identification, in B.K. Given and G. Reid *Learning Styles – a Guide for Teachers and Parents*. Lancashire: Red Rose Publications.

Restorative Practices Development Team (2003) *Restorative Practices for Schools*. Hamilton: University of Waikato.

Rice, M. and Brooks, G. (2004) *Developmental Dyslexia in Adults: A Research Review*. London: NRDC.

Riddick, B. (1996) *Living with Dyslexia*. London and New York: Routledge.

Riddick, B., Wolfe, J. and Lumsdon, D. (2002) *Dyslexia. A Practical Guide for Teachers and Parents*. London: David Fulton.

Rigby, K. (2002) *New Perspectives on Bullying*. London: Jessica Kingsley.

Roaf, C. and Lloyd, C. (1995) Multi-agency work with young people in difficulty, *Social Care Research Findings,* No. 68, June. York: Joseph Rowntree Foundation.

Rogers, B. (1994) Teaching positive behaviour in behaviourally disordered students in primary schools, *Support for Learning*, 9(4): 166–70.

Rogers, J. (2007) Cardinal number and its representation: skills, concepts and contexts, *Early Childhood Education and Care*, 178(2): 211–25.

Rogers, W. (1994a) *The Language of Discipline*. Plymouth: Northcote House.

Rogers, W. (1994b) *Behaviour Recovery: A Whole School Approach for Behaviourally Disordered Children*. Melbourne: Australian Council for Educational Research.

Rogoff, B. (1990) *Apprenticeship in Thinking: Cognitive Development in Social Context*. New York: Oxford University Press.

Rosenthal, R. and Jacobson, L. (1968) *Pygmalion in the Classroom*. New York: Holt, Rinehart and Winston.

Royal National Institute for the Blind (RNIB) See it right checklist, www.rnib.org.uk/xpedio/ groups/public/documents/PublicWebsite/public_printchecklist1.pdf (accessed 30 April 2008).

Royal National Institute for the Deaf (RNID) (2004) *Inclusion Strategies*. London: RNID.

Russell, P. (1997) Parents as partners: some early impressions of the impact of the Code of Practice, in S. Wolfendale (ed.) *Working with parents after the Code of Practice*. London: Fulton.

Ruthven, K. (2002) Assessment in mathematics education, in L. Haggarty (ed.) *Teaching Mathematics in Secondary Schools*. London: RoutlegeFalmer.

Rutter, M., Maughan, B., Mortimore, P. and Ouston, J. (1979) *Fifteen Thousand Hours: Secondary Schools and their Effects on Children*. London: Open Books.

Rutter, M., Tizard, J. and Whitmore, K. (1970) *Education, Health and Behaviour*. London: Longman.

Salmon, P. (1995) *Psychology in the Classroom*. London: Cassell.

Salmon, P. (1998) *Life at School*. London: Constable.

Samuels, S.J. (2002) Reading fluency: its development and assessment, in S. Samuels and A. Farstrup (eds) *What Research Has to Say about Reading Instruction*. Newark, DE: International Reading Association.

Sarbin, T. (1986) *Narrative Psychology: The Storied Nature of Human Conduct*. New York: Praeger.

Schachar, R. (1991) Childhood hyperactivity, *Journal of Child Psychology and Psychiatry*, 32: 155–92.

Schifter, D. (2001) Learning to see the invisible, in T. Wood, B. Scott-Nelson and J. Warfield (eds) *Beyond Classical Pedagogy: Teaching Elementary School Mathematics*. Mahwah, NJ: Lawrence Erlbaum Associates.

Schön, D. (1983) *The Reflective Practitioner: How Professionals Think in Action*. New York: Basic Books.

Schön, D. (1987) *Educating the Reflective Practitioner*. London. Jossey-Bass.

Schweigert, F.J. (1999) Moral behaviour in victim offender conferencing, *Criminal Justice Ethics*, Summer/Fall: 29–40.

Shapiro, S. and Cole, L. (1994) *Behaviour Change in the Classroom: Self-Management Interventions*. New York: Gulliford Press.

Sharron, H. (1995) Behaviour drugs – headteachers speak out, *Special Children*, April: 10–13.

Shulman, L. and Shulman, J. (2004) How and what teachers learn: a shifting perspective, *Journal of Curriculum Studies*, 36(2): 257–71.

Singleton, C. (1991) *Computers and Literacy Skills*. Hull: BDA.

Singleton, C.H. (1991) A rationale for computer-assisted literacy learning, in C.H. Singleton (ed.) *Computers and Literacy Skills*. Hull: Dyslexia Computer Resource Centre, University of Hull.

Singleton, C. H. (1994) Computer applications in the identification and remediation of dyslexia, in D.Wray (ed.) *Literacy and Computers: Insights from Research*. Widnes: United Kingdom Reading Association.

Skinner, B.F. (1938) *The Behaviour of Organisms*. New York: Appleton Century Crofts.

Skinner, B.F. (1953) *Science and Human Behavior*. New York: Macmillan.

Smith, C. (2004) Confrontation in the classroom, in J. Wearmouth, R.C. Richmond and T. Glynn (eds) *Addressing Pupils' Behaviour: Responses at District, School and Individual Levels*. London: Fulton.

Smith, C.J. and Laslett, R. (1993) *Effective Classroom Management: A Teacher's Guide* 2nd edn. London: Routledge.

Smith, J. and Elley, W. (1997) *How Children Learn to Write*. Wellington: Longman.

Snowling, M.J. (2000) *Dyslexia*, 2nd edn. Oxford: Blackwell.

Special Educational Needs and Disability Act (2001). London: HMSO.

Stahl, S. (1998) Saying the 'p' word: guidelines for exemplary phonics instruction, in R. Allington (ed.) *Teaching Struggling Readers: Articles from The Reading Teacher*. Newark: International Reading Association.

Stanford, P. and Siders, J.A. (2001) E-pal writing! *Teaching Exceptional Children*, 34(2): 21–4.

Stanovich, K. (2000) *Progress in Understanding Reading: Scientific Foundations and New Frontiers*. London: Guilford Press.

Stipek, D., Salmon, J.M., Givvin, K.B., Kazemi, E., Saxe, G. and MacGyvers, V.L. (1998) The value (and convergence) of practices suggested by motivation research and promoted by mathematics education reformers, *Journal for Research in Mathematics Education*, 29, 465–88.

Sullivan, P., Mousley, J. and Zevenbergen, R. (2003) The context of mathematics tasks and the context of the classroom: are we including all students? *Mathematics Education Research Journal*, 15(2): 107–21.

Swanson, J.M., McBurnett, K., Wigal, T., Pfiffner, L.J., et al. (1993) Effect of stimulant medication on children with attention deficit disorder: a 'review of reviews', *Exceptional Children*, 60(2): 154–62.

Taylor, E. (1994) Syndrome of attention deficit and overactivity, in M. Rutter, E. Taylor and L. Hersov (eds) *Child and Adolescent Psychiatry: Modern Approaches*, 3rd edn. Oxford: Blackwell Scientific.

Treatment and Education of Autistic and Related Communication Handicapped Children (TEACCH) (1998) TEACCH Autism Program, www.teacch.com/ (accessed 6 May 2008).

Tew, M. (1998) Circle time: a much neglected resource in secondary schools, *Pastoral Care,* September:18–27.

Thomas, G. (1992) Evaluating support, *Support for Learning*, 5(1): 30–6.

Tod, J., Castle, F. and Blamires, M. (1998) *Implementing Effective Practice*. London: Fulton.

Tomlinson, S. (1988) Why Johnny can't read: critical theory and special education, *European Journal of Special Needs Education*, 3(1): 45–58.

Topping, K. (1996) Tutoring systems for family literacy, in S. Wolfendale and K. Topping (eds) *Family Involvement in Literacy*. London: Cassell.

Topping, K. (2001) *Thinking, Reading, Writing*. London: Continuum.

Topping, K.J. (1995) *Paired Reading, Spelling and Writing: The Handbook for Teachers and Parents*. London: Cassell.

Topping, K.J. (2001) *Peer-assisted Learning: A Practical Guide for Teachers*. Cambridge, MA: Brookline.

Tribble, C. (1996) *Writing*. Oxford: Oxford University Press.

Underwood, J.E.A. (1955) *Report of the Committee on Maladjusted Children* (Underwood Report). London: HMSO.

United Nations Educational, Scientific, and Cultural Organization (UNESCO) (1989) *United Nations Convention on the Rights of the Child*. UN, GA res, 44/25. Geneva: United Nations.

Visser, J., Cole, T. and Daniels, H. (2002) Inclusion for the difficult to include, *Support for Learning*, 17(1): 23–6.

Vygotsky, L.S. (1962) *Thought and Language*. Cambridge, MA: MIT Press.

Walkerdine, V. (1988) *The Mastery of Reason: Cognitive Development and the Production of Rationality*. London: Routledge.

Walshaw, M. (2004) The pedagogical encounter in postmodern times: learning from Lacan, in M. Walshaw (ed.) *Mathematics Education within the Postmodern*. Greenwich, CT: Information Age.

Warfield, J. (2001) Where mathematics content knowledge matters, in T. Wood, B. Scott-Nelson and J. Warfield (eds) *Beyond Classical Pedagogy: Teaching Elementary School Mathematics*. Mahwah, NJ: Lawrence Erlbaum Associates.

Warnock Report (1978) *Special Educational Needs, Report of the Committee of Enquiry into the Education of Handicapped Children and Young People*. Cmnd. 7212. Department of Education and Science. London: HMSO.

Waterland, L. (1985) *Read with Me*. Stroud: Thimble Press.

Watkins, C. and Wagner, P. (1995) School behaviour and special educational needs – what's the link? in National Children's Bureau *Discussion Papers 1: Schools' Special Educational Needs Policies Pack*. London: NCB.

Watkins, C. and Wagner, P. (2000) *Improving School Behaviour*. London: Paul Chapman.

Watson A., De Geest, E. and Prestage, S. (2003) *Deep Progress in Mathematics – the Improving Attainment in Mathematics Project*. Oxford: University of Oxford, Department of Educational Studies.

Watt, D., Sheriffe, G. and Majors, R. (1999) Mentoring black male pupils. Unpublished MS, City College, Manchester.

Wearmouth, J. (1986) Self-concept and learning experiences of pupils with moderate learning difficulties: a comparison between pupils in special mainstream schools, unpublished MA thesis, Institute of Education, London University.

Wearmouth, J. (1996) Registering: for what purpose? *Support for Learning*, 11(3): 118–23.

Wearmouth, J. (1999) Another one flew over: 'maladjusted' Jack's perception of his label, *British Journal of Special Education*, 26(1): 15–23.

Wearmouth, J. (2000) *Co-ordinating Special Educational Provision Meeting the Challenges in Schools*. London: Hodder.

Wearmouth, J. (2004a) Learning from 'James': lessons about policy and practice for literacy difficulties in schools' special educational provision, *British Journal of Special Education*, 31(2): 60–7.

Wearmouth, J (2004b) 'Talking Stones', an interview technique for disaffected young people, *Journal of Pastoral Care in Education*, 22(2): 7–13.

Wearmouth, J., Glynn, T. and Berryman, M. (2005) *Perspectives on Student Behaviour in Schools: Exploring Theory and Developing Practice*. London: Routledge.

Weavers, J. (2003) Dyslexia and mathematics, in M. Thomson (ed.) *Dyslexia Included – a Whole School Approach*. London: David Fulton.

Wenger, E. (1999) *Communities of Practice: Learning, Meaning and Identity*. New York: Cambridge University Press.

Westby (1991) Learning to talk-talking to learn: oral-literate language difference, in C.S. Simon (ed.) *Communication Skills and Classroom Success*. San Diego, CA: College Hill.

Wheatley, C.L. and Wheatley, G.H. (1979) Developing spatial ability, *Mathematics in School*, 8: 10–11.

Whitehead, D. (1993) *Factual Writing Think Sheets*. Hamilton: Seaforth Education.

Wilde, J. (1994) The effects of the let's get rational board game on rational thinking, depression and self-acceptance in adolescents, *Journal of Rational-Emotive and Cognitive-Behaviour Therapy*, 12: 189–96.

Wilde, J. (1995) *Anger Management in Schools: Alternatives to Student Violence*. Lancaster, PA: Technomic.

Wilde, J. (2001) Interventions for children with anger problems, *Journal of Rational-Emotive and Cognitive-Behaviour Therapy*, 19(3): 191–7.

Wiliam, D. (1999) Formative assessment in mathematics: part 2: feedback, *Equals*, 5(3): 8–11.

Wilkins, A.J., Evans, B.J.W., Brown, J.A., Busby, A.E., Wingfield, A.E., Jeanes, R.L. and Bald, J. (1994) Double-masked placebo-controlled trial of precision spectral filters in children who use coloured overlays, *Ophthalmic and Physiological Optics*, 14: 365–70.

Williams, H. and Birmingham City Council Education Department (1998) *Behaviour in Schools: Framework for Intervention*. Birmingham: Birmingham City Council Education Department.

Wilson, A. and Charlton, K. (1997) *Making Partnerships Work: A Practical Guide for the Public, Private, Voluntary and Community Sectors*. York: Joseph Rowntree Foundation.

Wing, L. and Gould, J. (1979) Severe impairments of social interaction and associated abnormalities in children: epidemiology and classification, *Journal of Autism and Developmental Disorders*, 9: 11–29.

Wood, D., Bruner, J. and Ross, G. (1976) The role of tutoring in problem solving, *Journal of Child Psychology and Psychiatry*, 17: 89–100.

Wragg, E.C., Wragg, C.M., Haynes, G.S. and Chamberlain, R.P. (1998) *Improvising Literacy in the Primary School*. London: Routledge.

Wray, D. (2002) Metacognition and literacy, in G. Reid and J. Wearmouth (eds) *Dyslexia and Literacy: Research and Practice*. Chichester: Wiley.

Index